W9-DCN-336

Also by Kevin Cook
....

Tommy's Honor

Driven

Titanic Thompson

The Last Headbangers

Flip

Kitty Genovese

The Dad Report

Electric October

Ten Innings at Wrigley

The Burning Blue

WACO
RISING

WACO RISING

DAVID KORESH, THE FBI, AND THE BIRTH OF AMERICA'S MODERN MILITIAS

KEVIN COOK

Henry Holt and Company
New York

Henry Holt and Company
Publishers since 1866
120 Broadway
New York, New York 10271
www.henryholt.com

Henry Holt® and Ⓗ® are registered trademarks of Macmillan Publishing Group, LLC.

Library of Congress Cataloging-in-Publication Data is available.

ISBN: 9781250840523

Our books may be purchased in bulk for promotional, educational, or business use. Please contact your local bookseller or the Macmillan Corporate and Premium Sales Department at (800) 221-7945, extension 5442, or by e-mail at MacmillanSpecialMarkets@macmillan.com.

First Edition 2023

Designed by Meryl Sussman Levavi

Printed in the United States of America

1   3   5   7   9   10   8   6   4   2

*To the memory of
the Branch Davidians
and ATF agents who died
at Mount Carmel*

Contents

WACO
RISING

Prologue

The FBI struck before sunrise. The Branch Davidians, holed up in their ramshackle retreat near Waco, Texas, always expected the final battle to come without warning. That's what the Bible predicted. Instead there was a brief warning, a wake-up call delivered over loudspeakers moments after 6:00 a.m. on April 19, 1993:

> *We are in the process of placing tear gas into the building.*
> *This is not an assault. This is not an assault.*

At 6:02 a.m., tanks broke through the compound's walls, filling the front rooms with tear gas. Some of the people inside screamed, some prayed. Some ran for shelter. Some strapped gas masks over their faces. Others grabbed rifles and started shooting at the tanks and federal agents outside.

"*Come out of the compound with your hands up,*" the loudspeakers blared. "*You are under arrest.*"

David Koresh was shocked. It wasn't supposed to go down this way. He had spent the night writing out his interpretation of the Seven Seals in the Bible's book of Revelation. As soon as he finished, he said, he would lead his people out. And now this—after two months of stalemate, a surprise attack.

Still, he stayed calm. Only a fool imagines he can foresee God's ways. The thirty-three-year-old leader, who ruled every facet of the Davidians' lives and slept with female followers as young as twelve, may have been zealous. He may have been reckless, rapacious, and vain, but he wasn't a fool. With his dimpled chin and shoulder-length hair—"Jesus hair," his followers called it—he had the look of a messiah. Koresh had pictured this moment, even prayed for it. Now it was here. The final battle was unfolding the way he'd told them it would, quoting Revelation: "*Behold, the devil is about to throw some of you into prison, that you be tested. Be faithful unto death.*"

Koresh rallied the others. The apocalypse was deafening, the FBI's loudspeakers booming at full volume. Helicopters circled in the dawn's early light. There was gunfire and wailing as tanks equipped with battering rams punched through walls. If Koresh ever needed proof of his preachings, here it was: American tanks crashing through walls, rolling toward American women and children.

There wasn't much time. After fifty-one days, the end of his standoff with federal agents was here. Or was it the end of the world?

1

Wandering Bonehead

Vernon Howell, who would later take the name David Koresh, was born in Houston on a sweltering morning in August 1959. His mother was fourteen years old.

Bonnie Clark told friends she was "sort of engaged" to the baby's father. Bobby Howell was a high school senior, a good kisser with a pickup truck. Bonnie dropped out of eighth grade to have their baby. The age of consent was seventeen, but a fourteen-year-old Texan could marry with parental consent. "Daddy signed the papers, but Bobby backed out," she remembered. "God had a plan for my life and Vernon's life, which didn't include Bobby."

Bonnie gave her son his father's name anyway. She named him Vernon Wayne Howell and raised him while working two or three jobs at a time. She waited tables. She worked in a nail salon. She cleaned houses and offices for a realtor. After a brief marriage to an ex-con who beat her, she lied about her age and worked as a waitress at a nightclub on a tumbledown block of Houston's Canal Street. With its mirrored walls and green neon, the Jade Lounge seemed posh to her. "A lot of prostitutes hung around," she recalled, "but they didn't work out of there."

The owner liked the lively new girl with the auburn hair. "My knight in shining armor," she called Roy "Rocky" Haldeman, a burly navy vet, the sort of proprietor who could break up a bar fight or win one.

By the time they married in 1965, Roy was thirty-six. Bonnie was twenty and pregnant again. She delighted her new husband by giving birth to a boy they named Roger. Haldeman sold his share of the Jade Lounge and moved the four of them to a farm near Dallas.

He didn't think much of his wife's first kid. For one thing, five-year-old Vernon was so hyper that Bonnie called him "Sputnik." For another, he stuttered. Worse yet, the boy was shaping up to be what his stepfather considered "a pussy." He cried every time he got dropped off at day care. "Roy would tell him not to cry," she recalled. "He said, 'Be a man!' Roy beat him on his butt and left it black and blue." Thirty years later, Koresh described those beatings to an FBI negotiator. His stepfather spanked him so hard, he said, "he made me fly like a kite."

School was no easier. The boy was dyslexic as well as hyperactive. Vernon flunked first grade twice. After that, a teacher told the eight-year-old he'd been assigned to special education, and for a moment he thought she meant he was special. Other kids disabused him of that notion by giving him a nickname: Mister Retardo. "When my mom picked me up after school that day," he recalled, "I busted out howling, '*I'm a retard!*'"

His boyhood took a turn for the better on the day of a middle-school sports festival. Even the special-ed students were expected to compete in one event or another, so a coach entered Vernon in a cross-country race. "I didn't know I could run fast," he recalled of the day he won a blue ribbon. But Vernon and his half brother used to chase each other around Haldeman's land. "We didn't have bikes or expensive toys. We built up leg strength racing, so when I ran against them city boys, I ran 'em ragged." He began to believe there might be something special about him, a touch of greatness.

He also had a God-given knack for shooting guns. Even Haldeman was impressed when his stepson drew a bead with a BB gun and hit squirrels between the eyes. As he grew his first whiskers, he developed other passions: for cars, girls, and, to Bonnie's surprise, God. He owed his interest in religion to Bonnie's mother, Erline Clark, a

Seventh-day Adventist who took Vernon to Sabbath services in Tyler, Texas, and gave him his first Bible.

Seventh-day Adventists celebrate the Sabbath from sunset on Friday to sunset on Saturday, the Old Testament way. They believe human history will end soon with the Second Coming of Jesus. Vernon preferred the rigor and drama of his grandma's religion to the chaos in the Haldemans' house, where his mother and stepfather drank, fought, and split up only to kiss and make up to the sound of grunts and thumps in the bedroom next to his. When they were on the outs they'd send him to stay with his grandma for months at a stretch. It took Vernon a while to make sense of the old-timey language in the Bible she gave him, but once he got the hang of the thees, thous, and shalts he was pleased to find all sorts of violence and sex in its onion-skin pages. By the age of twelve, despite his struggles in school, he could recite long biblical passages from memory.

Haldeman was a mean drunk who got meaner and drunker with age. Finally, Bonnie left him. Vernon claimed she slept with men for money after that, but she swore it wasn't so cut-and-dried as that. According to her, she paid their bills with help from "some rich boyfriends."

Vernon dropped out of the ninth grade with a grade-point average he once described as "you don't want to know." But he was good with his hands. He worked construction and made tax-free money fixing cars, motorcycles, lawn mowers, and power tools. Good old Vern could take a backfiring engine apart and put it back together so it purred. He did carpentry for friends "just like Jesus," said Bonnie, who cosigned for a Chevy pickup truck Vernon called his "chariot." She felt bad about partying her way through his youth to the point that she forgot much of it, and for letting her men beat him. Still she saw a silver lining in what she called the "whuppings" he endured as a child, including some she dispensed herself. "As far as disciplining children, he learned from all the wrong things I did," Bonnie said years later, when she became more religious. "I think God caused certain circumstances in his childhood for him to understand humanity."

She recalled "Mary," her son's first girlfriend, as a raven-haired temptress. The girl had dark hair all right, but her name was Linda. Sixteen-year-old Linda Campion was the one who introduced eighteen-year-old Vernon to sex. "My first love," he called her years later. "I was shy, still a virgin, and she was jailbait. We had the most beautiful relationship of carnal spirituality" in the bed of his pickup.

He didn't believe in using condoms. The Bible warns men not to spill their seed. The Bible said sex could make a man and woman "one flesh," not one flesh and a little bit of rubber. So he said a doctor had told him he could never have children. He was "sterile," he told Linda, a word he'd heard in a movie.

He was startled when she told him she was pregnant. But the more he thought about it, the more he liked the idea. "I was blown away at the thought that I'd have a child," he said. "Me, Mister Retardo—going to have a baby!"

Instead, Linda's father paid for an abortion.

Vernon stayed away from the Campions for a month, sleeping in his truck down the road from Linda's house. Finally, Dick Campion took pity on him. A middle manager at Texas Instruments, Campion wanted his daughter to be happy. "Stay with us," he told the boy, who moved into Linda's room and into her bed. Vernon considered their sleeping arrangements "weird. In the mornings her dad would knock on the door. 'Linda, time to go to school! Vern, are you going to work?'"

Soon Linda was pregnant again. This time her father welcomed the news, rattling on about love and family and a church wedding—until Vernon started to apologize for his role in her abortion. "I didn't know about it till after," he blurted. "Oh man, did I feel like a murderer."

Dick Campion's face turned red. He hadn't known who was responsible for Linda's first pregnancy. She had blamed another boy.

"So he kicked me out."

Vernon wasn't ready to move back in with his mother or his grandmother. He went back to sleeping in his truck, looking up at God's constellations, "talking to the heavens." Those conversations could be a joy on clear nights but weren't so inspiring when it rained. "I ended up cussing God out."

He spent three years working construction and doing odd jobs, living here and there, crashing at his grandma's now and then. He got kicked out of the Seventh-day Adventist church in Tyler, Texas—"disfellowshipped"—for having sex with a church elder's fifteen-year-old daughter. He smoked Camels, drank beers he liked to call "suds," and learned to play a guitar his mother bought him. "I taught myself to play before anybody ever tuned that guitar. Once it got tuned, I had to learn all over again." He loved Elvis Presley, the Mamas & the Papas, Johnny Cash, and later Uriah Heep and Foghat. Vernon pictured himself as a rock star, but at the age of twenty-one he was still a nobody with no place to call home. "A wandering bonehead," in his own estimation.

His wandering led him to a religious commune a hundred miles south of Dallas. The Branch Davidians, a splinter group of Seventh-day Adventists, lived there. On a dog-day morning in 1981, Vernon Howell drove up to their retreat ten miles east of Waco. He parked outside the chapel and went looking for Sister Roden.

2

A New Religion

Branch Davidians trace their roots to Victor Tasho Houteff, who dropped out of elementary school in his native Bulgaria and immigrated to America in 1907. Houteff never lost his thick Balkan accent, but he had plenty of good old American get-up-and-go. After settling in Rockford, Illinois, he worked his way from grocer's assistant to grocer to hotelier, then rode the Atchison, Topeka and Santa Fe railroad to Los Angeles. Soon Houteff joined the sales force for Maytag, a new company whose electric washing machines would help fill his pockets with commissions. He also joined the Seventh-day Adventist Church, whose members celebrate the Sabbath on Saturday, the seventh day of their week, and expect Jesus's second coming to be imminent.

Houteff railed against what he viewed as the weakness and worldliness of his fellow Adventists, who responded by kicking him out of their congregation. In 1935, at the age of fifty, he led three dozen followers to a tract of land near Waco, Texas, a medium-sized city on the muddy Brazos River. Like other Seventh-day Adventists, they believed that the end-times predicted in the book of Revelation, the Bible's violent final chapter, would occur in their lifetimes. But the Davidians, as he named his followers, claiming they were true heirs to the biblical House of David, toed a stricter line than other

Seventh-day Adventists. They lived communally and homeschooled their children. They avoided meat, tobacco, alcohol, dancing, and all music except hymns. Houteff dubbed their retreat "Mount Carmel" after the spot in Israel where the prophet Elijah was said to have performed a fiery miracle, calling flame from the sky to prove that Yahweh was truly God. As Davidians knew, the plain below Israel's Mount Carmel was called Armageddon.

The balding, smiling Houteff claimed to be a modern prophet. He interpreted scripture in twice-daily lectures, explaining how his Davidians' numbers would increase from 38 to 144,000, a number representing 12,000 for each of the twelve tribes of Israel, enough to lead them safely through the end-times. His message attracted hundreds of followers.

Two years after founding the sect, the fifty-two-year-old Houteff married Florence Hermanson, who is described in church records as his "helpmeet." She was seventeen. Houteff answered critics who charged that he was "robbing the cradle" by referring them to Abraham, who was said to be eighty-six when he sired a child by Hagar, a slave girl young enough to be his great-granddaughter. "Abraham, the father of the faithful, certainly took to himself a wife much younger," he declared. Florence would serve as her husband's assistant for twenty years, taking down his sermons in shorthand and typing them up.

Houteff died of a heart attack in 1955. His widow took over his role the next day, claiming that his gift of prophecy had passed to her. To prove it, she announced that the apocalypse would come before 1960. In fact, she said, Jesus would return to earth in fire and glory on April 22, 1959.

More than nine hundred Davidians gathered outside Waco in the days leading up to that fateful Wednesday. Some had sold homes and businesses to move to Mount Carmel. On Tuesday night, the eve of the predicted Second Coming, they built campfires and shared what they expected to be their last earthly meals. But midnight passed with no sounding of trumpets, nothing but the howls of coyotes and chirping of crickets. Sister Houteff led prayers. Wednesday's sun rose and set with no sign of the messiah. "Naming a date was Florence's fatal error," says Bill Pitts, a professor of religion at Baylor University who has spent decades studying the Davidians. "Hope faded, and the Davidians began to disperse."

Some held firm in their faith, awaiting the Second Coming through the summer and fall of 1959, raising cows and bartering milk for food and fuel oil. Florence Houteff, their failed prophet, left Mount Carmel in disgrace and disappeared from church records. She would live until 2008, leaving little trace but a grave marker in Vancouver, Washington, that identifies her as Florence Eakin, wife of a Vancouver businessman.

The Davidian remnant looked for a leader. One candidate had a plausible claim to some gift of prophecy: he'd tried to tell them Florence was wrong about the End of Days, but did they listen?

Born in Choctaw territory in 1902, Benjamin Lloyd Roden was five years old when his family's farm became part of the new state of Oklahoma. He grew up to be an oil field roughneck with the square jaw of a prizefighter. His family was Jewish, but Ben Roden was drawn to the evangelical Christianity sweeping the country in his youth. He married Montana-born Lois Scott, another religious searcher, in 1937. He was thirty-five; she was twenty. They attended a Seventh-day Adventist church in Kilgore, Texas, then joined the Davidians after moving to Waco. At that point, he began telling anyone who'd listen that Florence Houteff was a false prophet who didn't know the Second Coming from Shinola. The others ignored him but began listening after his prediction came true. How did Ben Roden know their leader was wrong about the apocalypse? God told him in a dream, he said. He'd been sound asleep when a great wind pulled him out of bed by the cuffs of his pajamas and shook him around the bedroom until he had a vision of himself leading a multitude, a new branch of the Adventist faith.

His sermons drew new believers to Mount Carmel. The Branch Davidians, he called them. Roden assured his followers that the end-times were coming soon, but he would not commit to a date.

He and Lois went on to have six children. Their oldest, George, turned forty in 1978. Ben told church elders that if he were to die before the world ended, George would succeed him as their "God-appointed leader." In a dream, God told him, "Let George do it," as a giant Texas longhorn bestrode the Earth.

George Roden made an unlikely heir apparent. Standing six foot three and weighing some three hundred pounds, he marched around his parents' seventy-seven acres in Tony Lama boots, jeans, and a black Stetson. He believed his dark mustache and goatee made him look intimidating. The .38 holstered on his hip helped, too. George had made a much-ridiculed run for president of the United States in 1976, vowing to bring law, order, and biblical prophecy to the White House. He collected enough signatures to qualify for a presidential primary that Jimmy Carter won with 419,272 votes. Alabama governor George Wallace finished second with 57,594, while 153 voters chose George Roden.

After Ben Roden died in 1978, George told the Branch Davidians, "I am your new prophet." That put church elders in a quandary. They weren't sure George was fit to lead his own life, much less a community of faith. When they said so, he cursed and spat at them. Some thought he might be possessed by demons. In fact, he suffered from Tourette's syndrome and took a handful of medications to control his outbursts. Under stress he would twitch, bang his fist, and yelp obscenities. When the elders expressed doubts about following a preacher who might lace a sermon with "shitfuck" and "cuntpiss," he insisted his medical condition had no bearing on his right of succession, which came directly from God. Who would dare dispute the God-given claim of Benjamin Roden's firstborn son?

His mother would.

Lois Roden had watched and listened while the elders debated George's claim. Now she stepped forward.

Lois had always been more than her husband's helpmeet. In some ways her knowledge of scripture surpassed his. In 1977, the year before Ben died, Lois had made news by proclaiming that the Holy Spirit is female. That third member of the Holy Trinity had appeared to her in "a vision of a shimmering silver angel in feminine form." In an era when TV and newspapers lavished attention on the Equal Rights Amendment and other signs of "women's lib," Lois Roden's claim was newsworthy. The *Dallas Times Herald* ran her photo—a lean, unadorned woman in a black frock, with gray hair and over-sized glasses that magnified her eyes, cradling a live white dove in her hands—under the headline "Holy Spirit Is a Woman." The other two members of the Trinity might be male, Sister Roden said, but a hundred generations of scholars and worshippers had missed the plain fact that the biblical word for the Holy Spirit, "Shekinah" in Old Testament Hebrew, is a feminine term. The Jews had known that, she said—Kabbalah held many references to this mother-sister figure.

To spread this good news, she needed a pulpit. Lois urged the elders to set aside her husband's succession plan and name her as their God-appointed leader.

"We searched our souls," says Clive Doyle, a Seventh-day Adventist who had heard of the Rodens' teachings and moved from his native Australia to join them. Doyle and the others looked on as George twitched and railed at his mother. "One interesting sidelight is how George cussed when his fits came on. He'd spit and call you the f-word, but something always kept him from taking the Lord's name in vain."

The elders acknowledged that Ben Roden had chosen George to be his successor. "We considered that," Doyle says. "We considered everything. What it came down to was, George was insane."

The elders took a vote. They named Lois the Branch Davidians' new prophetess, setting off a war between the Rodens.

After George and several gun-toting followers occupied Mount Carmel, Lois petitioned a state court for a restraining order against him. Judge Bill Logue of Texas's Nineteenth District Court granted it. George then sued his mother for stealing his prophetic birthright. The judge wasn't sure what to make of that claim. Logue, who presided over many of the Rodens' legal battles, called Branch Davidians "the most litigious bunch" he'd ever encountered. In private notes, he admitted preferring George's broad shoulders and ten-gallon hat to his mother's schoolmarmish appearance, describing Lois as "very homely. No makeup." He cut off both sides' testimony when it veered into religion. "They would go off the deep end of scripture," the judge recalled. "These were not mainstream Protestants."

George added Judge Logue to his growing list of enemies. Clive Doyle, who served as publisher of Lois's newsletter, *SHEkinah*, also made George's list after locking him out of their print shop. Furious, George used power tools to remove the print-shop doors and stop the presses.

In time, George Roden settled into an uneasy coexistence with his mother's followers. Lois took pity on him, allowing her son to live in a double-wide trailer on the property, and their community began growing again. By 1981 there was a core group of about a hundred living in trailers and rickety houses at Mount Carmel and well over a thousand other Branch Davidians scattered around the world, with clusters in England, Israel, Australia, New Zealand, and the Philippines. That was the year a disheveled, unshaven pilgrim came speeding up the gravel drive from Double-EE Ranch Road.

3

Sleeping with a Prophetess

Vernon Howell rolled in like blustery weather. He talked a mile a minute and had a habit of staring people down, then flashing a smile and hugging them. In his first meeting with Lois Roden, he said he'd heard about her teaching—what Adventist in Texas hadn't?—and thought it might be for him. He also confessed to being obsessed with sex. If there was no female willing to satisfy his urges, he admitted, he sometimes committed Onan's sin. He prayed to rise above fleshly desires, but the devil was hard to resist.

Sister Roden said he was welcome to stay but would need to tame his desires. The elders assigned him a room and a cot, and Vernon became a Branch Davidian.

He was devout in his own way but not devout enough to spend what was left of his youth bunking with a bunch of snoring, farting men. At first he did chores and washed dishes like the others. When Lois preached, he listened with rapt attention. "He followed her around like a lovesick puppy," another resident recalled. Over the next year, all his Bible study came in handy: he became Lois's prize pupil, quoting her favorite scripture verses, talking about his visions of the Kingdom to come. At some point—no living person knows exactly when—he joined the sixty-seven-year-old prophetess in her bed.

She said young Vernon had a spark to him. He'd picked up on her teachings faster than anyone else. Soon he was correcting the elders when they misquoted scripture. Now and then he'd make a sly reference to sleeping with Sister Roden, quoting Isaiah: "*And I went unto the prophetess; and she conceived, and bare a son.*" If he could impregnate her, he said, it would be a miracle "right up there with Abraham," who the Bible says sired a son with his ninety-year-old wife, Sarah. Vernon reckoned he had an advantage: "I'm only twenty-two. Abraham was a hundred when he did it!" He identified with polygamous patriarchs. "Abraham had more than one wife. David had more than one. Solomon had *a thousand*," he said. "How about that? Can you imagine Solomon taking all his wives to McDonald's? How much would *that* cost?"

He renounced music, rock and roll most of all. "The devil's music," he called it. Lois said no, he should follow his heart. Didn't the Bible say the sound of stringed instruments was pleasing to God? Didn't Psalms tell people to "make a joyful noise" and "come into His presence with singing"? What if Vernon Howell led young people to Jesus and the Holy Spirit with Christian rock and roll? Wouldn't that make it God's music?

Like his mother, Lois bought him a guitar. Soon he was singing and playing Christian rock, including songs he wrote himself. He couldn't read music, but picked out chords and committed them to memory. "Like a lot of guitarists, he just jammed and figured it out himself," one bandmate recalled. According to Branch Davidian Jaime Castillo, "David would say, 'If Satan can inspire musicians to write all those songs we all grew up with, don't you think God has the ability to inspire men to rock and roll?'"

With jeans hanging off his bony hips, with straggly hair and a screw-you sneer on his face, Howell looked the part of a rock musician. All he lacked was talent. "As a guitarist, he sucked," says David Thibodeau, a member of the band he formed in those years. "At least at first. Then he got better. That was his way. It was the same with cars, motorcycles, guns. He'd start by getting a feel for something, then work his butt off to master it. Here's a guy who started out with a Bible from his grandma and what does he do? Practically memorizes it."

Vernon's guitar became the first of a collection that would feature a pair of pure-white electric Charvel Jacksons he named Adam and Eve. He spent hours watching videos of guitar gods like Joe Satriani and Steve Vai. "He told us we were going to take over the Christian-rock scene and get famous, but that was his ego talking," Thibodeau says. "We were regional talent at best."

He was faring no better in bed. Months passed with no sign that he had impregnated the postmenopausal prophetess. Lois told him she'd conceived with him—a pregnancy test proved it, she said—but miscarried. Meanwhile her son George was still claiming to be the Davidians' true prophet, calling Vernon "a pervert and rapist." George sued; Lois countersued, eventually beat him in court, and tolerated George's angry fits as long as he didn't shoot anybody.

In 1983, the year she turned sixty-seven, Lois took Vernon with her to Israel, his first trip overseas. Like other evangelical Christians, they expected events in modern Israel to set the Last Days in motion. Vernon was developing a theory that had Jesus returning to Earth by 1995. But while he and Lois toured the Holy Land, her son commanded the pulpit at Mount Carmel. Peering down at the congregation, George railed at the creature he called "Vermin Howell," who he said spent nights "raping my mother" and practicing "a diabolical act," cunnilingus.

Whatever Lois and her young lover were doing in bed, it was about to end. Upon their return to Texas, Vernon told Lois that he had fixed his eye on someone else.

Rachel Jones was the daughter of a church elder. She was fourteen. Twenty-four-year-old Vernon said she reminded him of a girl described in the Song of Solomon: "*a little sister, and she hath no breasts.*" Years later, in a meandering phone call with an FBI agent, he would rhapsodize about Rachel's "long, beautiful hair," calling her "a *very* beautiful girl." In January 1984, with her parents' permission, he married Rachel in a civil ceremony in Waco. He assured her father that she wasn't too young for sex, pointing out that she was the same age as Vernon's own mother when he was born.

Lois Roden was heartbroken. During one Bible study, she had blurted about her carnal relations with her protégé, describing their union as part of God's plan to create a generation of leaders in time for the coming apocalypse. Now she slept alone.

Soon Rachel was pregnant. Late in her pregnancy, her husband returned to Israel with her—Rachel's first trip outside Texas. The part-time carpenter and his young wife planned a side trip to Bethlehem in hopes that their baby might be born there. Before that could happen, Vernon had a vision. Climbing Mount Zion outside the walls of ancient Jerusalem, he saw the universe whole and heard a booming voice, he said, as loud and clear as if God had the world's best sound system. The visitation filled him with "complete knowledge" of physics and astronomy, including the knowledge that angels traveled in UFOs.

Back home in Texas, George Roden was busy chasing Vernon's followers out of Mount Carmel, waving an M1 rifle. He sidelined his mother, now ailing with cancer, and started calling the property "Rodenville." He closed prayers by saying, "in the name of George B. Roden, amen." He took out an ad in the *Waco Tribune-Herald* declaring himself the Branch Davidians' rightful leader. The ad sparked a new lawsuit from his mother. George countersued, urging Judge Logue to reject all claims from Lois, who he said was "under the spell of V. W. Howell . . . She is not capable of managing the property, or even preserving her own life from these cut-throats, motorcycle gangs, rock and roll musicians, and Satan worshippers." If Vernon wasn't stopped, George wrote, there could be "a Jim Jones–type massacre" at Mount Carmel.

This was the first reference tying Branch Davidians to Jones's Peoples Temple, a sect that had established a commune in Guyana a decade before. In 1978, with federal agents looking into sexual and other abuses at Jonestown, the Reverend Jones led a last rite in which his followers drank grape Flavor Aid spiked with cyanide. News accounts called it "Kool-Aid," and "drinking the Kool-Aid" came to mean blind obedience to a leader's idea. Soon there were morbid jokes about the mass suicide at Jonestown. One asked, What do you call a picture of Jim Jones? Answer: the Last Sipper.

In fact, Jones never drank the Flavor Aid. He watched more than nine hundred of his poisoned followers until he was certain they were dying, then used a pistol to shoot himself in the head.

◇◇◇◇

Upon returning from Israel, Vernon and Rachel collected their belongings and left Mount Carmel. Rather than risk a shooting war with George, they decamped to forty remote acres in Palestine, Texas, ninety miles from Mount Carmel, along with two dozen of his followers. During the first weeks of their exile in Palestine, pronounced *Pal-es-teen*, they slept in tents and buses near a towering three-trunked pine they called the "Trinity Tree." The men removed the buses' seats to provide more living space. After that they spent weeks building eight-by-sixteen-foot plywood shacks that shivered in winter winds. A tin-roofed shanty served as a communal kitchen. "It was rustic, but fun," recalled Bonnie, Vernon's mother, who joined the Branch Davidians that year. "We'd have Bible studies under the trees, where the bus seats were arranged in a circle." She would drive back and forth to Dallas or Tyler to clean houses and offices, returning after midnight, "and I'd wash up. You can take a pretty good bath with a gallon of water."

Their commune lacked electricity, running water, even outhouses. "We lacked everything but faith," recalls Sheila Martin, a Boston-born Adventist who joined the group in 1984. Like Bonnie, she made do with sponge baths and the occasional shower under a water jug poked full of holes and suspended from a tree limb. The Davidians used buckets as chamber pots. Each morning they lugged the buckets to a clearing in the woods, where a shovel stuck out of the ground. "Someone would start off by digging a hole. We'd empty our bucket, cover that hole up, and dig another one. The next person would cover theirs and dig a hole for the next person."

Few believers complained. "We were *lucky*," Martin says. "We had some of the best Bible studies you ever heard."

Despite his scruffy look and the body odor he sometimes gave off—like everybody at Palestine—Vernon's zeal and mastery of scripture convinced the others he was the latest in a line of spiritual leaders dating back to the Old Testament prophets. During Bible meetings, they gathered around him for sips of grape juice and bites of a cracker, which they called "emblems" of Jesus's Last Supper, followed by an hour or more of Bible study. "Jesus is fixin' to return," he promised in his Texas twang. "*If* we pave the way." As for their exile from Mount Carmel, "This here is our home for now. Here's where we start building an army for God."

His followers were seeking an understanding of God's plans for the world and for them. Many would swear no other preacher came close to the way Vernon Howell could harmonize the Bible's often-conflicting messages into a satisfying whole. Nobody made scripture come alive the way he did. In a vast, confounding world, he gave his Branch Davidians a crucial role to play in the end-times that were just around the bend. He gave their lives meaning.

<><><>

Fifteen-year-old Rachel gave birth to a son in March 1985. They named the boy Cyrus after Cyrus the Great, the Persian king who freed the Jews from slavery in the sixth century BCE. Cyrus Ben Joseph Howell was a happy child with straw-colored hair like his mother's, hair his parents let grow until it spilled over his shoulders. Except for trimming his bangs to keep them out of his eyes, they would not allow Cyrus's hair to be cut through all eight years of his life.

That summer Vernon drove to New Orleans for the 1985 General Conference of Seventh-day Adventists, held at the Superdome. He buttonholed conference-goers outside the stadium, handing out pamphlets detailing how their religion was wrong. *I Am the Son of God*, one began. *You ministers will lament your foolishness. Your lost flock will tear you to pieces . . . PREPARE TO MEET THY GOD.*

His flyers convinced nobody. He watched Adventists wad them up and drop them, then remembered what Lois had said about music. He sped back to Palestine, a 430-mile trip he made in six hours, packed up his guitar and amps, and made it back in time for the conference's last day. "He set up on a walkway outside the Superdome," his mother recalled, "and played for the Seventh-day Adventists." Some of them stopped to listen. Some even took his pamphlets home with them.

Three months later, Lois Roden died of breast cancer. The elders had no doubt that Vernon was next in line, but George wouldn't give up. He still controlled the property at Rodenville, as only he called it, preaching fiery apocalypse. And he was still spoiling for a fight with Vernon, who was said to have problems at Palestine.

According to Bonnie, "Rachel was down in the dumps." Some of the women knew why: after Vernon and Rachel returned from Israel, he had told her that the voice he heard on Mount Zion commanded him to have a child with her little sister, Michele. "Rachel was devastated." Michele Jones, born on the Fourth of July in 1974, was eleven years old. Vernon claimed to be "surprised" to learn that God wanted him to "go into" her.

The girls' father, church elder Perry Jones, had no objections. Wasn't the Virgin Mary said to have been only twelve or thirteen when she was betrothed to Joseph? If God wanted both of Perry's daughters to bear Vernon's children, he wasn't going to say no. "Perry told me his younger daughter was happy" to be the prophet's choice, Thibodeau recalled, "but I heard from the women that Michele was very distressed." The issue was resolved dramatically—even miraculously, according to Rachel, who was already pregnant with a second child. Rachel saw in a dream that her husband "might be destroyed, even die," if he refused the divine command. She agreed to share him with her little sister.

One Davidian remembered Vernon's "approaching Michele in the dead of night." The word "approaching" was a euphemism. Describing the encounter later as if he found it amusing, Vernon told some of the men that he'd invited Michele, who had recently celebrated her twelfth birthday, into his bed "to get warm." When he tried to pull down her underwear, she resisted. He kept going, he said, because God told him to.

Michele would go on to have three daughters by him—Serenity Sea and a pair of twins, Chica and Little One, all named by their father—by the time she turned eighteen. Rachel had two: Cyrus and his little sister, Star, born in 1987. Soon Vernon would claim other mates, though Rachel would always be his only legal wife. He selected male followers—his "Mighty Men," he called them—to serve as his unofficial wives' legal husbands. (His mother described them as the women's "cover husbands.") Thibodeau, a drummer in his band, became Michele's legal spouse without ever sleeping with her. Another band member, Jaime Castillo, scoffed at talk that Howell was robbing cradles, insisting that Michele was "a big girl for a twelve-year-old, and she didn't have the little-girl mentality. Not all girls between twelve and thirteen years old are little girls."

◇◇◇◇

George Roden also married unofficially in 1987. As Amo Bishop Roden, his common-law wife, recalled, "I believe he's only been with two women in his life." She saw her husband as sincerely religious if troubled, particularly by his obsession with this Howell fellow. Later that year, George issued a challenge to Vernon: Which of them could raise a Branch Davidian from the dead?

George used a backhoe to dig a coffin out of the burial ground at Mount Carmel. Inside lay Anna Hughes, interred there since 1968. Then Roden phoned his rival, daring him to bring her back to life.

As Howell recalled, "He challenged me to a duel of resurrection. I said, 'Not today, George,' and I hung up the phone." If there was going to be a miracle-off, he was willing to let the other guy go first.

Three times George Roden tried to resurrect Anna Hughes. Failing that, he used the backhoe to carry her coffin to a maintenance shed. After that, George took to patrolling the grounds with his .38 and an Uzi submachine gun, warning his dwindling congregation to watch out for Vernon and his pack of heretics. Even longtime loyalists began to ask if his mental troubles were tipping into paranoia. George said no, he could see the future plain as day: Vernon Howell was planning a sneak attack on Mount Carmel.

He was right.

4

....

Madman in Waco

As soon as he heard of George Roden's efforts to resurrect Anna Hughes, Vernon huddled with Wayne Martin. A lawyer who had joined the Branch Davidians along with his wife, Sheila, and their five children in 1985, Martin had been one of the few Black members of his class at Harvard Law School. He suffered what he called "a spiritual crisis" after their son Jamie was stricken with bacterial meningitis, leaving the boy blind and disabled. "A judgment," Wayne called it. After that, he devoted his life and career to his religion.

Soft-spoken Wayne Martin wore his hair in a tightly trimmed Afro. He wore wire-rimmed bifocals. He was the only Branch Davidian that Judge Logue didn't view as a religious nut. Logue described him as "bright and well prepared, very much a gentleman," noting that the only Black attorney who often appeared in his courtroom wore a jacket and tie even on the hottest Texas afternoons.

Martin accepted Vernon Howell as a divinely inspired spiritual leader. After checking the relevant statutes, he told Vernon that under Texas law it was illegal to disinter a body without a permit. They went to the police, who agreed that it would be a crime if George Roden dug up a coffin at Mount Carmel. If there was evidence that such a thing had happened, they might investigate. Vernon said, "Come on,

I'll show you," but Waco's police had better things to do than help one religious kook score points against another.

Howell sped back to Palestine. "We need evidence," he said.

He and seven followers including Dave Jones, Rachel and Michele's brother, spent the next several days preparing for a nighttime raid. They cleaned and loaded their rifles. They bought camouflage fatigues, combat boots, and flashlights at Kmart. They packed cameras to take photos of Anna Hughes's body. Shortly after midnight on November 2, 1987, they blackened their faces with charcoal, loaded their gear into a van, and drove to a spot a half mile from Mount Carmel. From there they crept into the brush outside Roden's compound.

Roden kept several mastiffs tied up outside, watchdogs that barked and howled at the intruders. George came out in his underwear, toting his submachine gun.

"Who goes there?"

The invaders hit the deck. "We commenced to crawl on our bellies all the way out to Double-EE Ranch Road," Vernon remembered. Then they hunkered down for the night. At first light they sneaked behind the property and peeked into huts and sheds, looking for Anna Hughes.

Amo Roden had seen the long-buried woman in the maintenance shed. After twenty years underground, "Her hair was still there, but she was just a skull. Yeah, a skeleton, but her hair was still full."

Before the raiders could locate the corpse, the dogs' barking brought George out again. Vernon spotted him "with his black cowboy hat on, he's got his Uzi side-strapped to his right shoulder, just strutting as proud as could be."

Amo was in the kitchen of the Rodens' double-wide, heating a pot of beans, when the chatter of her husband's Uzi startled her. "I could hear the bullets whine," she said. Still she kept cooking. "The way I figured, if anybody lived, they'd probably be hungry."

Vernon and his men fired back. They later swore they were only trying to scare crazy George, not gun him down. In Howell's recollection, the skirmish "sounded like Vietnam. *Bam bam bam!* George's eyes get real big and he starts backpedaling his fat butt as fast as

I've seen any running back do it. I mean, beyond NFL pro! I says, 'Throw your gun down, George!' He hides behind this tree and then I hear *zap zap*. Uzi bullets sound like a jet going through the air. He's zappin' off rounds when we hear sirens in the distance. I'm thinking, 'Praise the Lord, here comes the sheriff's department!'"

A neighbor down the road had phoned 911. Amo kept clear of her kitchen window as gunfire continued. George got nicked in the thumb and belly by a raider's bullet that ricocheted off the stock of his Uzi. He would claim that the Israeli-made weapon saved his life, a sign that the God of Israel favored him.

One of Vernon's men, Stan Sylva, described a less dramatic scene. "We were not trying to kill George," Sylva testified later. "The tree he was behind was not real big, and George's stomach stuck out past it! We were firing over his head so we could keep him pinned down without hurting him."

At 10:21 a.m., six sheriff's deputies rolled up and disarmed the combatants. Vernon was annoyed to be forced to the ground, kicked by the deputies, and bitten by red ants running up his pants. Worse was seeing Roden go free while the raiders were indicted—not for trespassing or disturbing the peace, which Vernon might have copped to, but for attempted murder. They faced decades in prison.

During a ten-day trial in April 1988, the shaggy-haired prophet, dressed in a suit for once, made sure the gallery held rows of his supporters. Branch Davidian girls and women, including several he was sleeping with, sat in the gallery. Dressed demurely in their shapeless frocks, they whispered prayers during the proceedings.

At one point a prosecutor displayed segments of red fabric recovered from the crime scene, describing them as the invaders' "signaling devices." With Davidian Paul Fatta on the witness stand, the lawyer held up a shard of red flannel. "Isn't this the way you communicated in regards to the way you would move on the property?" he asked. "So you could flank Mister Roden and kill him?"

Fatta tried not to smile. The prosecutor had broken a cardinal rule of courtroom tactics: never ask a question if you don't already know the answer. "Do you really want to know?" Fatta asked.

"Oh, yes."

The piece of fabric the lawyer was waving, Fatta testified, came from a checkered shirt the raiders had torn into pieces while they waited for sunup. "We used them as toilet paper."

⬦⬦⬦⬦

Clean-shaven and soft-spoken in court, defendant Howell accepted his brief imprisonment during the proceedings. This trial, he said, was his cross to bear. Like Paul the Apostle writing to early Christians from a Roman prison, he was determined to make use of his confinement, working out his view of the world and his future. Citing Isaiah, he claimed to be a prophet *"brought as a lamb to the slaughter . . . and taken from prison."* Tyrants might jail him, he said, but they would learn a hard lesson.

His arrest had left George Roden in position to assume the prophet's role. Instead, incensed at the judge's allowing Vernon's raiders to present their case in court, Roden fired off a letter warning the judge and court officers that God would "send you herpes and AIDS the seven last plagues and shove them up you goddam bastards asses." Jailed for contempt of court, George claimed to be a victim of "a Communist conspiracy" aided by the pope.

While he was out on bail early in 1988, Vernon seized his chance to turn the tables. After lawyer Martin discovered that George Roden owed more than $60,000 in property taxes, Vernon turned to a few affluent Branch Davidians who helped him pay off the debt. In the spring of 1988 he and his followers, weeping and shouting praises to God, reoccupied the retreat. They found Anna Hughes's casket and put it to use in the trial, carrying it up the courthouse steps. In a macabre touch, Vernon tied a pink ribbon around the skeleton's neck "to dress it up."

To Roden's astonishment, seven of the eight raiders were acquitted of trying to kill him. Jurors deadlocked on attempted-murder charges against Vernon Howell, leading the judge to declare a mistrial in his case, and the man George Roden hated most went free. Some of the jurors hugged Howell on their way out of the courtroom. A month later the district attorney dismissed all charges against him.

Roden promptly sued Vernon and his followers for $10 million, claiming they were illegally occupying Mount Carmel and "besmirching" his legacy. After his suit was dismissed, he fired off a newsletter to everyone on the Davidians' worldwide mailing list, an all-caps account he called "HISTORY OF THE CONFLICT BETWEEN GEORGE B RODEN AND VERNON W HOWELL." Accusing church elders of denying his birthright because they "THOURLEY DETESTED ME," he claimed the elders had been "DOOPED," calling the raid a "TERRORIST ATTACK ON RODENVILLE, TEXAS" to determine "WHO WOULD BE THE KING OF THE WORLD."

◇◇◇◇

Thirty-five British and Australian converts moved to Waco that year. The new arrivals joined the Martins, Joneses, Vernon's mother, Bonnie, and more than fifty others in a redesigned chapel where they listened to Vernon's vivid discourses on the secret messages God had hidden in the Bible.

Between meals and Bible study, the Branch Davidians improved the buildings and grounds at Mount Carmel and tended the cows, sheep, goats, and chickens that made the retreat nearly self-sufficient. Some evangelized around town, handing out pamphlets and tapes of "Madman in Waco," the latest tune from Vernon's band. In a nasal whine he sang of *"a night in the darkness, risking our life for the Lord, helpin' the women and children . . ."* The prophet who bedded pubescent girls in his flock had written the song about George Roden, painting George as demon-driven. *"This is for the little children,"* he sang. *"God knows how it should be, stars and stripes a'flyin' till there's justice and liberty. There's a madman livin' in Waco, a madman livin' in Waco."*

He and his band, Messiah, played in Mount Carmel's chapel, where they hooked up amps and shook the walls. Sometimes they gigged at Cue Sticks, a pool hall behind the Kmart on Old Dallas Highway, where he and his posse had geared up for their raid on Rodenville. Steve Schneider, his right-hand man, served as the band's manager, handing out business cards embossed with the sword-and-starburst logo of "Messiah Productions." Howell often played a guitar painted with a garish image of himself nailed to a cross, surrounded by angels, with a half-naked Mary Magdalene at his feet. If a set went well, with the crowd dancing to "Madman in Waco" or the band's passable cover of the Knack's "My Sharona," he might buy pitchers of suds for the house. Most of their numbers were Christian rock tinged with metal. "We didn't have a playlist," drummer Thibodeau remembers. "David liked to wing it. We'd get up and play 'Madman in Waco,' which kind of served as our 'Brown Sugar.'"

Roden fired back with a newsletter to everyone on Mount Carmel's worldwide mailing list. "*The seed of the adulterer is a bastard*," he wrote. "*We know he is a rock'n'roller musician and a satan worshipper who use their tongues for sex. If you have ever seen the rock stars called KISS, you will see them jut out their tongues which is their symbol for oral sex.*" As for Vermin Howell, "*the rod he is using to rule the nations is his genitals, the rod below his belt.*" With Mount Carmel thriving, no one paid much attention.

Roden had had his fill of Waco. After his jail term was up, he packed his clothes, Bibles, and guns and left town, leaving his wife behind. "He went to Odessa to stay with Wayman Dale Adair," Amo recalled, "who he subsequently killed, which resulted in his scholarship to the laughing academy."

Adair, who went by Dale, had turned up at Mount Carmel a few years before, telling the others that George Roden was no prophet and Vernon Howell wasn't, either. He knew because he himself was the next true prophet. In Odessa, he and Roden split the rent on a month-to-month duplex. Dale got used to his roommate's tics while Roden, who believed himself to be a descendant of King David, tolerated Dale's anti-Semitic rants and Hitler salutes—until a voice told him that Vernon had sent Dale to kill him.

On October 15, 1989, Roden brewed a pot of coffee. He handed Dale a cup, waited while he finished it, and asked if he'd like another. Dale said yes, he would, but instead of refilling his cup, George gave him a whack in the head with a hatchet. He split his skull, then took Dale's own pistol and shot him with it.

Roden was found incompetent to stand trial for murder, due to mental illness, and committed to a hospital for the criminally insane in a town whose name must have rung cruelly in his ears: Vernon.

"Next thing I hear," Judge Logue recalled, "he's over there at Vernon State Hospital. They examine him every six or twelve months, and a psychiatrist says whether he's sane or not. Once they say the cotton picker is sane, he's back on the street."

Officially restored to competence, Roden was charged with Adair's murder. He represented himself in court, pleading not guilty by reason of insanity, and won the case. Acquitted but admittedly insane, he returned to the mental hospital for an indefinite term.

He escaped several times. Transferred to a psychiatric ward at Big Spring, Texas, he escaped again, turning up days later at the Israeli consulate in New York City, saying he was Jewish and that the Palestine Liberation Organization was trying to kill him. Shipped home to Texas, he wound up back at Vernon State Hospital.

Roden would outlive the man he hated most. After ten years at Vernon State, he would disappear from the hospital one night. Back in Waco, Judge Logue's phone rang.

"Judge, I hate to bother you," a court officer said. "It's George Roden. Seeing as how you're one of his chief enemies, we thought we'd better tell you he escaped."

Soon Logue's phone rang again. "Nothing to worry about—they got him." Searchers had found Roden hanging from a fence, dead of a heart attack. According to one Branch Davidian, "George was escaping, climbing the chain-link fence around the hospital, when he got his foot stuck. He hung there till his heart gave out."

◇◇◇◇

In August 1990, ten months after Roden killed Dale Adair, Vernon traveled to Pomona, California, one of several Davidian outposts he was visiting that summer. He made a side trip to the local courthouse, where, unshaven as usual, with his shirt unbuttoned far enough to show chest hair, he filed the paperwork required to change his name.

According to the petition he signed that day, he was changing his legal name from Vernon Wayne Howell to David Koresh because he was "an entertainer and wishes to use the new name for publicity purposes."

5

....

Planet Koresh

The Branch Davidians' flat, windy property measured seventy-seven acres, but they spent almost all their time in a two-acre compound some of them called the Anthill. They built it in two years after reclaiming Mount Carmel from George Roden in 1988. With Koresh overseeing the work, they turned what a neighbor remembered as "truckloads of lumber and sheet rock, hundreds of pounds of nails, miles of electrical wire, and enough sand and gravel to fill an Olympic-size pool" into a short-term home for him and 120 followers. Their plywood walls wouldn't need to last long because Jesus was coming back soon. Koresh laid out the floor plans and oversaw construction of what he dubbed "Ranch Apocalypse."

David Thibodeau, the resident smart-ass, had his own name for Mount Carmel. He called it "Planet Koresh."

The self-appointed prophet led a diverse group of more than a hundred. Many of his followers were Black, including a contingent of "Afro-Brits" who had picked up stakes in England and moved to Waco. There were Australians, Caribbean islanders, several Hawaiians, and others of Asian, Mexican, and Native American descent, plus Pablo Cohen, an Argentina-born Israeli the others called their "Taco Jew." To any Caucasians who didn't cotton to foreigners or Blacks, Koresh said, "Don't be flaunting yourself or what country you are from. Don't be flaunting your education or the color of your skin. God's not into that, and we won't tolerate it here."

A dented mailbox out front read BRANCH DAVIDIAN CHURCH, but there wasn't much mail for believers who saw themselves as a breed apart from millions of "mainstreamers" who went to church on Sundays. Koresh considered mainstream Christianity little more than a modern convenience. "You go to a religious social club once a week and act like a yo-yo. Stand up, sit down, stand up. Christianity two thousand years ago wasn't like that."

His preaching mixed biblical versification with homespun wisdom. "I reckon we're up against Babylon," he said, "and the odds ain't on our side!" For true believers, his Bible studies were better than any movie. Livingstone Fagan, one of the Afro-Brits, had been studying for his master's in theology at England's Newbold College when Koresh gave a talk there. "In three hours I perceived more Biblical truths than I had done in the eight years I'd been involved with organized religion," said Fagan, who moved to Texas to join Koresh's flock. According to another Davidian, Rita Riddle, "I learned more with him in one night than in a lifetime of going to church." Koresh made recruiting trips to Australia and Hawaii, often captivating his listeners with a dramatic new vision of Seventh-day Adventism.

His writings were strewn with errors—"maby" for "maybe," "manny" or "menny" for many, references to man's "mortle sole." But when his followers gathered on the tiers of Mount Carmel's chapel, each following along in his or her Bible as he preached, they were transfixed. As Branch Davidian Kathy Schroeder put it, "We believed prophecy was being fulfilled. To see the fulfillment of God's words, spoken thousands of years ago, was very exciting."

Sheila Martin: "He wove it all together, explaining it all. Was he a showman? Very much so. He told us and showed us that God was real, we could trust Him and we didn't have to be afraid, whatever was getting ready to happen."

Clive Doyle: "As David himself said, with his limited education he could never have had the knowledge he had. Not without help. I believe God was speaking through him."

David Thibodeau: "People talk about his charisma. Charisma my ass—he was a plain old country boy. People think we were a bunch of fanatics following this 'charismatic' leader, this radical who hypnotized us. It wasn't like that. He was just a dude, but he had a sort of genius for getting under your skin. Why did we follow him? Mainly because he had a deeper understanding of scripture than anyone I ever met."

Doyle: "People ask why we followed David Koresh. I say, What if you lived two thousand years ago? You're a fisherman. Jesus walks up and says, 'Follow me.' That's who we were."

Thibodeau: "Were we a cult? I don't like the c-word, but I can tell you that we were inspired. Can you imagine what that feels like? How good it feels to have a purpose in life?"

Koresh's teachings revolved around Revelation, the Bible's hair-raising climax, with its Marvel Comics images of God looking down from an emerald throne while Four Horsemen named Death, Famine, War, and Conquest gallop under stars falling from the sky. In the soon-to-come Last Days, he preached, a man would rise to shepherd a chosen few to the Kingdom of Heaven. That leader need not be a paragon of virtue, as Fagan and other religiously trained Davidians knew from their readings of scripture. The messiah could be a sinner or even a dyslexic former "retard," provided he could "open" the Seven Seals of Revelation, which meant interpreting God's plan for the end of time. Like King Arthur's pulling a sword from a stone, this was a task only one human could perform. "*I saw in the right hand of the one seated on the throne a book . . . sealed with seven seals,*" wrote John the Divine, the first-century evangelist credited with writing Revelation, "*and I saw a mighty angel proclaiming with a loud voice, 'Who is worthy to open the book, and to loose the seals thereof?'*"

Koresh never claimed to be a saint. He said he wasn't the original Jesus but a twentieth-century Christ, a "sinful messiah" for a sinful era. "If the Bible is true, then I'm Christ," he told a reporter who came digging around his Anthill. "But what's so great about being Christ? A man of sorrow acquainted with grief." Asked if he was brainwashing the other Davidians, he asked, "Doesn't Christ brainwash us? He gets rid of the filth and puts in the good."

He liked testing his followers' faith. One day he drove some of the women to a laundromat and dropped them off with a warning: "Do the laundry—don't you go shopping at Walmart." They got the laundry done with time to spare. "And yes, we visited Walmart," Sheila Martin remembers. "But we got back in time for afternoon worship. And he had the gate closed. He comes out and asks, 'Did you listen to me? Or did you have a nice vacation from God?' In a way it wasn't fair, but David had his rules." Life at Mount Carmel was "fun," she says, "as long as we were obedient."

Doyle recalls a Bible class in which Koresh told the youngest girls to give him their favorite dolls. All but one girl complied. "I wanna keep my baby!" she said. He collected the other dolls, then poured out a bag full of brand-new ones, the toys every girl wanted that year. "They all got a brand-new doll, all but the girl who held on to hers. David said, 'You didn't trust me. You made a choice against me.'"

◇◇◇◇

Waco firearms dealer Henry McMahon admired Koresh's work ethic. "At first he knew nothing about guns. At the end he knew more than I did," McMahon said. According to Thibodeau, "He loved taking weapons apart, cleaning and greasing them, reassembling them. It was a sensual pleasure, a feeling for the way things work." Koresh could strip a gun and reassemble it in seconds. He knew enough about night-vision scopes to prefer cheap but effective $750 infrared models to Starlight scopes that cost up to ten times as much. The scruffy prophet was the same way with car engines, often working under the hood of his gleaming black turbocharged 1968 Camaro, holding forth on Psalms or Revelation while country music played on the tape deck. His band played nothing but rock, but he liked to sing along with Merle Haggard or Randy Travis while he worked.

Thibodeau smiles at the thought of one of their moneymaking schemes from those days: "We discovered gun shows!"

Guns were part of life in Texas. With a population of 17 million and more than 65 million registered firearms, the Lone Star State had more guns than any other. In the early 1990s, with Congress debating new limits on gun sales, the Branch Davidians began attending gun shows all over the state. As arms dealer McMahon later told ATF agents, Koresh "bought guns as an investment. He believed that if federal gun-control proposals became law, prices for semiautomatic firearms purchased before the ban would double overnight." Koresh haggled over purchases, often insisting on mint-condition weapons still in boxes from their manufacturers. "He was buying guns to resell, not to use," McMahon said. Marketing their wares at gun shows, the Davidians sold secondhand Russian AK-47s, Israeli Uzis, gas masks, and ammo vests labeled "David Koresh Survival Wear." Hunting jackets made by Mount Carmel seamstresses came complete with dummy grenades sewn into the fabric to make them look extra-deadly. And when the price of AK-47s topped Koresh's most optimistic prophecy, shooting from $500 to $2,000, he and his flock cleaned up. Gun-show profits paid for a swimming pool at Mount Carmel as well as dirt bikes, go-carts, and a 52-inch wide-screen TV for the chapel.

After that, Koresh hosted movie nights, screening *Apocalypse Now*, *Full Metal Jacket*, and other Vietnam War films for his followers, young and old, "to get y'all ready for the battles ahead." According to a former Davidian, he called war movies "training films." Another favorite was *The Lawnmower Man*—"a cult classic," he called it, about a "retarded" hero with superhuman powers. He also loved MTV, "especially if Madonna was on," Thibodeau recalled. Koresh believed that after his preaching made him famous, his favorite pop star would join his harem at Mount Carmel. He claimed God had spoken to him in a dream, saying, "I will give thee Madonna."

◇◇◇◇

"Every time David went somewhere, at least five or six people followed him," his mother said. "Especially girls." He might take a few young women for a ride or drive some of the men to the Chelsea Street Pub in West Waco "to kick back and swallow some suds." A pitcher of Miller High Life later, he might let the men order another, instructing one of them to phone Mount Carmel and tell the women they were free to enjoy a wine cooler or two. He banned smoking entirely except when he lit up, justifying his Marlboro Lights with a description of God in Psalm 18: "*There went up a smoke out of His nostrils.*" Koresh alone decided who could break the rules and when.

On Friday nights the women welcomed the Sabbath by "dressing up a little," one follower said. "They wore their best sweaters, maybe a bow in their hair, even earrings." In Koresh's view, every Branch Davidian female belonged to him. When church elder Doyle's fourteen-year-old daughter, Shari, became one of the prophet's "wives," he wondered, "Is this God's will, or just horny old David?" Still he agreed to the match. As Doyle put it, "God asks his messengers to do some weird stuff."

Horny old David sometimes brought sex talk into the chapel. Gladys Ottman, a Canadian follower, recalled sitting in a circle during Bible studies when Koresh asked which of them masturbated or had tried oral or anal sex. He could preach against such "deviance" with a gleam in his eye.

He spoke of "reaping the virginity" of young girls to create generations of descendants whose numbers he pictured growing from twelve to twenty-four to forty-eight and then into the thousands. He also reserved the right to sleep with their mothers. Forty-eight-year-old Jeannine Bunds, whose nineteen-year-old daughter, Robyn, would bear him a son, was proud to join Robyn in the harem they called the "House of David." "He wouldn't do it unless you wanted it," she said. "He was a very appealing, sexual person." A registered nurse, she slept with Koresh and also delivered several of his children including Michele Jones's twins, Chica and Little One, who like all the rest were named by their biological father. Robyn Bunds believed that Koresh "carried God's seed." She agreed with Alisa Shaw, another of his bedmates, who said, "Not every woman is worthy of Koresh's loins."

For all Mount Carmel's racial diversity, there were taboos Koresh did not violate. One qualification for membership in the House of David appeared to be skin color: he chose no Black women as "wives." Not even pretty Novelette Sinclair, a Jamaica-born Canadian who admitted being sexually drawn to him, was invited into the House of David.

Still he claimed to be color-blind. He liked to point to the Afro-Brits and say, "The Blacks let me down. I hate Blacks." Then he'd point to the Hawaiians and Filipinos. "I hate the yellows. I hate the whites, too, all superior-like. I hate *me*. Don't you?"

Instead of hate, they regarded him with awe. Koresh considered that appropriate. As their prophet and messiah, he said, quoting the Song of Solomon, he was entitled to *"threescore queens, and fourscore concubines, and virgins without number."* He scolded the men: "You married guys have to stop fucking and put your mind one hundred percent on the message." Thibodeau told of how he "liked to fling taunts at us. 'I got all the women, aren't you jealous?' We'd chuckle awkwardly, ha ha. Then David would say, 'We're all God's guinea pigs. My lot's to procreate, yours is to tolerate.'"

"He said God had mates for us in the Kingdom," says Sheila Martin, who stopped sleeping with her husband once Koresh announced that Davidian men—all except him—must be celibate. "There were perfect mates for us in heaven, so we should not want the mates we were with. The Catholics had nuns and priests who saved themselves for God. That was what we should do." At one point Koresh blamed his followers for his stomach ulcers. "He said he was being punished because of us. We were failing him and failing God." Sheila's husband, attorney Wayne Martin, already blamed himself for the meningitis that had crippled and blinded their son Jamie. Wayne tended to put on weight and felt guilty about that as well. Redoubling his efforts to live a spotless life, he slept apart from his wife, in a different room on another floor, as Koresh commanded.

"It was not easy on David to have a bunch of wives," Koresh's mother, Bonnie, insisted. "It hurt Rachel in the beginning, but then God told her David was to take another wife. Rachel was cheated out of a lot of things. David used to tell me, 'Mama, she never had a wedding or honeymoon. Someday I'll give her a real wedding and a real honeymoon.'" In Bonnie's view, her son was saving Michele, Robyn, and other female followers from a life of promiscuity. "David took some wives," she said, "but they weren't out in the world sleeping around like they would have been."

Rachel, Koresh's lone legal wife, gave his other lovers advice on how to "bathe and perfume themselves" before joining him in bed.

Each new member of the so-called House of David received a

gold-plated Star of David to wear on a chain around her neck. Some girls were groomed for future membership from the age of three or four. As one Davidian remembered, "When I asked my mother why she let that happen to me, she replied, 'When my sisters and I were at Mount Carmel, we had to submit to the church elders. If we resisted, they held our hands over the fire until we submitted. That's just what it means to be born a girl.'"

◇◇◇◇

Steve Schneider, who served as Koresh's chief deputy, suffered a crisis of faith when his wife, Judy, joined the House of David. An affable, ginger-haired forty-one-year-old with a PhD in comparative religion from the University of Hawaii, Schneider always said he believed in David above all. Then his wife of ten years got pregnant by Koresh and changed her name to Judy Schneider-Koresh. "We were lovers for close on twenty years and never made a baby," the anguished Schneider said. "Now, suddenly, she's having his child."

"David saw the position he was putting Steve in," said Thibodeau. "It's almost like he liked it. Steve told me, 'For a moment I really wanted to kill him.' But when it got down to it, what did he do? Steve stayed loyal."

Another insider chose a different path. Marc Breault, pronounced *bro*, a tall, bushy-haired Australian who was legally blind, squinted at his Bible while claiming he could parse its meanings better than Koresh. "Marc thought David was wrong," Sheila Martin says of Breault, who had a master's degree in religion from Loma Linda University. "We thought David might kick him out."

Instead, Koresh urged them to hear Breault out. "If Marc's a prophet," he said, "God will show him the way."

Breault was beginning to look for a way out. It turned his stomach to sit at his computer, typing up one of Koresh's sermons in forty-point type the nearly blind man could read, while an underage girl walked by on her way to the stairs that led to Koresh's room. He thought, *"That little thirteen-year-old is going up there to make love to David."*

The longer Breault stayed at Mount Carmel, the worse he felt about his life there. Breault's wife, Elizabeth Baranyai, had annoyed Koresh by resisting his advances. She and Marc weren't about to break their marriage vows for any man. "I'm seriously starting to doubt whether God has ever talked to this guy," Breault told some of the others. After Koresh nullified all marriages between other Branch Davidians, Marc and Elizabeth left Mount Carmel for their native Australia. From there they launched a campaign to expose Koresh as a cult leader.

Their defection lit the fuse for all that came later. As Thibodeau put it, "In Marc Breault, David had his Judas."

6

The Sinful Messiah

The flagpole out front flew a blue and white banner designed by Koresh. The Branch Davidian flag featured the colors of the Israeli flag and a snake slithering through a Star of David. Why a snake? He cited Numbers 21:8: "*Make thee a fiery serpent, and set it upon a pole.*"

With operating expenses of about $15,000 a month in the early 1990s, he and his hundred-plus followers at Mount Carmel relied on contributions from Branch Davidians around the world as well as income from the Mag Bag, a Waco car-repair shop they ran, plus the earnings of lawyer Wayne Martin and Dave Jones, Rachel's brother, who had a job as a mailman. "David asked families to give $350 a month," Sheila Martin recalls, "but he wouldn't throw anyone out if they couldn't pay." The residents raised chickens and goats, preferring goat milk to cow's milk for religious reasons. On trips to the supermarket, "we would buy very frugally," one said. "Apples by the case, potatoes and onions, bananas galore."

Mealtime was communal. A sign on the cafeteria wall read, THIS IS NOT A RESTAURANT. IF YOU DON'T LIKE THE FOOD, F.U. "Breakfast was oatmeal, bread, bananas, sometimes eggs, and millet," Thibodeau recalled. Sometimes there were graham crackers—a treat that gave Australian Graeme "Crackers" Craddock his nickname. When supplies ran low, they might make do with potato chips and Cheetos. Lunch, dished out at one o'clock sharp, "was usually a simple salad, maybe some soup and beans, but when Juliette Martinez and her mother, Ofelia Santoyo, were preparing lunch, they treated us to delicious burritos, roast chicken or grilled fish." Red meat, considered unclean, was never on the menu. Spartan suppers, served at six, often consisted of popcorn, bananas, and anything left over from lunch. Bonnie remembered eating popcorn "just about every night. We'd have soup or fruit salad, watermelon or maybe just bananas." On special occasions, Koresh let them have ice cream or soft drinks. Sometimes he dished out the ice cream himself. The Davidians also stockpiled army-surplus MREs (meals ready to eat) to sell at gun shows or eat when groceries ran low. Thibodeau described the freeze-dried military meals as "rations of spaghetti and meatballs or tuna casserole that tasted like mud when eaten cold, or slime when warmed." But nobody came to Mount Carmel for the cuisine.

Davidian women homeschooled the children. They did not stint on discipline. A wooden paddle known as "the Helper" hung from a hook in the cafeteria. Parents kept other paddles to use on misbehaving children, "the flat kind that didn't leave bruises," one mother said. The men rigged an outdoor shower under a tree, but women were not allowed to disrobe outside—they had to take sponge baths. With water scarce, Koresh haggled with a Waco merchant for a 1,500-gallon polyethylene water tank the men installed behind the main building. Gray-haired Roy Haldeman, back together with Bonnie after years of fights and reconciliations, helped. More favorably inclined toward the prophet Koresh than he ever was with his wayward stepson Vernon, he trucked the tank "to the water company," Bonnie recalled, "and we'd pay to fill that thing up with water because our well wasn't working." Roy drove the full tank back to Mount Carmel, "and everyone went down and filled their water jugs."

Steve Schneider compared living at Mount Carmel to "camping indoors." Only the kitchen and cafeteria had running water. There were no toilets; residents relieved themselves in outhouses or plastic buckets. Their dorm-style rooms featured bunk beds and had no closets. Blankets or sheets hanging from nails served as doors between rooms. The Davidians marked their belongings by pinning them with name tags or writing their initials on them. The few who had valuables they couldn't afford to share kept them locked in their cars parked outside, if they had cars, or left them with relatives outside the compound.

They slept in a three-story stack of rooms they called "the tower." Built atop the cement-walled space that had once held the Rodens' printing press, the central tower was a warren of spartan spaces with plywood walls and ladders between floors. Adult men, no longer allowed to sleep with their wives, bunked on the ground floor. Mothers and children occupied second-floor bedrooms while childless women occupied the topmost level along with Koresh, whose bedroom was the largest of all. A set of stairs led to the prophet's room.

Residents listened to music and news on battery-powered radios. They read by oil lamps and Coleman lanterns, and plugged holes in walls and windows with towels or straw. Koresh lectured them about fire safety but never fixed the walls and windows. During cold spells, they slept in sweaters and coats, keeping the lanterns on all night.

"We weren't there for comfort," Sheila Martin says. Along with other mothers she minded the children, helped look after the livestock, grocery shopped, cooked, and cleaned. "And I was joyous about it." At twice-daily meetings in the chapel, with its bare walls, tiered seating, and a stage, where his band sometimes jammed, "David required us all to bring our Bibles. His rule was simple: no Bible, no study. 'Don't look at me. Look at the Word,' he'd say. 'That's where you'll find peace, guidance, and your salvation.' And he preached, sometimes for hours and hours. But David made preaching more of a conversation—with us and with God."

Some nights a dinner bell called them to the chapel for Bible study. If the spirit moved Koresh, the bell might ring at midnight or one in the morning. They'd file in with their Bibles, some of the children rubbing sleep from their eyes. Even toddlers were expected at Bible studies. They might yawn their way through part of the lesson, "but David kept it interesting, just by the way his voice went up and down," Sheila says. "He always gave us something new, something to make scripture come alive."

Koresh was fond of Sheila's son Jamie despite the boy's occasional wailing during Bible studies. Blind, disabled Jamie was the size of a three-year-old at the age of ten, often in pain, curled into himself. "One night he cried and cried," his mother says. "People were staring at us. David took Jamie from me and held him in his lap. He said, 'You guys need more healing than this child.' And Jamie calmed down. David was starting the Bible study when Jamie smiled and laughed, and David said, 'Wait, don't laugh yet. Let me get to the funny parts!'"

His preaching shifted from Revelation to conspiracy theories that anticipated those of the decades to come. There were secret societies at work behind the scenes, Koresh said. The Merkabah, a chariot mentioned in Kabbalah, was a prehistoric UFO. "And now we see them again. Angels don't really have wings. They don't need them. They go in spaceships powered by the refraction of light."

The Branch Davidians didn't celebrate Christmas 1991 or any other Christmas. Passover was the main event on their calendar—not that Koresh ever hosted a traditional seder. "David thought rituals were bullshit," Thibodeau says. "If we have the truth, why do we need a performance?" Instead, they reflected on God's saving Israel while Egypt's children died, listening to Koresh describe the oncoming day when history would end in glory for the chosen few who followed him.

His mother described life at Mount Carmel as "hard work. But every once in a while we had a hoedown. David's band played and we'd just sing and dance."

◇◇◇◇

After Marc Breault and his wife split from the others, Breault sent long letters from Australia to friends at Mount Carmel, encouraging them to leave. His letters warned that Koresh was a false prophet and pedophile. The Davidians took them to Koresh. "David would read Marc's letters aloud," Sheila Martin says. "He'd ask us, 'Is Marc right? I mean, how do you know I'm not deceiving you right now?' He wanted us to make up our own minds."

Day-to-day life went on as before. The men finished building a swimming pool—not a suburban-style pool with a diving board but a DIY rectangle dug with shovels and a rented backhoe, lined with cement and filled with water from a nearby pond. They added chlorine and used an electric motor to filter the water. Men and women used the pool separately so as not to tempt each other. Golden-haired Cyrus Koresh, who resembled a young Thor, refereed swimming contests. Thibodeau called the boy "a natural leader, the crown prince."

Excavating the pool had left a mound of dirt behind the main building. Koresh would place tin cans on the dirt pile for target practice. "His focus on guns was unique to him. Adventists traditionally preach and practice nonviolence," says Baylor religion professor Bill Pitts. "They take 'Thou shalt not kill' literally. During World War II, they worked as medics, refusing to carry guns." Koresh was different. Quoting the Old Testament prophet Nahum, he exhorted believers to "*keep the munition, watch the way, make thy loins strong, fortify thy power mightily.*" He said God's chosen people had every right to defend themselves. He wanted every Davidian man, woman, and child to know how to handle a gun, making every shot count, just like his brother-in-law Dave, Rachel and Michele's big brother. Dave Jones could shoot the bullet-sized gold medal out of a Campbell's soup can.

One day Koresh led church elder Clive Doyle to the dirt pile. He handed Doyle a rifle. "Let's see what you can do."

Doyle had never fired a gun. He squeezed off a few shots before Koresh took the rifle back. "You're wasting bullets."

During one target-practice session with Eddie Goins, a local musician, Goins pressed Koresh about rumors that he was sleeping with dozens of women. Koresh said he was "populating the earth with perfect people." Goins asked, "If you're God, man, why not just zap them here?" Koresh had a ready answer: "It's fun the old-fashioned way."

Heather Jones was seven years old when her father, Dave, the expert marksman, gave her to David Koresh. After that, like other children at Mount Carmel, Heather was expected to see Koresh as the only important adult in her life, and she impressed him by being a better shot than some of the grown-ups. "I liked learning about guns," she says, "and I could shoot, too."

Like Marc Breault, Heather's mother had left Mount Carmel after

Koresh told his followers that husbands and wives owed their loyalty only to him. "Before my mom left," Heather says today, "she gave me a Betsy Wetsy doll. David said, 'No, no.' He had me put my Betsy Wetsy on a stump and shoot it to pieces." After proving herself a crack shot, she asked when she'd get to see her mother again. "And David gets down in my face with his piercing eyes, and he says, 'Why would you want to see a devil?'"

Heather was one of the girls being groomed as Koresh's future "wives," but she was afraid of him. Her mother had prepped her for private studies with the prophet. "She teased my hair and put lipstick on me." She knew her first menstrual period "was going to make me a candidate for baby-making with him," like her aunts Rachel and Michele. "A lot of the other girls, it just melted their heart—the idea of having his child. But I told my mom I didn't want to."

Her room in the tower wasn't far from his. "I knew I was on his radar. Other kids got to spend time with their dads. Not me. Looking back, he was grooming me to be a wife, which I thought was gross."

By the time she turned nine, Heather was well acquainted with the Helper. "I got spanked for walking pigeon-toed. It hurt! He took me upstairs and put a chair in the middle of his room. Had me pull down my pants and lay across his legs. He had a big paddle as thick as a boat oar. David spanked me until he was finished. I kind of learned to wish myself somewhere else."

Soon, sitting gingerly with the others, she heard Koresh tell them Judgment Day might be coming sooner than they'd expected. Pacing in front of his amps, speakers, and guitar cases under the chapel's fluorescent lights, the only electric lights in the compound, he said, "The way things are shaping up, we may not get to Israel." Scripture said the Last Days would unfold in Israel, but now, with Breault lining up against him, history seemed to be picking up speed.

Koresh heard that Breault was in touch with government agencies. "Persecution is coming," he said.

◇◇◇◇

In May 1992, Special Agent Davy Aguilera of the Bureau of Alcohol, Tobacco and Firearms was assigned to investigate the Branch Davidians. A UPS driver had reported delivering a shipment of grenades to Mount Carmel. The package was actually a box of harmless grenade casings for Davidian women to sew into hunting vests, but to Aguilera, who ran the ATF's San Antonio office, grenades were grenades. He looked up Koresh's record and found an arrest and trial for the 1987 raid that wounded George Roden. That was enough to establish what Agent Aguilera deemed Koresh's "propensity toward violence."

The ATF had been founded as the Bureau of Prohibition in 1920. Its agents busted stills and speakeasies until Prohibition ended in 1933. After that, Bureau of Prohibition agents, including Eliot Ness, the G-man who took down Al Capone on tax-evasion charges, became members of the federal Alcohol Tax Unit. That agency added oversight of firearms in 1941 and of tobacco taxes a decade later, becoming the Bureau of Alcohol, Tobacco and Firearms.

Marc Breault contacted the ATF, offering to help investigate Koresh. He worked with an Australian tabloid-TV journalist, Martin Smith, on a story that set the tone for later coverage of the Branch Davidians. Breault said his friends at Mount Carmel had fallen under Koresh's spell: "They are a cult." He was still in touch with them, he said, and what he heard scared him. After Breault contacted the US embassy in Canberra, Australia, diplomats there wired the State Department in Washington, passing along his warning that Koresh was planning a mass suicide during Passover 1992 and would kill anyone who tried to arrest him.

Koresh got wind of Breault's predictions. He thought they were funny. After Passover passed with no bloodshed, he phoned the sheriff's office in Waco. "We're still here," he said. "I don't know what you've been told, but we're here."

The authorities went on relying on Marc Breault when it suited their purposes. Breault faxed diagrams of Mount Carmel's floor plans to the ATF in hopes the agency would raid the place. He described how Davidians broke gun laws by converting semiautomatic AR-15s— the gun the NRA called "America's rifle"—into automatic weapons. (Both semiautomatic and automatic weapons reload themselves. The difference is that semiautomatics fire once when the trigger is pulled, while automatics keep firing until the trigger is released or ammunition runs out. Most automatic weapons are illegal in the US.) Breault swore that Koresh was still planning to kill himself and his followers.

That spring, four ATF agents set up an outpost in a rented house across the road from Mount Carmel. "They moved in with hardly any furniture," one Davidian remembers. But the new neighbors brought cameras they aimed out their windows, "and they weren't too good at that. David could see the sun glinting off the lenses."

Koresh tried being friendly. "He said, 'Take a six-pack of beer over there and welcome them to the neighborhood,'" Doyle recalls.

Doyle did just that. He lugged a six-pack across Double-EE Ranch Road to the rented house. "I knocked. Then this fellow opens the door a crack and says, 'You can't come in. I've, um, got my girlfriend here!' And slams it." Doyle left the beer on the porch. "Then he opens the door, grabs the beer, and shuts the door again."

Before long, the Davidians' new neighbors came up the gravel drive to introduce themselves. The men said they were students at Texas State Technical College, though they looked to be in their thirties or forties. Their government-issue sedans looked like unusual wheels for college students. The ATF's undercover agents also had a hard time describing what college courses they were taking. One said he was majoring in philosophy, an unlikely choice at a trade school.

Koresh gave them a tour of the property, even invited them to join him shooting targets on the dirt pile out back. One of the so-called students jogged back to the rented house and returned with a rifle. He didn't know much about guns, he said; he'd just picked this one up at a flea market.

Koresh said, "Let me see it." He stripped the gun down and slapped it back together.

"You didn't buy this at a flea market," he said. "This is a sniper rifle."

ATF special agent Robert Rodriguez was in charge of the outpost across the road. His job was to infiltrate the Davidians' property for evidence of illegal weapons. The broad-shouldered Rodriguez had a cover story: he identified himself as Robert Gonzalez, a fortyish trade-school student who wanted to learn more about the Davidians' beliefs.

"David was aware that Robert was probably an undercover agent," Koresh's mother said. But he liked "Robert Gonzalez," who was a good listener and a pretty good shot with a pistol or rifle. Thinking he might convert him, the Davidians' leader turned on the charm when Robert stopped by to shoot, sip a beer, or talk scripture.

"You know what? For a cult leader, I'm a nice guy," Koresh said.

◇◇◇◇

In August 1992, three months into the ATF's investigation of Koresh and his followers, six federal agents approached a cabin at Ruby Ridge in Boundary County, Idaho. They were there to serve a warrant on a minor gun charge. The cabin belonged to Randy Weaver, an army veteran and former Green Beret. Weaver was also a survivalist and white supremacist. His offense: selling an undercover agent a sawed-off shotgun that was shorter than the limit under federal law. When he resisted the agents, a shootout erupted. A US marshal shot Weaver's fourteen-year-old son, Sammy, in the back as the boy tried to run away, killing him. Kevin Harris, a family friend of the Weavers, shot and killed a deputy marshal. During the eleven-day siege that followed, FBI and ATF agents surrounded Weaver's cabin. When he and Harris emerged to visit a shed that held Sammy's body, an FBI sniper shot Weaver through the armpit. He and Harris ran back to the cabin where his wife, Vicki, held the door with one arm while cradling their ten-month-old baby, Elisheba, with the other.

The sniper fired again. His bullet passed through Harris's chest and killed Vicki Weaver. Her body lay under the kitchen table for a week before her husband surrendered.

To Koresh, the incident at Ruby Ridge proved that the government would stop at nothing to disarm Americans. During a Bible study that summer, pacing in front of the drum kit and amps on the stage in the chapel, he challenged Branch Davidians to *wake up*. "What are you going to do six months from now," he asked, gesturing toward the walls and windows, "when all this is surrounded with tanks?"

Thibodeau spoke up. "*Tanks?* That's paranoid, David."

Koresh smiled. "Was Ruby Ridge a dress rehearsal? Are we next?"

Thibodeau wasn't sure. As he knew as well as anyone, Koresh liked to cast everything in the most dramatic terms. Still, they both noticed military helicopters flying over Mount Carmel that fall, circling like vultures.

The ATF needed evidence of gun violations to justify a search warrant. Special Agent Aguilera hoped to find proof that the Davidians were converting semiautomatic rifles to fully automatic "assault weapons." Finding none, Special Agent Rodriguez reported hearing rumors that Koresh was sleeping with underage girls. Aguilera urged a judge to issue a warrant based in part on "sexual abuse," though pedophilia was outside ATF jurisdiction. The ATF would later add the claim that there was reason to believe the Davidians were running a methamphetamine lab. In reality it was the previous tenants in the agents' own cabin who had a meth lab and who left behind flasks and Bunsen burners that the ATF used as evidence against the Branch Davidians.

Aguilera's petition for a search warrant cited "circumstantial evidence that its members were indeed converting semiautomatic weapons to fully automatic without having paid the proper fees." That was true. Automatics fetched higher prices at gun shows. Converting rifles from semi- to fully automatic was a crime; violators could be found guilty of possession of a firearm without proper registration. In the affidavit supporting his request for a warrant, Aguilera added that "an informant," likely agent Rodriguez, "observed at the compound magazines such as the *Shotgun News* and other related clandestine magazines." *Shotgun News* was a bible of the firearms trade, with 145,000 subscribers in gun shops, pawn shops, and sporting goods stores nationwide.

The ATF got its search warrant. Thibodeau claims it was "not coincidental" that the agency had a congressional budget hearing coming up. "They looked like shit after Ruby Ridge. They needed a big win."

In June 1992 Mark England, a reporter for the *Waco Tribune-Herald*, took an interest in Koresh and the Branch Davidians. He started looking into the subject after Marc Breault contacted him from Australia, calling Koresh a dangerous cult leader. The thought of a gun-toting, child-abusing cult ten miles from downtown Waco grew more pressing in light of that summer's standoff at Ruby Ridge. England phoned Mount Carmel and spoke to Koresh, who said he and his Davidians were just good Christians minding their own business. After Ruby Ridge, he said, Americans had to stand guard against government forces that might want to confiscate their guns.

Spy magazine mocked "ATF Follies" like shooting Vicki Weaver and spending a reported $18,650 for every illegal firearm the agency seized, but the *Tribune-Herald* took a different tack. During an editorial meeting, the paper's top editor, Bob Lott, called Koresh a cult leader whose influence was "a dangerous and sinister thing the public should know about." Lott assigned England and another reporter, Darlene McCormick, to the Koresh beat. The two of them spent months researching a story that became a series of articles with a title borrowed from one of Koresh's names for himself: "The Sinful Messiah."

Deadline Pressure

Reporters England and McCormick interviewed Koresh on the phone but didn't speak to the other Branch Davidians, relying mostly on Marc Breault and other ex-followers who viewed Koresh as a fraud. "His legal name is David Koresh," they would note at the top of their first report, then proceed to call him Howell the next 367 times they referred to him. Such word choices reflected newspaper policy: at the direction of top editor Bob Lott, the *Tribune-Herald* described the Branch Davidians not as a denomination, faction, or sect, but as a "cult."

As the writers prepared their report, federal agents were rehearsing a raid at Fort Hood, an army base seventy miles away, under the supervision of Green Berets. Their operation plan was code-named Trojan Horse. Ground-level agents considered the code name lame. Among themselves they called the plan "Showtime."

With dozens of ATF agents checking into local motels and staging training exercises nearby, the *Tribune-Herald* writers knew their story wouldn't be exclusive for long. After they pressed editor Lott to run their exposé before they got scooped, he moved the paper's publication date from March to February 27.

The twenty-seventh fell on a Saturday, a sleepy Sabbath for the Branch Davidians. There were more than a hundred men, women, and children at Mount Carmel that day. At least a dozen of the forty-one children there had been fathered by Koresh, a first seeding of the 144,000 descendants he hoped to generate.

Under the headline "The Sinful Messiah," the *Tribune-Herald's* front-page story began:

> If you are a Branch Davidian, Christ lives on a threadbare piece of land 10 miles east of here called Mount Carmel.
>
> He has dimples, claims a ninth-grade education, married his legal wife when she was 14, enjoys a beer now and then, plays a mean guitar, reportedly packs a 9mm Glock and keeps an arsenal of military assault rifles, and willingly admits that he is a sinner without equal.

Quoting Breault and other former "cultists," England and McCormick's story featured anonymous complaints that the man they called Howell "abused children physically and psychologically; boasted of having sex with underage girls in the cult; and has had at least fifteen so-called 'wives.'" He was said to rule Mount Carmel "by virtue of the Branch Davidians' belief that he alone can open the so-called Seven Seals in the Bible Book of Revelation, setting loose catastrophic events that the Branch Davidians believe will end mankind and propel Howell and his followers into heaven. Former cult members, though, said Howell is headed in the opposite direction."

After detailing Koresh's "marriages" to teenage and preteen girls and more speculative accounts of his supposed "mind-control techniques," the reporters ended their story with a quote from Koresh: "'We're doing what we're doing and nobody's going to stop us,' Howell said."

◇◇◇◇

Koresh read the story aloud inside the chapel at Mount Carmel, surrounded by his followers. "Well, at least they got the last part right," he said. He warned that they should expect an attack: "It's going to be soon." He had expected the end-times to begin with God's chosen people—him and his Branch Davidians—returning to Israel, but his preaching was nothing if not flexible. "It looks like God has other plans," he said.

Events were speeding up. After the government's preparations for a major operation led the *Tribune-Herald* to go to press, the story's publication spurred the ATF to accelerate its action plan. According to one ATF insider, the agency got wind of the newspaper's schedule from a former Secret Service agent who was working for the *Tribune-Herald*'s parent company. Special Agents Aguilera and Rodriguez knew that raiding Mount Carmel, with its stockpile of weapons, might be like kicking a hornets' nest, but with the newspaper saying, "Authorities have not acted on the complaints" of child abuse, sexual abuse, bigamy, mind control, and weapons violations, there was no time to waste. A sidebar to the "Sinful Messiah" story was headed "The Law Watches, But Has Done Little."

TV and radio reporters rushed to catch up with the *Tribune-Herald*'s reporting. Not long after dawn on Sunday the twenty-eighth, a cameraman for Waco's KWTX-TV, Jim Peeler, set out to cover a rumored ATF raid on Mount Carmel. He stopped to ask a mail carrier for directions to Double-EE Ranch Road. As it happened the mailman he met was none other than Dave Jones—Rachel and Michele's big brother, Koresh's sharpshooting brother-in-law. Jones told Peeler how to get to Mount Carmel. The cameraman thanked him and warned him to stay away from the cultists' compound, where the shooting might start at any minute. An ATF assault "is going to be soon," he said. "You better get out of here because there's a National Guard helicopter over at TSTC [Texas State Technical College], and they're going to have a big shootout with the religious nuts."

Jones raced back to Mount Carmel, passing a Jeep loaded with men in black tactical gear and riot helmets. By that time their friend Robert Rodriguez, aka Gonzalez, had knocked on the compound's steel front doors. He'd brought Koresh a copy of the Sunday paper. The second installment of "The Sinful Messiah" series carried the headline "Religion Student Marc Breault Is Introduced to a Bizarre Texas Cult."

Again, Koresh read quotes from the story out loud.

Howell told the gathering that God had commanded him to have sex with a fourteen-year-old girl in the cult.

He would act like he knew every sentence in the Bible . . . to uphold anything he wanted.

Howell did seem a throwback to the 1960s, with flowing brown hair that curved gracefully to below the shoulders, wire-rim glasses, a beatific smile and easy talk of peace and love. Younger Branch Davidians gravitated to Howell's persona and his passion for rock music. Howell's almost celestial knowledge of the Bible mystified the older cult members.

Koresh didn't seem angry. He liked seeing his name in the paper, even if they did keep calling him Howell, and couldn't complain about the bits describing his "flowing brown hair" and celestial knowledge.

That morning a half-mile-long convoy of ATF and military vehicles, including a pair of tarp-covered cattle trailers, had rolled north from Fort Hood, an hour away. Why cattle trailers? The men planning the raid thought the Davidians might mistake them for farm vehicles that had taken a wrong turn. In fact the trailers, pulled by pickup trucks, held seventy-six heavily armed federal agents in riot gear, equipped with flash-bang grenades and zip-tie handcuffs. According to Texas journalist Dick Reavis, "They planned to burst from the trailers in a run, neutralize the dogs, batter down the building's front door, and arrest Vernon Howell a.k.a. David Koresh. Some fifty agents had been assigned to enter the front door, including a contingent of female raiders whose job was to restrain and calm Mount Carmel's women and children." Some also packed candy they hoped would "appease the kids" Koresh was said to be holding captive.

Around 8:00 a.m., the convoy arrived at Bellmead Civic Center in Waco, which served as a staging area for the upcoming raid. The agents found coffee and doughnuts waiting for them. There were also several dozen Happy Meals from McDonald's—perks for them to offer Davidians who surrendered. By then, ATF snipers had taken positions on low hillsides near the compound. The agency referred to them as "forward observers."

Undercover agent Rodriguez, still looking over the newspaper with Koresh, was shocked to see Dave Jones arrive with news of a raid: "*It's on! They're coming.*" The man the Davidians knew as "Robert Gonzalez" thought his cover might be blown. "I was pretty shaken," he remembered.

Koresh offered him a handshake. "Good luck, Robert," he said. With that, Special Agent Rodriguez fled the compound. As Thibodeau recalled, "Robert turned and hurried out, and I sensed from the way he hunched his shoulders that he half expected to be shot in the back."

Rodriguez jumped in his unmarked SUV and barreled up the drive. He switched on his siren and banged the horn to alert the other agents in their house across the road that the Davidians were on to them. He rushed inside the house and phoned his superiors: "They *know*!" The ATF had been counting on surprising Koresh; now the element of surprise was gone. Rodriguez pleaded with his bosses to call off the raid, but they were determined to stick to the plan. They had already put the nearest hospital and an ambulance service on alert in case there were casualties. After weeks of briefings, rehearsals, and drills, they weren't about to send eighty vehicles and more than a hundred agents back to Fort Hood.

An hour passed. "Everything was quiet," Rodriguez said later. He thought his bosses were about to make a dangerous mistake. "I went outside, and sat down, and I started to cry."

Sheila Martin remembers the same lull. "After Robert left, David told all of us ladies to go to the chapel. He said the police were coming. I thought he was talking about a police car or two. We held each other and prayed and put our trust in God."

At the Civic Center, the raiders were told that Koresh knew they were coming. "Our op plan said we'd call it off if we lost the element of surprise," recalls former ATF agent John Risenhoover. Instead, he and the others piled into the cattle trailers, standing three abreast, clutching the center rail and trying to stay on their feet during the bumpy fifteen-minute ride to Mount Carmel. Rather than the usual pre-raid banter, there was "an eerie quiet," one of them says. According to Risenhoover, "Nobody expected a shootout. We had a Jonestown mentality: Get in there fast, before they kill themselves." Risenhoover carried a nine-millimeter pistol, twenty zip-tie handcuffs, "and a roll of duct tape. The duct tape was so I could tape David Koresh's mouth shut, so he couldn't tell them all to commit suicide."

Koresh called the others together. In church elder Clive Doyle's recollection, "David said, 'We just got a report that some law enforcement agency is coming out. I want you all to stay calm. I'll go down to the front door and talk to them.'"

8

....

Showtime

The raid began with three National Guard helicopters sweeping in from the east with the sun behind them. They were meant to distract the Davidians from the government's next move: the cattle trailers barreling up the drive to Mount Carmel.

The Davidians heard helicopters first. It was 9:45 in the morning.

"They're coming," Koresh said. "But I want to talk it out with these people, so don't anybody do anything stupid."

He started for the double front doors along with his white-haired father-in-law, Perry Jones, who had to hurry to keep up with his daughters' husband. Outside, the cattle trailers pulled up on the driveway. The seventy-six heavily armed ATF agents in riot gear jumped out and advanced on the building. Two four-man teams shouldering twenty-foot aluminum ladders jogged to the sides of the central tower for an assault on the building's upper floors.

Special Agent Roland Ballesteros was tasked with serving the search warrant. As Ballesteros approached the picket fence in front of the compound, he expected the Davidians to "make a stand based on their religious beliefs," he testified later. "We anticipated we would be met with force." Instead he saw Koresh ten yards away, unarmed, waiting to meet him.

Ballesteros aimed his shotgun at the Davidians' leader. "I instinctively yelled at him: 'Police! Search warrant! Lay down!'" he recalled.

Other agents shouted, "*Get down! Lay down!*"

Koresh ignored them. Peering out over a small army of black-jacketed federal agents in helmets and bulletproof vests, he asked, "What's going on? There's women and children in here!"

Ballesteros could barely hear him. He had a radio link in one ear, a sound-muffling earplug—to keep from being dazed by flash-bang grenades—in the other. He had expected the skinny sect leader to lie down as ordered or reach for a gun, not talk back. Again he yelled, "Search warrant! Lay down!"

Instead, Koresh smiled. Then he ducked back inside as the agents advanced. "And that," church elder Doyle recalls, "is when all hell broke loose."

Special Agent Ballesteros hit the deck at the first sound of gunfire. He recalled hearing "twenty, thirty, I don't know how many bullets" coming from the building. "I sustained a bullet wound to my left hand." It left his thumb hanging sideways. Another agent, one of the last to pile out of the cattle trailers, heard shots before her boots hit the ground.

Both sides would claim the other shot first. It is possible, even likely, that the shots that triggered the gun battle were aimed not at Ballesteros and his assault team or at the Branch Davidians, but at the dogs penned outside the compound.

The Davidians kept half a dozen Alaskan malamutes as pets. The children looked after the dogs, which resembled huskies but were larger. Full-grown malamutes weigh eighty to ninety pounds. Several of the Davidians' dogs were still pups, less than a year old, but were already bigger than many of the children. During briefings, Ballesteros and his team had been told to expect "attack dogs" that would need to be "neutralized." Thus the raid's first wave of bloodshed was a hail of bullets directed at the dogs.

"I heard gunfire from the front of the house. I thought agents were probably killing the dogs," one ATF agent told investigators later. Another recalled shooting and killing a dog that was "barking offensively."

Four of the malamutes were littermates. The agents would state that their reasons for shooting them included the fact that the dogs were baring their teeth. "Then they shot the mother, who was chained to the flagpole," Doyle said. The mother's name was Fawn. "She was no threat to anyone. She was barking at them for killing her kids, and so they shot her, too."

Davidian Kathy Schroeder was diapering the youngest of her four children when the shooting started. She told her older kids to put their shoes on—they might need to run. Graeme "Crackers" Craddock, a former physics teacher from Melbourne, Australia, believed the ATF's attack proved Koresh had been right all along: the Last Days were at hand. Ready to wage holy war, Craddock grabbed his nine-millimeter pistol and AR-15 rifle and threw an ammo belt over his shoulder.

Forgetting Koresh's command not to do "anything stupid," his followers rained bullets on the federal agents outside, who shot back. Inside the front doors, Perry Jones crumpled to the floor, screaming, "I'm shot!" Outside, Special Agent Kenny King, an ex-marine and Vietnam veteran, led three raiders up a ladder to the roof. They had no radio link to Ballesteros and the others, no way to know how the raid was progressing as gunfire sounded below and behind them. Their instructions were to enter and occupy Mount Carmel. The ladder got them to the roof of the lower part of the compound, near a second-floor window in the tower's exterior wall. Before they could reach the window, bullets came through the wall. King was hit by a round that passed through his right elbow and chest. He lay stunned and bleeding on the roof while the agent behind him, Todd McKeehan, a Gulf War veteran from Tennessee, took a bullet that killed him. King crawled toward the gutter, taking more shots in the legs and buttocks, and then executed a spider drop, a hand-over-hand maneuver that eased his fall to the courtyard behind the tower. He landed with a thud, still exposed to shots from inside. Any of a dozen Davidians could have shot him; none did. King would survive.

Special Agent Dave Millen used a multipurpose Halligan tool to break a second-story window. Shot in the helmet and bulletproof vest, Millen slipped back down the ladder to relative safety. Special Agent Conway LeBleu, a thirty-year-old father of two from Louisiana who was still on the roof, took a bullet to the temple, just under his helmet. LeBleu died in seconds, still clutching his twelve-gauge shotgun.

Special Agent Bill Buford broke a second-floor window and tossed in a flash-bang. Buford, another Vietnam War combat veteran, was one of the assault team's senior agents. He had played college football at Kansas. As head of the ATF's Little Rock, Arkansas, office, Buford had helped organize the raid. He and the other planners had expected the Davidians to be gathered in the chapel that morning, praying. "We were going to go in there, we were going to kick a little booty, then we were going to ease out and be home before noon," he told *Texas Monthly* years later. Now he and two other agents, Keith Constantino and Glen Jordan, clambered through the window after the flash-bang. Despite the hour—just short of 10:00 a.m.—it was dark inside. As his eyes adjusted, Buford saw Scott Sonobe, a diminutive Filipino the Davidians called "Snow Flea," wielding an AK-47. Agent Constantino dropped Sonobe with a round that passed through his hand and into his right leg. Sonobe fled into the shadows.

Buford and his team "were receiving a tremendous amount of fire through the walls," he recalled. There was so much gunfire through Mount Carmel's thin walls that the shots "sounded like popcorn." As he and Constantino fired blindly, their fellow agent Jordan went down, crying, "I'm hit!" Jordan had been winged by a nine-millimeter round that probably came from Buford's pistol, the first instance of friendly fire during the raid.

In Buford's account, "Shots started coming up through the floor. The first round that hit me got me square in the butt and lodged in my thigh." He asked Jordan, "Can you move? We need to get out of here." With Constantino firing through the walls and floor, the three agents retreated through the window. "I pulled myself down to the edge of the roof and rolled off," Buford remembered. "When I hit the ground, I broke a bunch of ribs. I thought I'd been shot in the chest." Like Agent King, he was still a target for Davidians firing from inside the building. Buford spotted Special Agent Rob Williams shooting back, providing covering fire for his boss. Williams, whose twenty-seventh birthday was coming up the next day, "shot at a Davidian who had shot at me," Buford said. "But in doing so they were able to see where he was, and he was shot." A Davidian bullet struck Williams's face, killing him.

Agents Lowell Sprague and Steve Willis took cover behind a green Dodge van parked near the front door. Bullets hissed through the air around them. Sprague told Willis to keep his head down. "Careful!" he shouted, pointing to a fist-sized hole a bullet had just made in the van—a sign of the high-powered weapons the Davidians were shooting at them. The New Orleans–born Willis, who raced sports cars in his spare time, stayed low, but he was in the wrong spot as a fifty-caliber round from the compound tore through the driver's side of the van and then through its back window, striking Willis and killing him instantly.

The Davidians had a growing body count of their own. Australian Peter Gent had climbed to the top of Mount Carmel's empty water tower after the first shots were fired. Gent's twin sister, Nikki, had two children by Koresh and was pregnant with a third. At the sound of gunfire he poked his head out of the hatch at the top of the silo-shaped tower, the highest point on the property. Within minutes he was dead. The round that killed Gent, a semi-jacketed hollow-point bullet of the sort favored by law enforcement, entered his upper chest and came to rest at a spot the McLennan County coroner described as inches from his heel. After the raid the Davidians would point out that a bullet entering a man's chest and lodging near his foot could only come from above—from one of the government's helicopters. The ATF would insist that its aircraft were unarmed, a claim that was true as far as it went. There were no guns mounted on the National Guard helicopters that the agency borrowed for the raid on Mount Carmel. The agents inside the helicopters were another matter: they had weapons of their own.

"Peter was working," Thibodeau recalled of his friend, "standing on scaffolding and ladders" inside the water tower, "chipping away rust . . . he stuck his head and upper body out of the hatch at the top of the tower to see what was going on and was hit in the chest. He was unarmed."

In the next few minutes the well-armed Davidians turned their guns on the helicopters overhead. None of the agents inside was hit, though one—Special Agent Philip Chojnacki, who ran the ATF's Houston office—reported a bullet whizzing past his head. Two of the three helicopters landed in a nearby field so their pilots could inspect them for damage.

Government snipers shot at the compound from hidden positions. Several were stationed in the rented house across Double-EE Ranch Road, firing over their fellow agents' heads. One of the sharpshooters was former marine David Sullivan. In another agent's account, Sullivan "sat at a breakfast table in the undercover house across the road from the compound, sipping coffee and firing his .308-caliber scoped rifle at cult gunmen in the upper windows of the compound almost three hundred yards away. Sully was cool under pressure." Yet he wasn't much help that morning. "The snipers would brag that they shot sixteen or seventeen Davidians," says Dave DiBetta, one of the raiders who heard rifle rounds from the undercover house whistling over his head. "They were blasting away, but they weren't dialed in. Hell, they didn't hit anyone!"

Sheila Martin, huddled in a second-floor dorm room with her children, saw sunlight through holes in the walls. Her blind, disabled ten-year-old, Jamie, lay on a couch near the window, where she had put him "so he could hear the birds." Now bullets were coming through the window and the wall and "Jamie was screaming at the top of his lungs." Sheila crawled to the couch and gathered her son in her arms. "His face had blood on it, but he wasn't shot, thank goodness. He got nicked by glass from the shot-up window." She carried the wailing boy to the far side of the room, where they hid under a mattress with her other children.

Jaydean Wendell led her four kids to the relative safety of a hallway. "Stay here," she told them. Her husband, Mark, was on a different floor with the other men, but she didn't need to consult with anyone before taking action. Wendell had been a police officer in her native Honolulu. She returned to the bedroom she shared with her kids. She grabbed a rifle, climbed onto a bunk bed near a window, and shot at the agents outside. Her children would find her splayed on the top bunk, dead from a bullet to the chest.

By then Wayne Martin had phoned 911 from his Mount Carmel office, directly below the spot where his wife and children hid under a mattress.

"What's your emergency?" the operator asked.

"There are men around our building shooting at us," Martin shouted at his speakerphone. "*Shooting* at us!"

"Just a moment." The operator transferred the call to Lieutenant Larry Lynch of the McLennan County Sheriff's Department.

"This is Lynch."

"They're shooting at us in Mount Carmel! Tell them there are women and children in here and to call it off!"

Lynch heard gunfire over the phone. "Oh shit! Hello, who is this?"

"*Call it off!*"

"Hello?"

But the Davidians' lawyer wasn't talking. Martin was watching the apocalypse outside his office window.

The son of a New York City transit worker, Wayne Martin had earned a master's degree in library science from Columbia University, a two-year program he finished in a year. After graduating from Harvard Law School, he'd served as a professor and law librarian at North Carolina Central, a historically Black college in Durham. Then Sheila convinced him to move to Texas with their children. Both were devout Seventh-day Adventists who found Koresh more compelling than any preacher they had ever heard. Wayne set up a one-man law practice at Mount Carmel, handling contracts, real estate transactions, divorces, and custody cases for outsiders, giving most of his earnings to Koresh. A city councilman who befriended him described Martin as "well-prepared, mild-mannered and polite." That was high praise for a Black man in Waco's nearly all-white legal circles, but the same friend added that Martin was "maybe a little paranoid-ish. He thought the government was keeping tabs on him, wiretapping him."

The government wasn't just keeping tabs on him today. It was coming after him and his family, just as Koresh had predicted. Martin could have told his city council friend that even paranoid people have enemies.

The 911 dispatcher came back on the line. "Did he hang up?" she asked Lieutenant Lynch.

"No, he's on the line," Lynch said. "I hear shots."

They listened to gunfire on the open phone line. "I hope they get the kids out of the way," the dispatcher said.

Inside the compound, Heather Jones climbed out of her bunk bed as bullets came through the walls. Nine-year-old Heather, mailman Dave Jones's daughter, shared a room with Judy Schneider, one of Koresh's many "wives." She recalls hearing Judy shout, "Get down!" as she shoved Heather to the floor and covered her with "blankets and pillows and suitcases—anything we had in the room." Then Judy handed her two-year-old daughter, Mayanah, to Heather. Chubby-cheeked Mayanah was Judy's child with Koresh. Heather huddled with the toddler under blankets and luggage. Peeking out, she saw Judy carrying a gun to the window to shoot at the raiders. Seconds later, Judy flew backward and fell, squealing in pain. There was blood all over the floor.

A floor below them Perry Jones, all ninety-eight pounds of him, lay with his arms curled around the bullet wound in his stomach. Livingstone Fagan, one of the Afro-Brits, reached for Jones's arm. "When Livingstone started to lift him, Perry let out a shriek," Doyle remembered. Jones begged for something to ease the pain, "but no one had much of anything. I remembered a sample pack of aspirin or Tylenol had come in the mail. I went and got it and said, 'Perry, this is all I can find.'" Two over-the-counter pain pills for a through-and-through wound.

The Davidians' firepower turned out to be a match for that of the ATF. "It was a war zone," one agent said. Another swore that the fighting got so fierce he couldn't hear his own pistol firing.

Back at the McLennan County Sheriff's Office, Lieutenant Lynch heard a dial tone. Lawyer Martin had hung up. Lynch called back and got Martin's answering machine. He tried again. Now Martin picked up, shouting, "Call it off! Tell them to pull back!"

"Who is this? Wayne?"

"It doesn't matter! I'm under fire! We want a cease-fire!"

The line went dead. Next Lynch called Texas State Technical College. He reached a security guard, who hurried to the ATF's command post on the school's campus and told the desk agent to phone Lynch at the sheriff's department. Moments later, Lynch was on the phone with an agent in the ATF's "undercover house" across Double-EE Ranch Road from Mount Carmel. The agent radioed Ballesteros and the other raid-team leaders, saying somebody inside the compound wanted a cease-fire.

Lynch reached Wayne Martin again. He said he was working on a cease-fire. "Pass the word!"

For the moment, the Davidians held their fire. So did the raiders. Lynch and Martin kept talking, trying to wring peace from the firefight. "If they don't back off," Martin warned, "we're going to fight to the last man."

"I understand, Wayne. Just remain calm . . . everything's going to be fine."

Martin, peeking through his office window at black-clad ATF agents, said, "I'm as calm as they are."

◇◇◇◇

At 10:34, the 911 operator fielded another call from Mount Carmel. She asked the caller to identify himself.

"David Koresh," he said. She transferred the call to the lieutenant.

"This is Lynch."

"*Lynch?* That's sort of a funny name."

"Who am I speaking with?"

"David Koresh, the notorious. What'd you guys do that for? How come you try to be so *big* all the time? There's a bunch of us dead. There's a bunch of you guys dead. Now, that's your fault."

"Let's try to resolve this. ATF is pulling back."

"Why didn't you do that first?"

"All I'm doing is handling communications," Lynch said. "I can't give you that answer, David."

"Yeah? Well, let me tell you something. In our great country here, the United States, God has given us a rich history of patriotism. We're not trying to be bad guys. The thing of it is, God is sitting on the throne. I know this sounds crazy to you."

"No, no—"

"But you're going to find out sooner or later. There are Seven Seals in his right hand." While gunshots popped outside, Koresh began expounding on what he called the Bible's mysteries, quoting Revelation 22, "*Behold, I am coming quickly, and my reward is with me.*" Connecting that line to other verses, he asked the lieutenant, "What reward did Christ receive in heaven from his father? He received a book with Seven Seals."

Lynch broke in. "Can I interrupt you for a minute?"

"Sure."

"All right. We can talk theology, but right now—"

"No, this is life and death," Koresh said.

"That's what I'm talking about."

"Theology *is* life and death."

9

Cease-fire

The line went dead. Lynch stayed in touch with the ATF while Wayne Martin told Koresh and the others to hold their fire. The next time Lynch picked up the phone, he heard gunshots.

"That's not us shooting, that is them!" Martin shouted.

"Are you ready to come out and give up?" Lynch asked.

"When they stop firing!"

"God almighty," Lynch muttered, thinking of the *Tribune-Herald* stories that seemed to have spurred the deadliest shootout in ATF history. "*Damn* that fucking newspaper." He told Martin to "tell the others not to shoot. Get the word out." They might see ATF agents moving toward Mount Carmel, "but don't let someone fire on them. All they're doing is removing the wounded people. *Please emphasize that*. Don't let someone start firing."

Martin left his office to pass Lynch's message to Koresh and the others. While he was away, the 911 operator came back on the line, speaking privately to the lieutenant.

"Hey Lynch?" she said. "Between you and me—"

"Yeah?"

"Both of the guys on the roof are dead." She meant LeBleu and McKeehan.

"Both of them?" he said.

"Yeah.

"God almighty! Shit."

Lynch spent an hour juggling phone lines, coordinating between senior ATF agent Jim Cavanaugh outside Mount Carmel and Wayne Martin inside. Soon most of the raiders had pulled back from the front of the compound. Others circled to the rear, where they entered the first-floor gymnasium and took positions under a passageway leading to the second-floor bedrooms. They were crouched in defensive positions when a shadowy figure appeared on the passageway. It was Koresh. A volley of gunfire spun him around, one round grazing his left wrist. A bullet went through his lower torso, chipping his hip bone and exiting through his lower back. Getting shot, Koresh said later, felt "like a 250-pound man kicking you in the side. It took everything in my power to just feel, to crawl . . . everything was getting numb." The ATF agents would swear he shot first.

Koresh crept to shelter in the women's quarters on the second floor. Kathy Schroeder was kneeling beside him when Neil Vaega, one of his followers from New Zealand, brought news that gut-shot Perry Jones looked to be done for. Clive Doyle went to check and found Perry "so delirious that he wants something done to put him out of his misery." Doyle hurried back to the prophet sprawled in the hallway, propped up on pillows, looking half in shock himself.

"Tell him to hang in there," Koresh said. "We're going to get help."

Peter Hipsman, too, was pleading for a merciful death. A lapsed Catholic from Chester, New York, Hipsman was one of the bubbliest Davidians, the one who entertained kids with silly songs and a wacky Donald Duck impression. Shot twice in the raid's first minutes, he was moaning from wounds that looked fatal. According to Schroeder, Koresh conferred with Steve Schneider and told Vaega to put both men out of their misery. When Vaega returned minutes later he said Perry had gone quickly, but not Peter Hipsman. "It took two shots to finish him off."

Sporadic shooting continued while Lynch and Wayne Martin worked out a tentative truce. At one point the raiders got word through their radios: "ATF agents, stand down. Do not engage." By then they had been joined by officers from the Texas Department of Public Safety and local police and sheriff's departments. "Every ATF agent hearing that message had the same reaction: 'Fuck you!'" Risenhoover recalls. "We'd been under blistering fire with our law-enforcement brothers. Nobody wanted to turn tail and run."

Finally, shortly after noon, both sides held their fire while the raiders retrieved their casualties: four dead and twenty wounded, including an agent whose chest was bruised by a bullet that bounced off the pistol in its pouch in his Kevlar vest. One of the wounded was Agent Kenny King. Shot six times, King had lain on the ground for more than two hours before his fellow agents reached him.

By then, six Davidians were dead: Winston Blake, a former baker from Manchester, England, shot in the raid's first moments while wearing a GOD ROCKS T-shirt showing Koresh playing guitar; and Michael Schroeder, shot by ATF agents while trying to return from his job at the Mag Bag; as well as Peter Gent, Peter Hipsman, Perry Jones, and Jaydean Wendell. They would be remembered by their families and friends, but the lost lives of agents LeBleu, Williams, Todd McKeehan, and Steve Willis—gunned down by illegally armed "cultists"—carried a different significance. To the government, the deaths of four ATF agents turned Koresh and his followers into cop killers. That fact had an inescapable consequence: if and when Koresh surrendered, he could count on being put on trial for the murder of four federal law enforcement officers and sentenced to life in prison or death by lethal injection if convicted.

◇◇◇◇

The agents, hiding behind handheld shields, their own vehicles, and the Davidians' parked cars, shouted back and forth. "Cease fire! Only shoot if they shoot at you!" Two of them braved their way to Special Agent Eric Evers, who lay bleeding in a ditch. "We sloshed through the mud" and around a fence, the ATF's Chuck Hustmyre would tell *Texas Monthly*, "and when we looked around it, we saw two Davidians pointing rifles right at us. I thought, '*That's it. We're dead.*' But they didn't shoot. I left my pistol in my holster and kept my hands away from my side and yelled, 'We're supposed to pick up the wounded guy.' They started gesturing with their rifles and shouting, 'Hurry the fuck up!'"

Jim Peeler, the cameraman who had asked Dave Jones for directions that morning, saw undercover agent Robert Rodriguez banging the hood of his car, crying, "I told them! I told them!" Soon Peeler's KWTX-TV colleague Dan Mulloney paid a price for resisting ATF agents' demand for his videotape of the raid. "The agents grabbed him and started smacking him—just beating the total crap out of him," Peeler recalled. "Emotions were running really high."

Thibodeau, watching from a window, unscathed, felt a surge of pride. The retreating federal agents "had such pained expressions as they walked away. They couldn't believe the outcome, obviously. They couldn't believe they had lost."

ATF raider DiBetta agrees: "We went back to the main road, looking like a defeated army." Another former agent, Tom Crowley, recalls retrieving McKeehan's body from the roof. "We carried him down the ladder," he says, "and took care not to let his body touch the ground. We didn't set him down till we were off the property. We didn't want his body touching that fucking place."

While the agents tended their dead and wounded, Lynch kept Wayne Martin on the phone. "Talk to me now. You sound upset."

Martin surprised him with sudden regret. Not for the carnage on both sides of Mount Carmel's flimsy walls, but for failing to live up to his faith. "We've been a burden to him," the lawyer said of Koresh. Just as Martin blamed his spiritual flaws for his son's crippling illness, he now blamed himself and other Davidians for failing to meet Koresh's high standards. "We've learned truths from him that nobody else could teach us, and in spite of it all, we couldn't follow a few simple rules he gave us. And so we feel responsible."

"What have you not done?"

"Well, take a look at me. I'm overweight. I'm not supposed to be that way. I was supposed to get in shape . . . but I still came up short."

Lynch asked Martin what he thought would happen next.

"We're looking at our options at this point."

"What options?"

After a pause, Martin said, "We want God to come and help us."

◇◇◇◇

The prophet lay on bloodied pillows, shivering, eyes rolling up in his head. The others thought he might die any minute. Thibodeau recalls talk that Koresh was thirty-three years old, the same age as the crucified Jesus, bleeding from wounds in his side and his hand. "Yeah, we read some significance into that," Thibodeau said.

But Koresh rallied. Lying in a hallway an hour after getting spun off his feet by the bullet that passed through his side, he called for his guitar and strummed a few chords. "They don't kill me that easy," he said. When one of the elders mentioned the lives they had lost, Koresh sounded a reassuring note. "Nobody else has to die. God said this is enough. In other words, God has accepted these people, and that's it."

He said he wanted to call his mother. Bonnie had moved to Tyler with his stepfather, Roy Haldeman. Someone brought a phone down the hall to Koresh. The phone was connected to a jack in another room by a hundred-foot extension cord. Bonnie wasn't home to take his call, so he left a message on her answering machine: "Hello, Mama, it's your boy. They shot me and I'm dying. But I'll be back real soon, okay? I'm sorry you didn't learn the Seals, but I'll be merciful, okay? I'll see y'all in the skies."

◇◇◇◇

Wayne Martin was shouting at his speakerphone. The ATF had promised to call off its attack, but now several more helicopters swept in from the southwest—from Waco. Martin railed at the feds until Lieutenant Lynch got a word in. "Those aren't ours!" he said. "They're TV helicopters."

By then the standoff was national news, with the Cable News Network at the head of the pack. In an era when cable TV was relatively new, CNN had scored ratings coups with coverage of the 1986 explosion of the space shuttle *Challenger*; the rescue of "Baby Jessica" McClure, who fell into a well in Midland, Texas, the following year; the fall of the Berlin Wall in 1989; and other breaking events—coverage the three broadcast networks, with their schedules of afternoon soap operas and prime-time dramas and sitcoms, couldn't match.

That evening, Koresh was on national TV. "They came all locked and loaded," he told CNN anchor David French in a phone hookup. "I opened the front door as they were running up. They were in complete combat uniform and they started hollering. I fell back and the bullets started coming through the door . . . I was hollering, 'Go away, there's women and children here. Let's talk!'"

Soon he was live on Dallas's KRLD radio, saying, "I ain't budging, and I ain't scared." When station manager Charlie Seraphin broke in to ask if he felt any sympathy for the ATF agents his people had killed, Koresh said yes, he did. "My friend, it was *unnecessary*."

"Are you getting enough to eat, David?" Seraphin asked.

"Although I am a ravenous bird from the East, I'm not eating too much. I'm sipping a little orange juice. I'm okay." His reference to a bird came from the book of Isaiah, a chapter predicting a cataclysm: "*Calling a ravenous bird from the east . . . I bring near my righteousness; it shall not be far off, and my salvation shall not tarry.*"

◇◇◇◇

Within hours the Federal Aviation Administration declared the area around Mount Carmel a no-fly zone. All civilian aircraft, including TV helicopters, were banned from the area. ATF agents kept TV, radio, and newspaper reporters hundreds of yards from the scene.

Koresh and Martin stayed in touch with Lynch and the raiders by phone. They worked out an agreement: if radio station KRLD broadcast a message from Koresh, he would send out some of the children the ATF was calling his "hostages."

At 8:55 that night, after the station aired twenty minutes of his preaching on Revelation's Seven Seals and the looming apocalypse, two little girls emerged from Mount Carmel. Six-year-old Angelica Sonobe and her three-year-old sister, Crystal, were the daughters of "Snow Flea," who had traded bullets with ATF agents, and Floracita "Sita" Sonobe, his wife. Sita led her daughters out, hugged them, and returned to the compound. The girls were hustled into federal custody. An hour later, Sita brought out the preschool daughters of Livingstone Fagan. Again, she returned to her husband and the others waiting inside.

The day of the raid ended with a crescent moon over Mount Carmel. About 120 Davidians, nearly as many ATF agents, curious neighbors, and a growing number of TV, radio, and newspaper reporters settled down for an uneasy night.

One of the onlookers was Vic Feazell, the McLennan County prosecutor who had sought to convict Vernon Howell of attempted murder for his shootout with George Roden six years before. Feazell, no Davidian sympathizer, was appalled by what he called the ATF's "storm-trooper tactics." He thought he knew what was going to happen next.

"The feds are preparing to kill them," Feazell told the *Houston Chronicle*, a quote that appeared in the next morning's newspaper. "That way they can bury their mistakes."

David and Goliath

An advance unit of the FBI's elite Hostage Rescue Team (HRT) arrived in Waco on February 28. Other agents sometimes called the HRT the agency's "ninjas." By that night there were fifty HRT agents on the scene, along with SWAT teams from field offices all over Texas. They were there to take command from the ATF, which had now botched its second high-profile assignment in six months. First Ruby Ridge, now this mess at Waco.

The FBI categorized the standoff as a "complex hostage barricade rescue situation" despite the fact that there were no hostages or barricades at Mount Carmel. Hostage/barricade rescues call for a sequence of actions that FBI agents had employed many times before. The job is to seal off the scene and convince hostage takers to surrender. The HRT and SWAT agents surrounding Mount Carmel knew that the vast majority of such incidents are resolved in six to eight hours. They had no reason to expect this one to be different, at least at first.

It would turn out to be utterly different. As Edward Dennis, a former US assistant attorney general, later assessed the situation at Waco, "Koresh made no threats, set no deadlines, and made no demands. Koresh and his followers were at Mount Carmel, where they wanted to be, living in conditions only marginally more severe than they were accustomed to." While an impartial observer might see the Davidians' children as hostages, unable to make their own decisions, the adults inside saw themselves and their children as members of a religious minority attacked by government forces sent to disarm and even kill them. They used a biblical term to describe the ATF, FBI, and National Guard forces surrounding them: Babylon.

Special Agent in Charge Jeffrey Jamar took over leadership of the FBI command post on the Texas State Technical College campus, a nine-mile drive from Mount Carmel. One colleague described the six-foot-four Jamar as "a big man with broad shoulders, so intimidating that subordinates tried to avoid him." A cowlick falling over Jamar's forehead might have suited a younger man, but the jowls connecting his cheeks to his neck made him look all of his forty-nine years. His job was to keep the Waco standoff from turning into another Ruby Ridge.

Jamar sent teams of agents to secure the perimeter. There weren't enough of them to cover every acre of scrubland surrounding Mount Carmel, but they made their presence clear. Church elder Clive Doyle spotted "agents all over the place. There were seventeen on one ridge beyond the swimming pool. If you looked through binoculars, you could see three different sniper positions near the dairy barn." In the hours before sunrise on the first of March, some of the Davidians tracked the agents' movements by using the night scopes on their rifles. "We knew we were surrounded."

◇◇◇◇

Gary Noesner had dreamed of being an FBI agent since his boyhood in Atlantic Beach, Florida. At the age of twelve, he saw J. Edgar Hoover on TV's *The Mickey Mouse Club*, describing the heroics of G-men like Eliot Ness, who brought down Al Capone, and Melvin Purvis, who tracked down John Dillinger and Pretty Boy Floyd. Noesner joined the Bureau right out of Florida Southern College and worked his way up from desk duties to the Hostage Rescue Team. He was calm, affable, direct—the very model of a hostage negotiator, which he became after seven years in the FBI.

He'd been shopping at a hardware store near the FBI Academy

in Quantico, Virginia, the morning of Sunday, February 28, when his beeper went off. Noesner barely had time to pack a bag before reporting to the local airstrip and boarding a government plane that whisked him to Texas. Within hours of leaving Virginia, he was shaking hands with Jamar at the Bureau's command post in Waco.

His first on-scene briefing convinced him that David Koresh "sounded like a charismatic con artist—perhaps more accurately described as an antisocial personality or sociopath." Noesner had two short-term goals. He wanted to convince Koresh to trust him, and to secure the release of more kids as fast as he could. The total rose to six the next morning, when the Davidians sent out two of the four children of Jaydean Wendell, the slain ex-cop from Hawaii. Thirty-seven children remained inside the compound.

That evening, Noesner took command of the negotiating team that would deal directly with Koresh. It was time to say hello. He put on the headset connecting him to Mount Carmel and took a deep breath. "Hi David. This is Gary."

"Gary, huh?" Koresh sounded calm, even friendly. "Who'd you say you were with, Gary?"

"The FBI."

Noesner said he'd heard Koresh was wounded. How was he doing?

"A little pain, a little pain." After a brief lecture on scripture— "the harmony of what the prophets have been shown must be harmonized"—Koresh promised to send out two more children. He asked for nothing in return. As with the others, he said, the children would leave Mount Carmel two by two, like the creatures Noah saved in the book of Genesis.

"I have your word on that?" Noesner asked.

"You have God's word on that."

Koresh made good on his promise. In the early-morning hours of March 1, he arranged to send out former policewoman Jaydean Wendell's other two children, eight-year-old Jaunessa and her baby brother, Patron. A little after eight that morning, a white government car pulled up beside the empty water tower that still held Peter Gent's body. At 8:22, Sita Sonobe, wife of the wounded Snow Flea, emerged again, blinking in early-morning sun. Leading Jaunessa by the hand, she carried five-month-old Patron to the white sedan and handed him over to a federal agent. The car pulled away for the fifteen-minute drive to the FBI's command post. By the end of the day, half a dozen more Davidian children between two and eleven years old would join them on the outside.

Over the phone with the FBI, Koresh made a cryptic reference to the Bible. "There's a little secret with these children," he said. "Read Psalm eight. Bye-bye."

The eighth Psalm refers to children and infants (*"out of the mouths of babes and sucklings"*) before referring to a siege: *"you have established a stronghold against your enemies."*

As Noesner recalled, the children leaving Mount Carmel "came out with little notes pinned to their jackets saying things like, 'Please send me to my aunt Sophie in Des Moines.' Well, we didn't do that." Instead the FBI put the children on the phone to their parents and relatives inside the compound. "We let them know that their kids weren't going anywhere. We were waiting for them to come out and resume custody."

But the Davidians left inside had no intention of abandoning their home or their leader. Almost without exception, the adults shared Koresh's determination to stick to their guns and their faith. The children had no choice in the matter, though some of the older ones shared their parents' belief that the siege proved Koresh had been right all along. Hadn't David told them bad men would come after them one day? He had told them that even children would have to fight back—not for themselves, their families, or even for God, but for *him*. As the sun climbed over the water tower on the morning after the raid, the Davidians presented a unified front. Koresh spoke for them when he gave the agents on the phone a promise: "We ain't comin' out."

That vow left Noesner and Jamar worrying that Koresh might be planning a Jonestown-style mass suicide. Koresh swore he had no such plans, and on that count, at least, Noesner believed him. As the negotiator knew, sociopaths tend to harm others, not themselves. But there was more to it than that: the more he wheedled and dickered over the phone, the clearer it became that the Davidian "prophet" believed he had a chance to convert the FBI men to his way of thinking.

"I've always loved law enforcement," he told Noesner, "because y'all risk your lives every day." After several minutes of holding forth on the Seven Seals, he assured the negotiators that they still had time to save their souls. The Seals, which occupy a mere three chapters of the book of Revelation, not even two full pages in the King James Bible, describe the coming apocalypse. To "open" the Seals meant to fully comprehend and explain them, an act that would set the Last Days in motion. Koresh intended to do just that. If the negotiators hoped to understand "what's happening in this crazy world," he said—and avoid spending eternity in hell—they'd better listen to him.

◇◇◇◇

"Time is always in our favor."

That maxim from the FBI's hostage negotiation training manual holds true in almost every case in which agents encounter armed criminals holed up in banks, schools, apartments, churches, and other settings where they must calculate the risks of intervention against the chance to save innocent lives. Yet Noesner suspected that this case might be an exception to the rule. The "hostages" had no desire to be saved, except in a spiritual sense. Hunkered down in their retreat, where they were accustomed to doing without electricity or running water, the Branch Davidians were armed to the teeth and provisioned with military rations that might last them a year. All they wanted was to be left alone. Unfortunately for them, as Noesner well knew, that was no longer an option—not with four federal agents dead.

At a March 1 press conference, ATF spokesperson Sharon Wheeler presented her agency's view of the raid. "I don't believe we were outmaneuvered or outplanned," she announced in a twang as Texan as Koresh's. "The problem is that we were outgunned. They had bigger firearms than we had."

As she spoke, agents were moving reporters and cameras farther away from Mount Carmel, ostensibly for their own safety. The media perimeter went from several hundred yards from the Davidians' fortress to more than two miles. "From then on," one TV correspondent said, "all we and the rest of the world could see was a long-distance view of the compound." Soon after the FBI took command, reporters felt the growing federal commitment through the soles of their shoes: the ground shook as Bradley and M1 Abrams tanks rumbled toward Mount Carmel. Eventually the federal armor at Mount Carmel would include nine Bradleys, two Abrams, and five modified tanks known as combat engineering vehicles (CEVs). The 68-ton Abrams tanks, the largest and most powerful in America's arsenal, had played a decisive role in Operation Desert Storm during the Gulf War in 1991, destroying Russian-made Iraqi tanks from more than a mile away. Each one weighed more than a fully loaded railroad car. Their arrival seemed to confirm the Davidians' suspicions. Seeing the press perimeter pushed into the distance made matters worse. They had hoped media coverage might help keep Babylon at bay.

Inside Mount Carmel, the Davidians examined the damage from the previous day's raid. They found holes in the front walls that matched bullets' paths. Some of the ATF's nine-millimeter rounds "went through two, three, four walls," Koresh told the negotiators, "and right out the back." Outside the compound, some members of the media were already questioning the government's actions. The *New York Times* noted that the raid had been the costliest and deadliest in ATF history. One agent on the scene called it "inexcusable." Once the Davidians started shooting, he said, "the raid should have been aborted. Instead, we walked right into it." The *Washington Post* referred to the Davidians as a cult but also quoted a local pastor who wondered why the ATF would stage such a spectacle. "Why didn't they get him when he was out alone?" The locals were used to seeing Koresh jogging and running errands around the neighborhood. "Personally, I think they wanted a show of force. They underestimated a religious leader," the pastor said.

CNN had particular interest in the showdown at Waco. Its typical ratings were dwarfed by those of the three broadcast networks, but CNN's numbers leaped when breaking news led millions of viewers to tune in for ongoing coverage of dramatic events, sometimes for hours at a time. The life-and-death spectacle at Mount Carmel proved ideal for daily recaps and live updates that kept viewers watching.

The cable network was at the forefront of the unfolding drama from the start with its live phone interview with Koresh after the raid. But CNN and the Davidians would both get a surprise that added insult to Koresh's injury.

At 1:30 p.m. on March 2, the FBI cut off Mount Carmel's phone connection to the outside world. The phones still worked but now led only to the FBI command post. Up until then, the Davidians had been talking to family and friends outside as well as the press. Their phone service had always been spotty, thanks in part to a puppy that liked to chew on phone cords; it took several hours before they realized they were cut off.

At 4:45 that afternoon, the Justice Department officially removed the ATF from command of "the incident at Waco." From that point on, the FBI was in charge. Chief negotiator Noesner settled into the Bureau's command post in a windowless airplane hangar on the technical-college campus, the site of a former air force base. He commandeered a private room where a supervisor—often Noesner himself—would sit near the man on the phone, listening in and passing him suggestions on index cards. Another member of the negotiating team made sure the tape recorder was working properly. A fourth agent took notes, keeping track of key points in their discussions with the Davidians—usually Steve Schneider and Koresh, who did most of the talking.

At 4:48, as arranged, Koresh sent two more children out to the white sedan waiting by the water tower. By then, shivering through waves of pain and dizziness, he thought he might be dying. Annetta Richards, a Davidian who had worked as a nurse, cleaned the seeping wound in his side and took his blood pressure. She reported a worrisome number: "Eighty-five over forty." Someone came up with a bottle of aspirin, but Koresh refused it. Instead, he rubbed garlic on his wounds. Soon he rallied again. This time the catalyst was anger.

The Davidians had discovered that their phone line led only to the FBI. Sitting up straight to take the phone, Koresh railed at Jim Cavanaugh, the negotiator he liked best, the one who called him "buddy." Cavanaugh was ATF, not FBI, and had helped lead the raid.

"You guys—" he said, voice rising. "You guys are telling the public of this country that you don't want any blood." He instructed

Cavanaugh to "tell those boys they better get our lines back operate-able, or they're going to go to bed every night with the knowledge that they're the ones that killed these little children." It was the first time he'd made even a veiled threat involving the children.

"Okay, David."

"You tell these boneheads, these bureaucrats, whatever they are, to *open our lines up!* Tell them guys if what they want is a big fight, then *come on!*"

"David, no, we don't want to fight."

Moments later, Schneider put one of the children on the line.

"Are you going to come and kill me?" the little girl asked.

"No, honey," Cavanaugh said. "No. Nobody's going to come kill you."

Koresh took the phone back. "This is in your hands now, *buddy.*"

Cavanaugh kept him talking, promising to pass the word up the chain of command, reminding Koresh that he too answered to higher powers. "I'm just the guy that's talking to you." The son of a New Jersey fireman, Cavanaugh was a holdover—a sixteen-year ATF veteran working with Noesner's FBI team because Koresh seemed to trust him. "I've got all kinds of bosses and commanders and generals around here," he said. "I've got guys with gold leaves and badges like you wouldn't believe. All heavyweights. I mean, think about me. I get pressure. I've got the news, I've got the governor, I've got the *vice president—*"

Koresh said, "You're my voice, then."

"I'm not tricking you," Cavanaugh said.

Koresh confided that his wounds might be fatal. He had "a hole in the back that's bigger than the hole in the front." If he died that night, he said, one of his regrets would have to do with the way the press was describing him. Maybe Cavanaugh could set them straight. "Listen, Jim," he said, "there's nothing that hurts me more than being called a cult leader. I'm not a cult leader. I'm a Bible teacher." After a lengthy discussion of Jesus's suffering on the cross, Koresh sounded ready to give up the ghost.

That alarmed Cavanaugh. "If you live, you can spread the word," he said.

"I cannot. They'll lock me up in jail for a hundred years."

While they talked, the tanks outside had rolled closer to the parked cars and picket fence in front of Mount Carmel. That angered Koresh: "If they want to fight, we'll fight!"

"We are not coming in," Cavanaugh assured him. "We are not coming in. We are not coming in."

"If you're going to keep moving closer and closer to our rear ends, then finally we're going to turn around and we're going to slug you. I mean, this is a great nation, but it's not bigger than my God. I'm the little guy, you're the big guy. The Goliath. I'm the David. Remember that. And Goliath does get his head sunken in with a rock. Think about that."

Cavanaugh promised to think about that. Again, he swore the tanks would not attack, imploring Koresh to stay calm while they moved closer. Schneider, less combative in his talks with Noesner's team, may have urged Koresh to wait and see.

The tanks moved forward again, and again stopped.

The Davidians held their fire.

◇◇◇◇

That evening, after a tense night and long workday, Agent Cavanaugh went back to his motel room. Special Agent Henry Garcia, the FBI's night negotiator, took his first turn on the phone. His shift consisted mainly of a torrent of preaching from Koresh.

"The sun and moon and stars is darkened. Heaven departs as a scroll," Koresh declared, paraphrasing Revelation, "and the great men of the earth cry to the rocks and mountains to hide them from the face of the reality that they would not know." His evangelizing gave Garcia little room to interrupt. During one long stretch, Koresh preached about Assyrians, Nebuchadnezzar, bellies of brass and legs of iron, the holy hills of Zion, Habakkuk, Nahum, Persia, Micah, mighty angels, and seven thunders. The FBI transcript shows Garcia saying nothing but "Um-hum" or "Uh-huh" twenty-eight times in a row, with one "Right" thrown in for good measure.

After more than an hour, the negotiator asked the preacher how he was feeling.

"Pain," Koresh said. "A little pain. When I cough, oh man—never mind!" Yet he was clearly enjoying his hours with a captive audience. That night he sent out four more children. The last two, released at 11:05 p.m., included Sheila and Wayne Martin's disabled son, Jamie, wounded by flying glass during the raid. Ten-year-old Jamie weighed less than forty pounds and couldn't walk. His mother carried him to the car waiting by the water tower.

"It hurt to let my Jamie go," Sheila remembers, "but I knew I'd see him again. In this world or the next."

Koresh surprised the negotiators with an offer that seemed impulsive: if they arranged for him to deliver a nationwide broadcast, he and his followers would surrender. Using hand signals, Noesner encouraged Garcia to indicate that they were receptive.

"Okay, David," Garcia said. "Let's see what we can do."

Noesner thought the idea might end the standoff. Later, after consulting his superiors and an FBI profiler, he had Garcia make the offer: if the FBI arranged a broadcast that would send Koresh's voice and his message to millions of Americans, would he lay down his weapons and bring his people out? "We're trying to get some time on the national Christian Broadcasting Network, which has several thousand radio stations across the country," Garcia said.

Koresh was intrigued. As midnight approached, he agreed. Schneider passed the word to the other Davidians: "Get ready to leave. We'll all go out tomorrow."

Koresh fell asleep. The men around him took the good news as a reason to party. "Our pent-up feelings burst out," Thibodeau recalled. "We expected to be leaving Mount Carmel the next morning, so we felt free to indulge our appetites one last time, and broke into our cache of hard liquor." Gorging on desserts, smoking cigarettes, guzzling whiskey, they spent the wee hours "shouting and singing, praying at the top of our voices, making a hell of a racket. Everyone was blissed out."

At the FBI command post, Garcia and the other men on Noesner's team celebrated with handshakes and backslaps. The incident at Waco was almost over.

11

Wait

It was midnight in Phoenix, where the Christian Broadcasting Network was based, when the FBI began phoning CBN executives' homes. Some of the broadcasters were rousted from their beds. They quickly agreed to air an hour-long special the next day: Koresh's message to the world.

At 1:20 a.m. Waco time on Tuesday, the second day after the raid, Koresh sent out two more children. One was Natalie Nobrega, the eleven-year-old daughter of one of the Afro-Brits. The other was seven-year-old Joanne Vaega, whose father had put Perry Jones and Peter Hipsman out of their misery. That brought the number of children released to sixteen.

Koresh spent the predawn hours of March 2 on the phone with Henry Garcia. At one point Garcia interrupted a long harangue on Psalms and Revelation to remind him to record his message for CBN. The FBI needed the recording soon, Garcia said, in order to get it on the radio during "drive time" that morning, when commuters were on their way to work.

Koresh corrected him. He said drive time was between 5:00 and 6:00 p.m., when people were driving home.

"Prime time in radioland," Garcia said, "is when everybody is going *to* work."

But Koresh fancied himself an expert on radio programming as well as scripture. "Ask the producers and they'll tell you the opposite."

Garcia changed the subject to the preamble Koresh had promised to add to his message. Koresh was unfamiliar with the term. Told that a preamble was a short statement at the start—in this case stating his vow to lead his people out of Mount Carmel after his message aired—he promised to record one. Garcia emphasized how crucial the preamble was to his FBI bosses. Koresh was unmoved. "Your bosses, your bosses! I mean, this is not Burger King management. *You're* the negotiator."

"Well, I don't have all the power. I still have bosses." One of their stipulations, Garcia said, was that an adult Davidian would bring out the tape. That way it wouldn't get damaged, he said, and Koresh agreed.

After hanging up the phone, Koresh recorded an hour-long audiotape. He chose Mount Carmel's oldest resident to take it out to the FBI.

It was a chilly morning, temperatures in the forties inside and out. Catherine Matteson, seventy-seven years old, was huddled in her bunk when "someone woke me up and said David wanted to talk to me." Matteson had been a Davidian since 1960, more than twenty years before Vernon Howell arrived. After decades of following the Rodens, she had no doubt that David Koresh was the new Christ.

"I made this tape," he told her. "I'd like you to take it so it can be played on prime time."

She asked if her friend Margaret Lawson could go with her. He agreed. Lawson was seventy-five, and as Koresh admitted later he doubted the two elderly women would be any help if the rest of them wound up fighting the authorities. He handed Matteson the only copy of the fifty-eight-minute audiotape, and at 8:10 that morning the two gray-haired women emerged from the retreat along with two more of Wayne and Sheila Martin's children. Matteson had barely handed over the cassette when she and Lawson were arrested and handcuffed. They were truly hostages now, threatened with long prison terms unless they got on the phone to Mount Carmel and urged others to follow them out. They refused. Asked to help the government's efforts by drawing floor plans of Mount Carmel, they refused.

The Davidians inside the compound sang and prayed. They packed their few belongings in suitcases, gym bags, backpacks, grocery sacks, and pillowcases. They helped the children put on their coats. Many of the children were scared that the bad men outside would shoot them. Steve Schneider, Koresh's second-in-command, arranged a task to distract them from their fears.

They had been left with eleven malamute puppies after ATF agents shot the other dogs. The pups, their eyes still shut, had been too small to go outdoors. Schneider told the children to find a cardboard box and keep them safe and warm until it was time for them all to leave.

Koresh had a showman's idea of how their exodus would play out. "Women and children first, and then guys, each one with his hands up," he said. "And then four of you carry me out on a stretcher. That will be good TV."

◇◇◇◇

Koresh's broadcast began at 1:32 that afternoon. The Davidians gathered around radios to listen. He opened with his prearranged preamble: "I, David Koresh, agree upon the broadcasting of the tape to come out peacefully with all the people immediately." After that he said, "What we're trying to present today may in some ways shed a better light in regards to my situation and my predicament here at Mount Carmel." Then he launched into a long monologue about the looming apocalypse, the Seven Seals, and "the testimony of Jesus Christ." He spoke of God's emerald throne and "cloven tongues of fire." Finally, toward the end of his speech, energy flagging, he took a long, ragged breath. "It's funny," he said. "People always like to build the sepulchres of dead prophets and garnish their tombs, but they hate and kill their living prophets."

While Koresh and his followers listened to his radio sermon, the FBI prepared for the Davidians' exit. Three prison buses and eight ambulances pulled up behind the tanks outside Mount Carmel. One of the ambulances was armor-plated, a bulletproof vehicle dispatched specifically to keep Koresh safe from any angry observer or ATF agent who might want to take a shot at him. Next, a government truck dropped a pea-green army stretcher at the foot of the driveway near their bullet-pocked front door. Schneider and another Davidian, Greg Summers, hurried to bring the stretcher inside. Summers, a longhaired Australian, was legally married to one of Koresh's many "wives," who had a one-year-old daughter with Koresh and was now pregnant by him again. Koresh called Summers one of the insiders he relied on, his Mighty Men.

As the broadcast wound down, Schneider and Rachel Jones Howell took turns on the phone while Koresh listened to the end of his sermon. Nothing pleased him like the sound of his own voice. Rachel gave the negotiators an approximate head count of the Davidians who would be coming out: forty-seven women, forty-three men, and twenty children.

More than seven hundred federal, state, and local law enforcement officers kept watch over Mount Carmel, waiting for them to come out. As Supervisory Special Resident Agent (SSRA) Byron Sage, a member of the FBI brass, recalled, Koresh "guaranteed us" that as soon as the Christian Broadcasting Network finished playing his tape, "he would come out and bring everyone with him. Frankly, he thought he was dying, and he was milking it for all it was worth . . . This was his launchpad to everlasting fame. He had been some obscure, wackadoo preacher on the high plains of Texas, and now, all of a sudden, he was the messiah."

Koresh's sermon ended at two thirty. In closing, he said, "We made an agreement with the ATF agents—that if they would allow me to have national coverage with this tape, that all the people here at the facility—'compound' as y'all call it—will give ourselves over to the world, give ourselves out to you. This is what I promised, and this is what we're going to keep. Thank you very much. God bless you."

He was pleased with his performance. Soon after it ended, he got back on the phone.

"Hey, your message got out great," negotiator Cavanaugh told him.

Koresh agreed. "At least now people realize I'm not as crazy as they thought."

Cavanaugh was ready to talk him through the next step: the Davidians' surrender. Instead, Koresh handed the phone to Steve Schneider. An hour went by. Schneider said Koresh was leading his people in prayer.

"What are you saying?" Cavanaugh asked. "Are you ready to leave now?"

"Yeah, pretty quick," Schneider said. "We're just getting a last few things together."

"If you see an armored ambulance pull up, you can call me."

"Okey-doke. Appreciate it, Jim. God bless you. Bye."

◇◇◇◇

Two hours passed. Three. Agent Cavanaugh asked Schneider why they hadn't come out yet.

"Honest truth—everyone's quiet," Schneider said. "They're just waiting."

The world was watching. The hundreds of law enforcement agents outside were outnumbered by a media contingent clustered in an area nicknamed "Satellite City" for its banks of news vans mounted with satellite uplinks, an area peopled by nearly a thousand reporters, photographers, TV and radio correspondents, producers, and technical personnel representing ABC, CBS, NBC, CNN, PBS, Fox TV, the BBC, and other outlets. Zoom lenses focused on the blue and white Davidian banner on the flagpole outside Mount Carmel, the tanks parked nearby, the compound's windows blocked by mattresses and hay bales. Mike Cox, a Texas Department of Public Safety spokesman, called the press contingent "probably the biggest media turnout" in the state since the 1969 Apollo moonshot brought hordes of reporters to Houston, "maybe the largest since the Kennedy assassination."

Still there was no sign of movement. Cavanaugh complained to Schneider: "He gave us his word. We had an agreement. After the message was played—"

"But what if a higher power speaks to you? What do you do?"

That sounded ominous to Cavanaugh. He said, "This was not our agreement, Steve."

"Look, I know you don't believe there is a supernatural power that speaks audibly to a person."

"No."

"But if there is a God in this universe," Schneider said, "then there's laws of man and there's laws of God. And this God that has led him all his life says for him to wait."

"To *wait?*"

"He says his God says that he is to wait."

"Let me talk to him."

Rachel took the phone. "He's weeping right now," she told Cavanaugh. "He's not going to talk."

Cavanaugh asked if she could lead the others out. "Well, I'm not exactly sure how to use the right words," she said. "I'm not a good spokesperson. We believe only he can open the Seven Seals, and God told him to wait, and that's what we're doing."

"David and I made an agreement," Cavanaugh told her. "He also made an agreement with the world on the radio. As soon as the tape played, everyone would walk out peacefully."

Steve Schneider came back on the line. "Okay, okay—"

"I have commanders," Cavanaugh said, "and they are losing trust. They're starting to doubt me. I've got to have some movement *now*."

"He says his God says he should wait."

"Yeah, Steve, but—"

"Is this being taped, by any chance?" Schneider asked.

Cavanaugh lied. "No." He pressed Schneider: "We've kept every single part of our bargain. We moved the snipers back from the fence. We've never, ever, broken our word."

"I believe that," Schneider said.

"And now I feel really let down by you and David."

"God is saying, 'Wait.' He prayed, and there was a voice that said nothing else to him but 'Wait.'"

"You've gotta show me something," Cavanaugh said. "Something like a time—like if I give you a few more minutes, then you'll come out."

"Let me go talk to him."

A few minutes later, Schneider came back with bad news. "David can't go against God." He said Koresh was speaking darkly of "a snare for Babylon," another line that worried the negotiator.

Cavanaugh kept him talking. They were at a pivotal moment, he said. If Koresh broke his promise to lead his people out, "Who's going to believe him the next time?" If the prophet went back on his word, "He will lose. All the good you got from that broadcast, he's going to lose it."

Schneider left the phone again to relay the message. Koresh, lying in his bed of sheets and mattresses fifty feet down the hall, sent a message back.

"He thinks the world of you," Schneider told Cavanaugh. "He says, 'Just fear God and wait.'"

Schneider sent word to the other Davidians: "We're not going. God told David to wait." Back on the phone to the FBI, he said they weren't coming out.

Angry and frustrated, Noesner handed a note to his negotiator, who delivered it verbatim: "We delivered on our end of the bargain. We did everything you asked."

Schneider said, "I understand. But God has the final word."

◇◇◇◇

That night, Ted Koppel's top-rated *Nightline* program led with images of the firefight three days before. "Today, an agreement to surrender. Was it made in bad faith?" Koppel asked. "Tonight, the standoff continues. Will it end in more bloodshed?" He described "a convoluted story that seems to be in the process of ending. But already, just about everything that could possibly have gone wrong in this bizarre tale about a heavily armed religious cult—just about everything that *could* go wrong *has*." *Nightline* correspondent Tom Foreman, reporting from Satellite City, called the military vehicles at Mount Carmel "a strategic display of power," adding that the press, miles from what Koppel called "cult headquarters," felt sidelined and stonewalled, "like the story is almost in another state."

On the phone to the FBI, Schneider voiced similar concerns. "I can't talk to the outside world," he said. "The press are so far back that you guys could come and blow us away and you could give any kind of story you wanted."

All three broadcast networks had led their nightly news programs with coverage of the standoff in Texas. *Time* magazine, *Newsweek*, and *People* were preparing cover stories on what was fast becoming the media event of 1993. Ratings for Koresh's radio sermon provided one measure of the story's drawing power. Along with the Christian Broadcasting Network, Dallas's KDFW-TV had carried the broadcast that afternoon. When the ratings came in, they showed that 40 percent of TV households in the Dallas–Fort Worth area had tuned in—more than watched *Jeopardy!* or even *The Oprah Winfrey Show*. The station's news director crowed, "I finally beat Oprah for an hour!"

12

A Gathering Storm

National traumas almost always have two consequences: investigations and jokes. "Other than that, Mrs. Lincoln, how did you like the play?" Twentieth-century calamities brought Pearl Harbor jokes, JFK jokes, Vietnam jokes. The 1986 *Challenger* disaster that helped establish CNN as a prime source of breaking news led to space shuttle jokes. "What does NASA stand for? Need Another Seven Astronauts." Seven years later, Koresh and the Branch Davidians became the most joked-about Americans of 1993.

One quip said his harem had a "prophet-sharing plan." What drove Koresh crazy? "The guy's got twenty mothers-in-law!" A new ice-cream flavor called Mount Carmel? "It's chock-full of nuts, but you can't get it out of the carton." Even New York governor Mario Cuomo had a one-liner on the subject. Asked if shoppers would return to lower Manhattan in the wake of February's bombing of the World Trade Center's parking garage, Cuomo said, "Where would you rather shop, Waco?"

Texas Department of Public Safety spokesman Mike Cox collected Waco jokes. His favorite compared Koresh to the Dallas Cowboys' lordly coach: "It's not against Texas law to impersonate Jesus—Tom Landry's been doing it for years."

◇◇◇◇

On March 3, the FBI towed several office trailers into place near Mount Carmel. On the phone with the FBI, Koresh reminded the negotiators that all this mobilizing had been avoidable. "You guys could have arrested me anytime. I jog up and down the road every day, and you ain't carrying weapons when you're jogging, are you? Y'all just wanted to play cowboy."

He kept asking to speak to Robert Gonzalez but was told the ATF agent he'd befriended had been reassigned. "We've had difficulty finding Robert," negotiator Cavanaugh said. "He's not in town anymore." In fact, as an FBI insider confided almost thirty years later, the negotiators didn't want Koresh speaking with the man he knew as Gonzalez—ATF agent Robert Rodriguez. Neither agency trusted the distraught Rodriguez not to say the wrong thing.

Koresh insisted he had not broken his promise to surrender after his nationwide radio sermon. That was God's doing, not his. "I'm dealing now with my father, not your bureaucratic system of government," he told Agent Cavanaugh. "Listen here. 'In the storm of the clouds of dust at his feet, he rebuketh the sea and maketh it dry. Carmel, the flower of Lebanon, languisheth.' The mountains quake and the hills melt. The earth is burned. So this is a worldwide event." He preached over the phone for an hour, connecting Old Testament prophecy to events in Texas in 1993, while Cavanaugh followed along in a Bible his boss had provided. "A lot of empires think they're really tough, don't they?" Koresh asked. "The Bible says, '*Chariots shall rage in the streets. Spoiling and violence are before me.*' You don't know what's going on, Jim, do you? You're wondering what this is all about."

This was the way he often ran daily Bible studies, expounding his way down a long, winding path to a leading question. It was how he made sure his followers were paying attention. Now he had another captive audience.

"They're fixing to get what?" Koresh asked.

Cavanaugh took a guess. "Correction?"

"A big whupping from God!"

"Right. Okay."

But mild agreement wasn't enough for the prophet when his mood darkened. After another biblical exegesis, he threatened Cavanaugh and everyone else outside Mount Carmel's walls. "Jim," he said, "let me tell you something about my father. He wants your butt. He wants to wipe this world out. It's proud, it's arrogant, it's corrupt, it's rotten."

"I'm just trying to get the innocent out," Cavanaugh said.

"You don't realize there's guns a billion times bigger than yours pointed at you. You don't know what's fixing to happen."

Cavanaugh, who would later call Koresh "diabolical," tried humoring him. "I think I'm getting a feel for it. It's really a little clearer." They discussed the release of Mark Jones, whose brother and sister were staying behind. Following the previous day's departure of Kim and Daniel Martin, lawyer Wayne and Sheila Martin's youngest children, Mark would be the nineteenth sent out. That was sign of good faith, as Koresh saw it. It was also good tactics, in his view. Like elderly Catherine Matteson and Margaret Lawson, children might be a hindrance if the standoff came down to a final battle with Babylon.

Koresh said he would send Mark Jones out with a box full of puppies, the litter of the malamute lying dead by the flagpole. "You killed my favorite dog," he reminded the negotiator.

"I'm sorry."

"You better watch out," Koresh added. "There might be a bomb in there."

Cavanaugh laughed. "A puppy bomb!"

Mark Jones came out at 4:26 that afternoon, carrying not a box but a squirming bag full of week-old pups. He also brought a wad of cash—a thousand dollars Koresh had tucked into his pocket, instructing him to give it to the FBI "for expenses"—another sign of good faith, as Koresh saw it.

Federal agents gave twelve-year-old Mark gentler treatment than Catherine Matteson and Margaret Lawson received the day before. They made him drop his backpack but returned it after making sure it wasn't booby-trapped. Then they gave him a ride in one of the tanks. Half an hour later, he was sitting on negotiator Cavanaugh's lap, talking to his family inside the compound.

"Jim's nice," he said. "They gave me a soda and a candy bar."

That had been a tactical error on the FBI's part. The Davidians, with their strict dietary practices, believed too much sugar made kids hyperactive. Kids at Mount Carmel got sugary drinks only on special occasions, with Koresh's permission.

Sita Sonobe took the phone to tell the boy, "Don't eat pork."

Next Mark spoke with his little sister. "Jim says come out," he told Heather. "It's okay, come out. Nobody's going to hurt anybody."

"I don't know," she said. "Is it nice there? Is it a house?"

"It's kind of like an airport," he said of the hangar the FBI had commandeered. "Come see me when you can. They're really nice."

The next voice was Koresh's. "Oh, they'll be *nice*," he told Mark. "People in the world are nice, they just don't know what we know, right? They don't believe in the Seals."

Steve Schneider spent much of that evening haggling with Noesner's team about the dead dogs in their pen by the flagpole. "They're starting to smell," he said. The negotiators agreed that the agents outside would allow two unarmed men to come out to bury the dogs. The Davidians kept their part of the bargain, but the snipers stationed outside Mount Carmel—who had permission to fire on any Davidian wielding a weapon—were not informed of the agreement. Now two men came outside carrying objects that looked like rifles.

Their "rifles" were shovels. At that moment a jumpy sniper could have triggered another battle, but the sharpshooters held their fire. The men tried digging graves for the dogs, but the ground was too hard, so they dragged the dogs' bodies far enough from the compound's front doors to cut the stench—closer to the tanks. They released a hunger-mad goose that had spent four days penned with the dead dogs.

Clive Doyle took on a more harrowing task. Someone had to bury the Davidians killed on the day of the raid. Doyle and the other elders chose a patch of bare ground in an underground part of the compound that served as a tornado shelter. "I was surprised that the bodies were not stiff," he recalled. "I had the idea of rigor mortis causing bodies to stiffen up and stay that way, but they don't. They get limber again." He tried digging four holes, but again the ground was too hard. He decided on a single, larger grave. That choice led to an awful geometry. The grave he dug was narrowest at the bottom, so he put former policewoman Jaydean Wendell, the smallest of them, there. Perry Jones, the second smallest, was next, followed by funny-song singer Peter Hipsman, and finally the biggest body, that of Winston Blake, one of the Afro-Brits, who had been shot in the head in the raid's first moments. "By then I was worn out and I got some help to fill the hole in. We ended up with a mound, and we put a wheelbarrow upside-down on top" to mark the spot until they had time to make a cross to mark the grave.

◇◇◇◇

The tanks moved closer. Koresh complained: "You are on our land." Cavanaugh said tank placement was outside his jurisdiction, but he would see what he could do. That evasion seemed to satisfy Koresh, who asked about "the second guy" he'd talked to on the day of the raid. Kind of a jerk. "Was his name Gary?"

"Gary, yeah," Cavanaugh said with Noesner listening in.

"Oh boy. That guy needs to go back to school. Talk about pushy!"

For a moment, Cavanaugh was enjoying his job. "I don't like him either," he said, relishing the dig at the lead negotiator.

"A real tough guy! And how does that work out? Being a tough guy just makes the crazy guys tougher."

◇◇◇◇

That night, Special Agent Garcia relieved Cavanaugh, strapping on a headset and saying hello. Koresh, fresh from a nap, said he felt his strength returning. He was sipping chicken broth, grape juice, and orange juice. He said the Davidians had "two hundred cartons of orange juice" socked away. He repeated that he couldn't believe the ATF had chosen to ambush him when he could have been arrested on a jog or trip to Walmart. The raid was a terrorist act, he said, but aspects of it had been "beautiful. Yeah, that one girl was breast-feeding her baby." He meant Judy Schneider-Koresh, who claimed she'd been nursing her two-year-old when bullets started flying. In fact she had handed her daughter to Heather Jones, then grabbed a rifle and hurried to the window to shoot back—a secret Heather would keep for years. According to Koresh, federal bullets "made two or three little gouges" in Judy, "but she's okay, like me. We're healers."

Again he asked to speak to "Robert Gonzalez."

Garcia lied. "I don't have any idea who he is."

"Maybe we should have taken Robert as a hostage." Koresh was joking, or was he? He went on to describe his view of the Bible as "one of the greatest socio-psychological formulas." In much the way an internet prophet named Q would stitch together doomsday scenarios a quarter century later, Koresh mixed Old Testament oracles, secret symbols, and science into a plausible recipe for impending disaster. God was a "highly technological being" who used UFOs as his advance scouts. God had arranged the universe to send messages to humans, if only we could decipher them. "I mean, there's a new constellation shaped exactly like an electric guitar, shining down on us. The Guitar Nebula! Do we really think all this is nothing but a coincidence?"

He went on for hours about angels, Ezekiel and Nebuchadnezzar, Shadrach, Meshach, and Abednego, nuclear war, the Second Amendment, and a coming Judgment Day when lightning would pour down like rain. "The clouds return, oh boy," he told Agent Garcia, describing the coming apocalypse, "a gathering of clouds just like it was two thousand years ago when the messiah was being killed. The clouds came, thunder in the heavens, darkness was over the earth. That's going to be repeated."

"Uh-huh."

The more Koresh talked, the more he seemed to believe he might convert at least one of the negotiators to his way of thinking. He was pretty sure he'd gotten his hooks into Robert, the sad-eyed ATF man.

"Would you consider Christ a political leader?" he asked Garcia.

The negotiator said he wasn't sure.

"If he was to come today in clouds of glory, your national leaders and all your great empire directors would have a United Nations council. The pontiff and leaders of all churches and governments would sit down and talk. What would *you* do?"

Garcia said he didn't know. Hours went by as he listened to what the negotiators called Koresh's "Bible babble." Some of them resented serving as the Waco wacko's listeners, but Garcia had a long fuse.

"You may be trying to pacify me—" Koresh said.

"Uh-huh."

"—but you will be judged."

"I believe you."

"Oh. If you believe me, are you ready to obey me?"

At last Garcia broke in. "*Listen* for a second!" He was hoping to talk about getting other children out of the compound.

Koresh cut him off. "Now you're talking like a Pharisee. You know, we have explosives here which could send those vehicles forty or fifty feet up in the air." Alluding to a rumor he'd heard on the radio, he said, "You don't know whether I've got all kinds of mines around the perimeter of this place!" But soon he calmed down, promising to release another child "at first light." Till then, he said, he would try to get some sleep.

During the night, Wayne Martin phoned the negotiators. FBI records describe him as "angry and militant." Martin said he wanted nothing from "your government" and predicted its downfall. Koresh had been chosen to rule over decadent America, he insisted, "establishing a new nation founded on the Seven Seals." He hung up at 3:12 a.m., then called back at 5:55 to warn the negotiators that they were speeding down a one-way road to hell.

◇◇◇◇

Eleven-year-old Kevin Jones emerged, bundled up against the cold, at 7:25 a.m. on March 4. Agents frisked him and drove him to the command post, where Cavanaugh patched the boy through to his aunt Rachel.

"They gave me something to eat. Donuts and Coke," he told her.

"Well, *that's* a real nutritious breakfast."

Nights had been wintry enough that the Davidians slept in coats and mittens. Agent Cavanaugh, back on the phone to Rachel, asked if they were using space heaters.

"Not anymore," she said. "Do you know what happens if a bullet hits one of those? The place will blow up."

"Yeah, be careful. No fires."

She said David had agreed to send out nine-year-old Heather Jones. Cavanaugh barely had time to say thanks before Schneider took the phone.

"I see your agency and other agencies like yours as Big Brother," Schneider said, speaking darkly of unseen forces behind "your government. I believe there is a Trilateral Commission, a Council on Foreign Relations, and the Illuminati. They're real organizations, with the Rockefellers and all these great merchants behind all these politicians, these puppets. Your agency is part of that whole thing, taking away the freedoms of America. More legislation, more regulation, more laws, so that ultimately a person has no freedom."

"Uh-huh."

"What you guys did with the Weaver case? That bothered me," said Schneider, referring to the family at Ruby Ridge. "Look at Bush and Clinton, both involved with the Trilateral Commission. I've always considered myself a conservative, someone who's not into taxes, who's into the freedom of people as long as they're not hurting their fellow man. But that's not what this country is degenerating to . . ."

Cavanaugh cut in. "Steve, let's talk about Weaver. He walked out of there safely, right?"

"How come his wife got killed? What about the boy—"

"That was a tragedy."

"Why did you guys do that?"

"Well, a US marshal was killed, wasn't he?"

"I heard they shot his dog first, and the kid—"

"I agree with you," Cavanaugh said. "It was a tragedy on both sides."

"I don't want to die and find myself in the wrong place," Schneider said. He meant hell. "Do you?"

Koresh returned to the phone to report that he had managed his first bowel movement since the raid. "Weird," he called it, complaining about the suppurating wound in his side. "It took me fifteen, twenty minutes to get up onto a one-foot-tall plastic pot to do a number two. I might as well have climbed Mount Everest!" With that he launched into a lecture about another oppressed prophet, describing Jesus's being "hauled before the magistrate." Agent Cavanaugh, recalling the Stations of the Cross from his Catholic boyhood, said, "I was an altar boy." He was hoping to make a connection with Koresh. Instead he'd made another tactical error.

"What's that?" Koresh asked.

Told that altar boys helped priests conduct Mass, Koresh said, "Catholics don't know the Bible." He went on: "I am *afraid* for you. You and all your teeny-tiny GI Joes around here, all your small little rinky-dinky helicopters, your small little rinky-dinky Land Rovers, your small little rinky-dinky *tanks!*"

"Hold on, David."

"They're gonna ransack us and put us in prison. But we're Americans, too, you know. We have bothered no one."

"You're going to get your day in court. I'm not a theologian, David. I'm just a policeman. I was hoping things would change today and you were still a man of your word."

"I still have full intentions of doing what I said," Koresh said. "But the thing of it is, I have a headquarters, too. You deal with your bosses, I'm dealing with my father. Martin Luther stood up and put his finger right in the face of *your church*. The government of that day was the Roman Catholic Church. Martin Luther was a cult leader." He linked Luther with John Knox, John Wesley, Thomas Campbell, and other Protestant leaders who broke away from Rome. "And you—you were an altar boy." Koresh said America had taken a step toward the coming apocalypse in 1960, when voters chose another former altar boy to lead the country. "We elected the first Roman Catholic president and God became very angry. Roman Catholicism, remember, is based on something Christ says would be an abomination." He meant the papacy, which he loathed. As for Jews, "They rejected Christ. A lot of people have strange ways of worshipping God, don't they? Especially the Jews."

Cavanaugh tried to change the subject. He asked about the children. Was Koresh planning to send more of them out?

Koresh said most of the kids still inside were his own. "This is my flesh and blood we're talking about now."

The agent apologized for Sunday's bloodshed. "Listen, I regret what happened. I wish in hindsight—"

"Oh, *I wish*," Koresh scoffed. Then he relented. "I'll give you a Bible study, then I'll send another kid out. Fair enough?"

<><><>

Heather Jones, the youngest of mailman Dave Jones's children, spent her last hour at Mount Carmel packing clothes and toys into a duffel bag. "Let me tell you something about Heather," Koresh was telling the FBI, describing the nine-year-old girl as "a real sensitive young lady." He didn't mention that Heather had been literally groomed to become one of his "wives." "Real cute, real pretty," he called her. "But sensitive. She cries real easy."

He put Heather on the phone.

"Do you want to leave?" Cavanaugh asked.

"I looked at David," thirty-eight-year-old Heather recalls today. Then, "I looked at my dad. He was nodding to me, mouthing, '*Yes—leave*.' Maybe to save me."

Dave Jones was so bashful that he'd never mentioned getting shot in the butt during the raid. Days passed before he let one of the nurses tweeze out the bullet. Now he gave Heather one of the few hugs she remembers from those days. "David always told us not to love our parents," she says. "I never hugged my dad till the very end."

Koresh stopped her on her way to the door. "You don't look very happy, Heather," he said. "You gonna put a smile on? You want a hug?"

"I was terrified," she says. "I was shaking, scared of David and what was outside. I thought they would shoot me as soon as I walked out that door." Instead, black-shirted agents "grabbed me and took my bag away. They took me to their headquarters," where Agent Cavanaugh put her on the phone to Mount Carmel.

"Hi Heather," Dave Jones said.

"Hi Daddy."

"How are you doing?"

"Sitting in a chair."

"God has many promises, Heather. Always remember that. Be a good girl. I'll see you, okay?"

Hard Bargains

Special Agent in Charge Jamar spoke at a March 5 news conference. He told reporters that President Bill Clinton was taking a personal interest in the standoff. The president had instructed the FBI "to wait as long as necessary to get Mr. Koresh and his followers out of the complex without violence, regardless of time and expense."

Texas governor Ann Richards had an even more personal interest. She was from Waco. Richards had told the ATF she wasn't sure federal forces should be using Texas National Guard equipment to raid a bunch of evangelical Christians in her hometown. Waco was known as Baylor's home, the birthplace of Dr Pepper, and the nation's leading producer of church pews. Governor Richards didn't want her hometown getting famous as a site of federal overreach. ATF deputy director Daniel Hartnett assuaged her fears with a letter assuring her that the Davidians were knee-deep in the drug trade. "Eleven members have prior drug involvement," he wrote. That was eleven out of more than a hundred, and their offenses were minor. Hartnett also cited "Koresh's possession of a methamphetamine lab within the compound." As he knew or should have known, Koresh and the Davidians had "possessed" the lab George Roden rented to a pair of meth cookers only long enough to clean it up.

Inside the compound, Koresh's wounds were bleeding again. He had been gaining strength, adding vegetables and spoonfuls of an iron supplement to his diet of broth and juice. Yet his wrist wound wouldn't close. The bullet hole in his gut leaked pus and blood. Coughing made him shiver in pain. He told the negotiators of his dark dreams about ravenous birds and helicopters. "If God wants me to live, I'll live," he said.

Had he died, the others might well have surrendered. "David was our leader," Thibodeau says. "We weren't going to follow Steve Schneider to the ends of the earth." Yet the FBI worried that Koresh's death might trigger the mass suicide the government hoped to avoid. Noesner's negotiating team arranged to send an agent to the front door with a first-aid kit. This gesture was portrayed as an act of charity in press conferences as well as in Noesner's memoir, *Stalling for Time*, with no mention of the fact that the first-aid kit held needles, forceps, suture thread, bandages, and a miniature listening device. From that point forward the FBI could occasionally eavesdrop on the Davidians, though transmission was spotty. Much of what the agents heard was indecipherable; they learned nothing useful. After that, they continued to plant bugs in shipments they sent to the compound, hiding them in the Styrofoam containers that insulated pints of milk for the children. The Davidians discovered some but not all of the devices, and presumed the government was bugging the packages it sent them.

Davidian nurses Annetta Richards and Julianne Matthews stitched up Koresh's wounds. The one near his hand soon scabbed over. The exit wound over his tailbone was slower to heal.

Daily life at Mount Carmel went on much as usual for the next few days. The Davidians avoided windows, though not one bullet had been fired from outside since the day of the raid. Breakfast might be applesauce and fig bars, followed by daily worship from eight to nine in the morning, a lunch of rationed beans or bread, and another worship session from two to three or four in the afternoon. If Koresh was in a voluble mood, Bible study might last until sundown. When that happened, many of them would be so drained by tension and meager rations that they crawled into bed for the night.

Water was scarce. The ATF raiders had shot up their white plastic water tank on the twenty-eighth. At the first rain, "we stuck buckets out of windows and secluded areas around the building where we couldn't get shot," Doyle said. They collected buckets of rain, straining it through paper towels for drinking water.

But they were running out of milk. Davidian women usually breast-fed their children until they were two or three years old, but several of the mothers stopped lactating during the siege, as can happen in times of stress. Koresh told the negotiators the children were hungry. Despite the Davidians' preference for goat milk, he said, they were willing to settle for cow's milk. "You need to help us out here," he said.

Noesner's team offered to send six gallons of milk if he sent out four more kids.

Koresh scoffed at the thought of trading children for the milk they needed to survive. "Go have a milkshake," he told the FBI, adding a jokey counteroffer: "We'll send you two kids for six gallons of ice cream." Then he signed off for the day, leaving Rachel to tell the FBI that her husband wasn't home. "He's gone to Waco to buy milk," she said.

◇◇◇◇

While Schneider, Koresh's earnest second-in-command, generally tried to get along with the FBI men, Koresh liked to keep them guessing. Sometimes he lectured; sometimes he hinted that he might lead his people out any day now. One thing that might prevent such a happy ending, he said, was the "biased coverage" he followed on TV. Like the conspiracy theorists of the century to come, he was convinced that the government was behind much of the "fake information" he saw on KDFW, CNN, and *Nightline*. He shook his fist at the TV when he heard himself called him a madman and rapist.

"Wrong!" he said. "I'm all the way pro-woman."

As if to prove it, he put Kathy Schroeder on the phone with the negotiators.

Schroeder, a thirty-one-year-old Floridian, was a member of the

"House of David," his harem. Her husband, Michael, had spent his days and nights at the Mag Bag car-repair shop three miles away. After hearing the news that morning, Michael Schroeder had hurried to Mount Carmel on foot with two other Davidians. They encountered ATF agents who thought they were escaping the compound rather than going the other way. Schroeder was carrying a Glock nine-millimeter semiautomatic pistol. During what ATF agents call "the second shootout," they killed him with six bullets, including two to the head and three to the back. They left his body where it fell.

When Koresh put Kathy Schroeder on the phone with the negotiators, she had just heard the news of Michael's shooting. Taking the phone, she said, "Hello. You killed my husband."

After a moment, the agent on the line said, "Kathy, let's get real here."

"Yeah, let's. You killed my husband, and all you want to do is bargain."

"Kathy, perhaps we're wasting each other's time. Put somebody else on."

"Are you going to bargain with human lives? There are babies here that need milk. Are you that inhumane, you can't just send us milk?"

"It's not that simple," the negotiator said. "Our concern is for the children first and foremost—"

"Right," she said. "The ones you don't want to send milk."

Koresh took the phone and struck a conciliatory note. "Hey," he said, "you've been enraged a lot of times, too, you know. Just don't burn our building down."

◇◇◇◇

On March 8, McLennan County sheriff Jack Harwell joined Noesner's team at the FBI command post. The peaceable sheriff in the white Stetson didn't carry a gun. He'd always left the Davidians alone as long as they kept to themselves. Koresh liked him.

"How you all doing in there?" Harwell asked.

Koresh said, "Fine, fine. We want milk." He complained that the negotiators "have done nothing but lie to us. Anytime Big Brother pushes me, I'm gonna push back."

Harwell said he understood. "But we've always got along."

"If *you* had called up and said you had a warrant for us, I'd have met you in town."

"I've laid awake thinking about that." The sheriff said he'd do what he could to get some milk sent in and made Koresh a promise: "No tricks."

Harwell made good on his word. In the next carefully choreographed handoff at the front door, the Davidians got six gallons of milk without releasing any more children. The milk helped but left the children, who were unaccustomed to cow's milk, burping and bawling with stomach pains. The shipment that held the milk jugs also carried a camera the size of a pea, but the spy camera wasn't much more use than the microphone the FBI had smuggled in with the first-aid kit. The Davidians, suspecting that anything the feds sent might be bugged, kept the milk and tossed the container holding the camera into a trash bin.

That morning, Clive Doyle and two other men crawled into the water tower to retrieve Peter Gent's body. Gent had been hanging from a ladder inside the tower for more than a week. Davidian Mark Wendell climbed through a hatch at the base of the empty tower, then went up the ladder, tied a rope around the body, and lowered it to the others. Gent's face "was just a mass of blood," Doyle recalled. They zipped the body into a sleeping bag. After another round of negotiations, the Davidians got permission to bury Peter Gent under a tree in front of the compound, where they hoped to move the other bodies now buried in the storm shelter, including that of Wendell's wife, Jaydean. When they were finished, they stuck a handful of plastic flowers into the dirt to mark Gent's grave.

◇◇◇◇

While Koresh napped, the negotiators tried to talk Schneider into replacing him or at least leading the others out "if something happens to David." Schneider refused. They tried the same tack with Rachel, who told them she was "a wife and mom," not a leader. "What I believe in is here," she said.

At 2:15 a.m. on Tuesday, March 9, the FBI turned up the pressure on the Davidians by cutting off their electricity. Their TV blinked off. Their walk-in refrigerator went dead.

The phone still worked, but Koresh refused to speak to the negotiators until power was restored. Schneider warned late-shift negotiator Henry Garcia that the small army outside—half a dozen tanks and more than three hundred federal agents—had yet to feel God's wrath. "We can take you out!" he said.

Like most of the others, Doyle hoped their ordeal would end soon. "I don't think any of us thought, '*Let's make them mad by staying in here as long as we can.*' But we had provisions to hold out for a long time." The fridge was full of food they began eating when the power went out, before it could go bad. For people who seldom overindulged, that brought a few days of pleasure. "Chicken salad was my favorite," Sheila Martin remembers. "That was special."

They also fortified the compound. Hostage Rescue Team agents watched through binoculars as the Davidians sawed firing ports through Mount Carmel's flimsy walls. The agents could see sunlight glinting off gun barrels inside. One agent compared guard duty at Waco to "sitting in the eye of a hurricane."

On the afternoon of March 9, an agent dropped a videotape outside the front door. Prepared by the FBI, the tape showed Davidian youngsters who had been released playing happily in their temporary quarters at Waco's Methodist Home for Children. Workers at the Methodist Home had been glad to discover that the kids showed no signs of physical abuse, and amused to see the children marveling at the first flush toilets they'd ever seen.

According to Justice Department records, the videotape was intended "to play on parental feelings for the children, and hopefully hasten the exit of the parents." The FBI restored Mount Carmel's electricity long enough for Koresh and his followers to watch it on the wide-screen TV in the chapel. But the tape backfired. The Davidians were aghast at seeing their children eating candy and guzzling soft drinks, jumping off furniture, acting hyper. Was the government trying to provoke them? The tape was the latest example of the FBI's failure to think along with the enemy. Instead of pleasing Koresh and his followers, it made them angrier.

"We need to get the word out," Koresh told the others. "*Our* message."

Within an hour, the Davidians spray-painted a bedsheet and hung it from an upstairs window. Its message: GOD HELP US WE WANT THE PRESS.

Soon someone in muddy Satellite City, with its population of almost a thousand, put up a sign reading, GOD HELP US, WE ARE THE PRESS.

14

....

Testimony

Koresh told his followers they could beat Babylon at its own game. "We'll make our own video."

Later on March 9, they pushed together a couch, chairs, and a potted plant to mimic the set of a talk show. Steve Schneider set a videocam on a tripod and interviewed Davidians.

◇◇◇◇

Lorraine Sylvia had a two-year-old daughter named Hollywood, fathered by Koresh. "David makes the Bible harmonize," she said in the grainy video. Asked if she was being held against her will, she said, "No one's holding a gun to my head."

"Is God talking to you?" Schneider asked.

"No, but God does speak to someone. David has proven himself to me. If he says wait, I'm going to wait."

◇◇◇◇

Sita Sonobe told of following her husband from Hawaii to Mount Carmel. At first, she said, "I always sat in the back" during Bible studies, "but the longer I listened—David set my ears ringing."

Her husband, Scott, known as Snow Flea, had been shot in the leg and hand during the raid, but sounded chipper ten days later. "I am *not* being held against my will," he said. "We're gonna be just fine, because God's in control."

◇◇◇◇

Nikki Gent dandled Dayland, her three-year-old son by Koresh, in her lap. Three months pregnant with her third child with the prophet, twenty-four-year-old Nikki was mourning her twin brother, Peter. "The ATF came in and shot my brother. He's buried out in front of the property now," she said. "I thought this was the country of freedom of speech. Freedom of religion."

"Is there anything you'd like to say?" Schneider asked.

"To my mom—Mom, I know you don't understand, and you're going to be heartbroken. But please, you always told me not to judge. In the end you'll understand."

◇◇◇◇

Derek Lovelock, the son of an RAF flier, hailed from Manchester, England. Lovelock said he'd found himself at the right place at the right time. "This is the end time. Prophecy is being fulfilled as it's written in Revelation."

Ofelia Santoyo, from Mexico, agreed. "Prophecy has to be fulfilled."

Kathy Schroeder told outsiders they should "read Revelation. It's all right there." Asked if anyone was holding her at Mount Carmel, Schroeder smiled. "Only God. We the people don't run this government anymore. *They* do, and they tell all the lies they want."

◇◇◇◇

Yvette Fagan recalled following her husband, Livingstone, from England to Texas to follow Koresh. Some of the others called them the best-looking couple at Mount Carmel, at least before David split up all the husbands and wives: talkative Livingstone, a lively, diminutive seeker with a master's degree in theology, and Yvette with her movie-star beauty and colorful African dresses. They had brought their two children and Livingstone's mother, Doris, with them. Now Yvette gave the camera a challenging look. She said, "Listen, I came here freely. I am a free agent."

"Where are your children now?" Schneider asked.

The question pained her. She looked away. "Out there. In Babylon." Six-year-old Renae and four-year-old Nehara had left Mount Carmel on the night of the raid. "I sent them out because they would die in this place. Those people came in here and shot up my bedroom with three children in the room! I sent them out for their safety. But now I am thinking they would be better off here. Even if they died, they wouldn't be in the hands of Babylon."

"Do you have anything to say to them?"

"To my kids: Remember the story of Daniel and his friends, Shadrach, Mishak, and Abednego. Those guys were taken into Babylon against their will, just like you. They were part of God's plan. God wants to work through you, too. You're out there for a purpose, kids."

◇◇◇◇

Judy Schneider-Koresh waved a scabbed hand. "As you can see, I was wounded when the ATF assaulted us," she said. The government bullet that left a purple gouge in her right index finger had passed through her right shoulder. She'd used tape and a pair of popsicle sticks to make a splint for that finger. Holding fidgety Mayanah, her daughter by Koresh, Judy listened while Steve, still legally her husband, coached her on the story they had chosen to tell.

He asked what she'd been doing when she got shot. "Were you nursing the baby?"

She nodded. "Just sitting there, and bullets start coming in!" It wasn't true, but for now they were looking past the commandment against bearing false witness. Judy went on to grouse about the FBI's tape of Davidian kids at the Methodist Home. "The video we saw of them running around crazily, eating candy, drinking soda pop—we were all quite upset. They don't eat candy. It's not good for your teeth or health."

Did she have a message for America? She sure did. "Before you judge us, make sure your own life is clean." Then, to her cuckolded husband, she added, "We're being stripped naked, so let's make sure that when that happens, Steve, you're ready to meet God."

◇◇◇◇

Koresh appeared in the video with several days' stubble on his face, sitting on the floor with his back to a wall. Too weak to stand, he introduced "my oldest son, Cyrus" with a wan smile, then asked the boy how old he was.

"Seven."

"Say hello to everybody."

"Hi." Cyrus waved to the camera.

Koresh ticked off his gripes against the government. "It's not against the law to buy firearms," he said, touching the tip of one finger. "It's not against the law to buy anything they sell at a gun show," he said, tapping another. Still he found himself surrounded by snipers and tanks. But he was not afraid. "Being an American first, I'm the kind of guy that'll stand in front of a tank. You can run it over me, but I'll be biting one of the tracks."

He wondered why the ATF had started this fight. "You could have arrested me going to town, going to Walmart," he said, his familiar refrain. "ATF—you boys are *wrong*. You want to argue with me? Catch me on the side of the road somewhere. But you come pointing guns in the direction of my wives and my kids and I'll meet you at the door." He paused. "And I'm sorry some of you guys got shot. But, hey, God'll have to sort that out, won't He?"

He closed with a wave of his good hand. "So we're gonna send this tape out. I do thank you guys. Sheriff Harwell, God bless you," he said, blowing a kiss. He was short of breath. "Anyway, God bless. Turn it off, Steve."

Schneider closed the hour-long tape by cutting away from Koresh. "*We're trying to work this out with you,*" Schneider said in a voiceover to the negotiators. "*We'll do the best we can. But remember, the God of David Koresh said to wait, and that's basically what we're doing.*"

◇◇◇◇

That night, a federal agent—watched and covered by many others—came to the front door to take the videocassette from Schneider. Noesner and his team watched the tape, took notes, and sent it up the chain of command. Unlike the Davidians, who hoped their video would reach millions, the negotiators had no illusions that anyone outside law enforcement would see it.

15

....

Tightening the Noose

Lead negotiator Noesner was willing to humor or flatter Koresh if it helped get more children out of Mount Carmel. Twenty-one had been released so far. Twenty more children remained inside. Most of them—twelve in the lowest estimate, seventeen in the highest—had been fathered by Koresh.

"You're dealing with my biological children now," Koresh said. "That's what we've come down to." Noesner knew it would take time to get some or all of them out.

He passed notes to whichever negotiator was on the phone. *Say yes. How's he feeling? Keep him talking.* As long as they were talking, nobody on either side was getting shot.

Unlike Koresh, however, Noesner had more than one boss. His immediate superior, Special Agent in Charge Jamar, reported to higher-ups who were getting tired of watching and waiting. They viewed the standoff at Waco as an ongoing national embarrassment. They wanted to know how soon Jamar was going to bring it to an end.

Noesner had lost face with Jamar when Koresh went back on his promise to bring everyone out after his radio broadcast. According to one agent, members of the FBI's tactical team had already viewed the negotiators as "a bunch of pussies." Now, with hard-liners like

Hostage Rescue Team commander Dick Rogers arguing for quick, decisive action, Noesner found himself bargaining on two fronts. As he saw his dilemma in the second week of March, "The internal battle over strategy was going to be as challenging as talking to Koresh."

Publicly, the government still endorsed the negotiators' approach. At a March 9 press conference, FBI spokesman Bob Ricks told several hundred members of the local, national, and international media that the Davidians had sounded more "belligerent" lately. He quoted Koresh: "We are ready for war. Let's get it on." While those words represented a droplet in the torrent of words Koresh poured over the phone every day, they made a lasting impression. Spokesman Ricks assured the press that war was the last thing the Bureau or the hundreds of law enforcement agents ringing the compound had in mind. "We are doing everything in our power to make sure that doesn't take place." At the same time, he hoped to give the press and public "a better understanding of what we are dealing with." Which was, in Ricks's portrayal, a suicidal cult leader who would welcome an invasion. "It is our belief that *he* believes his prophecy will be fulfilled if the government engages in an all-out firefight in which he is executed."

The *Waco Tribune-Herald* was among many outlets that focused on Koresh's quote. It ran a cartoon showing the bedraggled prophet with the muzzles of two tank barrels inches from his ears as he shouted, "Let's get it on!"

At the FBI command post, the internal battle over strategy heated up. Noesner entered a meeting to find Hostage Rescue Team chief Rogers sitting with Jamar, "both of them visibly angry" at Koresh and his stubborn followers. Rogers had supervised the botched siege at Ruby Ridge but seemed to have learned nothing from it.

"This joker is screwing with us," Rogers said of Koresh. "It's time to teach him a lesson. My people can get in there and secure that place in fifteen minutes." After more than a week of "coddling" outlaws who had slain four federal agents and wounded twenty, Rogers said they should "tighten the noose" until the Davidians gave up.

Noesner disagreed. "It's important not to overreact," he said. Yes, Koresh had broken his vow to come out. Yes, Koresh might be manipulating them. He might enjoy preaching to a captive audience of FBI agents. He might be getting off on being a national celebrity. "That's better than another firefight, isn't it?"

But the lead negotiator could tell which way the wind was blowing. Jamar provided another clue later that week. Tapping his finger to a map of Mount Carmel, he described how a 68-ton Abrams tank could plow through the Davidians' compound from one end to the other without slowing down. "He seemed excited," Noesner recalled. "The negotiators in the room were speechless. Had he forgotten about the women and children inside?"

Agents Cavanaugh and Garcia had manned the phone on twelve-hour shifts during the first week. As the siege dragged on, they shared the headset with half a dozen others, each working an eight-hour shift while three to seven other agents listened in, passed notes to the agent on the phone, transcribed their talks, monitored the recording equipment, and liaised with the tactical teams outside the compound. There were now so many negotiators on the line at various times, including four named John, that the Davidians had a hard time telling them apart. Both sides referred to the new arrivals as "John 2," "John 3," or "John 4."

The negotiators spent much of their time letting Koresh fill their ears with talk of everything from his school days to his views on biblical tyrants, Roman chariots, and flying saucers. He was listening to the battery-powered radio one day when he heard that the Guitar Nebula was "speeding toward us." He took that to be a good sign. He said he might surrender soon—but only if the agents who shot Perry Jones and five other Davidians during the ATF raid also faced arrest.

The FBI couldn't promise that. "You've got to understand," one of the Johns told him, "this is a multi-agency effort. If I were the boss, you and I could probably work this out." The FBI men on the phone had been instructed not to discuss the February 28 raid. As John 4 explained, "That was the ATF, and I'm FBI." Their seeming coyness kept them from aiding future lawsuits the Davidians might bring and from disparaging the ATF, which some believed had bungled the raid. Meanwhile the negotiators were getting "heat from above," John 4 said. "The bosses in D.C. look at TV or *USA Today* and they don't see anything happening. You need to give us something."

FBI technicians restored the Davidians' electricity long enough for them to watch the authorities' daily press briefing, then shut it off again. The Davidians answered with another bedsheet hung from a window. It read, RODNEY KING WE UNDERSTAND, a reference to the Black motorist beaten by Los Angeles police two years earlier.

◇◇◇◇

Inside Mount Carmel, "We made do," Doyle says. Koresh told his followers they were lucky despite their privations: "God's chosen people, that's us." Still, he warned that their ordeal was likely to end in flames. That sort of climax would fit the violent ends of Revelation as well as Babylon's purposes. As he asked one of the negotiators, "If you wanted to burn the place down, kill all the people, what evidence would be left?"

They all knew Mount Carmel was a firetrap. After dark, the Davidians relied on Coleman lanterns and candlelight. "We lined the front wall on the second floor with boxes of potatoes to block the rain and wind," Doyle said. They piled hay bales against windows and exterior walls to keep out the cold and block sharpshooters's views. There was less and less water that might douse a small fire. After days without rain to fill the buckets they hung outside, they rationed what they had left. Then Davidian Greg Summers hit on a clever way to replenish their water supply. The bullet-riddled polyurethane tank behind the main building was connected to a well. Summers used candles to melt some of the kids' green plastic army men and stuck them into holes in the lower part of the tank. When the plastic cooled, the toy soldiers plugged the holes. After that, the tank could hold hundreds of gallons of well water.

◇◇◇◇

On March 11, Koresh's mother hired defense lawyer Dick DeGuerin to represent her son. A media-friendly attorney in a bespoke suit and lizard-skin boots, sporting a short-brimmed white Stetson over his shock of blond hair, DeGuerin had already booked Bonnie on tabloid

The most familiar photo of David Koresh is a mug shot taken
after a 1987 arrest for attempted murder. (ATF)

Vernon Howell—not yet
known as David Koresh—
dropped out of high
school and started a
Christian-rock band.
Rachel Howell Koresh held son Cyrus
while Bonnie Haldeman dandled her
granddaughter in 1987. Koresh ruled
every aspect of his followers' lives;
when they lived up to his demands, they
got ice cream. (Photos courtesy of
Associated Press and Charles Pace)

ATF agents raided Mount Carmel on February 28, 1993.
(Associated Press and ATF)

Tanks rolled in as the siege began. "T-shirt Hill" was the place to find supporters of both sides as well as Waco souvenirs and a former US Army sergeant, Timothy McVeigh (top row center), a Koresh fan. (Associated Press)

An aerial view of Mount Carmel during the siege, with the pool and water tower at lower right. (ATF) The Branch Davidians appealed to the outside world with bedsheets hung from windows. The FBI blasted noise and pointed spotlights at them. (Associated Press)

On April 19, 1993, tanks broke through the compound's walls to "insert" tear gas. Shortly after noon, fire destroyed Mount Carmel. After the fire, the ATF flew its flag near the remains of the vault where women and children died. (Associated Press; center photo FBI)

Alex Jones, who helped turn Waco from a town into a cause, exhorted Capitol rioters on January 6, 2021. (Associated Press; patch courtesy of Dennis Wayne at Chiefmart.com)

Clive Doyle spoke at
a memorial service.
Heather Jones (above
right) and Sheila
Martin (right) stayed
in Waco, where Koresh
still has followers.
(Associated Press)

They Will Not find David's Bones! HE is Alive!!

TV shows that paid for interviews. Stepping out of a chauffeured car at Satellite City, he declared that he'd come all the way from Houston to represent David Koresh. The Davidian leader and his mother might pay his steep fees, he said, with a book advance and movie deal he would negotiate.

The *Tribune-Herald* dubbed DeGuerin "the messiah's messiah," but Koresh wasn't sure what to think of this self-appointed savior who looked like the richest tourist at a dude ranch. Koresh didn't want anyone calling him a sellout. He admitted fancying the finer things in life—his guitars, his '68 Camaro with its 500 horses, his Harley-Davidson with its scarlet gas tank, his "wives"—but swore that getting his message out meant far more than money. It offended him that Bonnie had taken payment from TV producers. The thought of merchants hawking Branch Davidian souvenirs "makes me sick," he said.

Koresh said he would consider meeting DeGuerin outside the compound if the feds would allow it. That gave him another topic to haggle about, along with children, milk, electricity, extension cords, and the negotiators' souls. When he pressed Noesner's men about their beliefs, most of them assured him that they were Christians, too. He told them they were risking their souls by representing the government against God's chosen few. "How will you answer for that? Huh?" In the next breath he'd sound a more obliging note. "I want to serve your laws where they coincide with God's laws," he told one of them. "America, of all the nations, is the closest to God's laws and the basic principles of common sense." He said he was pretty sure they could resolve their differences without more killing. "But I guess we'll have to see, won't we?"

◇◇◇◇

Kathy Schroeder returned to phone duty that day—bad news for the negotiators. The woman some Davidians called "Sarge" Schroeder was upset about seeing her little boy Bryan, who had gone out with other children ten days before, on the video the FBI had sent in. In the tape, Bryan sat in a corner looking forlorn while the other kids played. One of the Johns assured her that the social workers at the

Methodist Home were taking good care of all the children. "Still, Kathy continued to rail at us," Noesner recalled.

He wrote a note for the man on the phone: *Bryan needs a hug from his mommy.* In a gentle voice, the negotiator said, "You know, Kathy, I think what Bryan really needs now is a hug from his mommy." That made an impression. Kathy Schroeder agreed to leave Mount Carmel the next day.

She stepped out of the front doors on the chilly morning of Friday, March 12. She was promptly arrested, handcuffed, and delivered to the Methodist Home for a tearful embrace with three-year-old Bryan. After that, she was taken to jail.

But there was more to her story than a note about a hug. As Schroeder revealed later, Koresh had caught her smoking cigarettes, breaking his rules. "Get out," he said. By banishing Kathy Schroeder, he made a new enemy. Like Marc Breault, she would turn against him.

◇◇◇◇

The next morning a cold front sent temperatures into the twenties. With no electricity to run space heaters, the Davidians huddled in parkas and sleeping bags. Their breath fogged the air as they shared potatoes and crackers for breakfast. Koresh got back on the phone with the negotiators while others peeked through windows and holes in walls, keeping an eye on the tanks and heavily armed agents outside.

Thibodeau recalled the siege's second week as "a time when negotiations were harmonious." He thought the FBI was "being reasonable, considering everything that had happened. But at a certain point we realized that their word meant nothing. The negotiators would tell us one thing and the guys in the tanks did the exact opposite."

The agents outside "were mooning us," Doyle says, "dropping their pants, yelling profanity, giving us the finger."

"It showed how they hated us," Sheila Martin recalls. "Anyone would have wanted to fight back."

The tanks inched closer. FBI and ATF agents erected chain-link fences around the compound. The Davidians asked why—they weren't trying to escape. The negotiators explained that the fencing wasn't meant to keep them in but to keep reporters and nosy tourists out. The negotiators gave their word that the government had no plans to attack. They were not informed of a message their agency had sent to the US Army. According to an army memo filed on March 11, the FBI "requested Army provide refresher training on an expedited basis for HRT personnel in use of 40-mm grenade launchers."

16

....

T-shirt Hill

On March 12, Janet Reno put one hand on a Bible, raised her right hand, and swore to "support and defend the Constitution of the United States against all enemies, foreign and domestic." She had been briefed on the situation at Waco before her swearing-in as President Bill Clinton's attorney general.

America's first female attorney general had a particular interest in cases involving children. As state attorney for Florida's Dade County, she had mounted a much-publicized "crusade" against child abusers. As attorney general, she said, she intended "to do everything I possibly can to protect American's children from abuse and violence." Briefed on the crisis at Mount Carmel, Reno recalled being told the Bureau "had information that babies were being beaten. I specifically asked, 'You really mean babies?' The answer was, 'Yes, he's slapping babies around.'"

The Davidians were firm believers in corporal punishment. "Spare the Helper, spoil the child," some said. Marc Breault and several other disgruntled ex-Davidians claimed Koresh himself had dispensed the worst spanking they'd witnessed when he paddled Wisdom, his ten-month-old son by Robyn Bunds, until the boy's bottom bled. That 1991 incident, which Breault often described after breaking with Koresh, was probably the source of the FBI's "babies being beaten"

report. Though there were no signs that any of the twenty-one Davidian children released after the raid had been physically abused, the
FBI made child abuse a prime focus of Reno's briefings.

From her first day on the job, Reno faced mounting pressure to
end the standoff. She pored over briefing books, news reports, and
memos from experts inside and outside the Department of Justice.
She followed TV coverage of the siege, which showed Mount Carmel
behind newly erected fences, lit up by stadium lights that blazed all
night long. Per DOJ records, "the FBI began to illuminate the compound with bright lights to disrupt sleep, to put additional pressure
on those inside, and to increase the safety of the Hostage Rescue
Team." From then on, airline passengers on night flights to and from
Dallas could spot a blaze of light to the south.

On March 15, the Monday after Reno took office—the Ides of
March—one of Koresh's fondest wishes came true. He appeared on
the cover of *Time* and *Newsweek*. Seeing images of the covers on
TV, he asked the FBI for copies. The negotiators stalled. They had
read the articles. *Newsweek* called the Davidians a cult. *Time*'s cover
paired Koresh with Sheik Abdel Rahman, the Islamic terrorist behind
the recent World Trade Center bombing. Both magazines cast Koresh
as a dangerous pedophile—"the wacko from Waco"—who might
lead his cultists to a Jonestown-style mass suicide. Other publications
mentioned his supposed interest in "human sacrifice," a suspicion the
Washington Post would trace back to his nemesis Marc Breault, who
didn't mind conflating the fact that Davidians would sacrifice their
lives for Koresh with images of satanic rituals.

"We're working on it," the negotiators said of delivering the magazines. After that, demanding copies of *Time* and *Newsweek* replaced
asking for undercover agent Robert Rodriguez, aka "Gonzalez," as
Koresh's most frequent request.

Steve Schneider could have told the FBI men that it didn't matter
what the magazine stories said. Koresh was mainly concerned with
how he looked in the pictures. In his view, *Time*, *Newsweek*, and
the TV networks could pervert his story as much as they wanted—
in fact he expected it—but as long as they sent his picture and at
least a little of his message out to the world, he was thrilled. Every

sparrow's fall and magazine lie was part of God's plan, so why not enjoy the ride?

Koresh was getting his strength back. He could stand. He could walk. In one account he was even starting to feel horny again. Behind the walls of his compound, Koresh was King David taking seven wives. He was Jonathan Edwards preaching fire and fury. He was Billy Jack, the peace-loving '70s movie hero who kicked butt when he had to.

Soon he was daring the snipers to shoot at him. "Koresh routinely made himself openly visible to our tactical teams," said one FBI agent. "He would literally sit on a window ledge and eat a bowl of ramen noodles. At night, he liked to serenade us and play guitar solos. He was the king in his kingdom, and he was in no hurry to come out."

◇◇◇◇

The FBI turned to Bible scholars for advice. James Tabor, a Texas-born professor of religion at the University of North Carolina, claimed the government had misunderstood the Davidians from the jump. "A person familiar with biblical texts could have perceived the situation in wholly different terms from the government's 'hostage rescue' scenario," he said. From the Davidians' perspective, "their group had been wantonly attacked by government agents they understood to be in opposition to both God and his appointed prophet, David Koresh." Tabor and Phillip Arnold, a colleague who ran a religious think tank based in Houston, offered to serve as liaisons between Koresh and the FBI. To them, his "Bible babble" was at least intelligible.

FBI spokesman Bob Ricks brushed them off. He said, "Nobody can understand what this man is saying." So Arnold went around the FBI. He discussed the book of Revelation on a radio show that was a favorite of the Davidians. Within hours Steve Schneider was on the phone: "David wants to talk to that man."

Noesner agreed to send a tape of the radio show but would not put Arnold on the phone. Koresh was incensed. After weeks of preaching to negotiators who claimed to be Christians but couldn't name the Ten Commandments, he dreamed of talking scripture with experts like himself. But in Noesner's view, the scholars were amateurs. They might be sincere or they might be opportunists looking to get their names in the paper and make tenure, but they had no experience dealing with armed opponents during a standoff worthy of *Dog Day Afternoon*. They might say the wrong thing and set off a shootout. More likely, the professors might talk scripture with Koresh and tell the world he wasn't as crazy as the FBI said he was, making him a sympathetic figure to Christians all over the country and the world. Noesner knew enough about the Bible and enough about con men to see how Koresh turned scripture to his purposes when it suited him. "We could see how easily he altered his stated beliefs to serve whatever seemed to be in his interest at the moment," Noesner recalled. "Arguing religion with him would be a fool's game."

Cut off from the scholars who wanted to reach him, Koresh resumed his rants. "We're Christians," he told the negotiators. "Christians who follow Jesus and mind our own business. None of our neighbors complained on us. Tell me why you need tanks and something like seven hundred federal agents to pull me in on a misdemeanor weapons charge."

◇◇◇◇

Park Dietz, a professor of psychiatry at UCLA who often served as an expert witness in murder trials, offered to help the FBI. Without meeting Koresh or speaking to him, Dietz diagnosed him as "a psychopath," a cult leader "with antisocial and narcissistic personality traits that enabled him to become a master of manipulation." Syracuse University's Murray Miron studied Koresh's pronouncements—mostly Bible quotations—and declared that they bore "all the hallmarks of rampant, morbidly virulent paranoia." Like Dietz, Professor Miron had never been within a mile of Koresh, yet the FBI took his views seriously.

Rick Ross, a freelance "cultbuster" from Phoenix, was a different story. Ross hurried to Texas and moved into a Waco hotel to be near the action. He appeared live from Satellite City on CNN and CBS, insisting he could "deprogram" the Branch Davidians. He claimed the FBI was relying on him for advice. Peppering the agency with offers to negotiate personally with Koresh, Ross was such a persistent self-publicist that the Bureau made a point of disavowing him. According to its own account of the siege, "The FBI did not 'rely' on Ross for any advice whatsoever during the standoff. The FBI interviewed Ross only at Ross's request, and politely declined his unsolicited offer of assistance."

Another outsider had a better claim to understanding Koresh. Marc Breault, watching TV coverage from Australia, phoned and emailed the FBI to warn yet again that the Davidians were planning a mass suicide. According to FBI records, he also offered "to debate Koresh on a radio program to prove that Breault knew more about the Bible than Koresh." Bureau officials heard him out but kept Breault at arm's length, recalling his prediction of a mass suicide the year before.

The Bureau had two in-house professionals urging their superiors to keep watching and waiting. In a series of memos, agents Peter Smerick and Mark Young, a pair of behavioral scientists working as profilers, argued that "Negotiators should acknowledge part of Koresh's worldview, namely the existence of a 'conspiracy' against the Branch Davidians, and the Davidians' right to defend themselves." Second, they wrote, Noesner's team should "create the illusion that Koresh could win in court and in the press, that he would not go to prison, and he would attract many more followers if he came out." They stressed that the government's prime concern was "to insure the safety of the children inside the compound, and to facilitate Koresh's peaceful surrender." Smerick and Young admitted that the FBI might face the prospect of "eventually taking physical action against the compound." If such an attack took place, they predicted, "Koresh and his followers will fight back to the death, to defend their property and their faith, as they believe they did on February 28," the day of the raid. If the worst happened, "the FBI would be criticized if children were killed in such an attack."

There is no evidence that Attorney General Reno saw their memos. Still, her inclination was to exercise as much restraint as possible. Asked about having a sniper shoot Koresh the next time he showed his face, Reno said she didn't want federal agents "to shoot someone who was not shooting at them."

◇◇◇◇

Inside Mount Carmel, Koresh's followers blocked windows that hadn't already been blocked. At night, white beams from the FBI's stadium lights shot through the Davidians' firing ports and through bullet holes and cracks in the walls, streaking through dim rooms and hallways lit by candles and lanterns. With the power shut off, the Davidians finished their perishable food, then turned to canned beans, trail mix, and MREs. They rationed water for drinking and took fewer sponge baths. "We didn't smell great," Thibodeau remembers. "I guess our faith was as strong as our smell." They conserved batteries by having one person listen to the radio, take notes, then tell the others what was going on beyond the chain-link fences. "The news kept getting crazier," says Thibodeau.

Each day hundreds of curiosity seekers and peddlers joined the reporters, news junkies, FBI supporters, and Koresh fans on the blacktop roads near the compound. A rise about three miles up the road became known as "T-shirt Hill" for the vendors who congregated there. Others called it "Mount Carnival." Vendors built shacks or hawked souvenirs and refreshments from their cars, vans, pickups, and campers. Some of the T-shirts read LET'S GET IT ON or RANCH APOCALYPSE: WE AIN'T COMIN OUT. Some featured photos of Koresh from the *Tribune-Herald* or the national magazines. One design showed Koresh playing guitar over the line GOD ROCKS. Other T-shirts were pro-law enforcement: I SUPPORT THE ATF. Or jokey: MY PARENTS WENT TO MT. CARMEL AND ALL I GOT WAS THIS STUPID AK-47. One vendor sold T-shirts reading, WACKO WACO STAND-OFF, and said, "I sold my first shirt to an FBI agent." Another called out to prospective customers: "God is telling you to buy this shirt!"

One day a preacher stood amid the hubbub, condemning vendors for profiting off the suffering of believers. A gray-bearded pilgrim carried a sign reading, NO GESTAPO TACTICS. Another protester's sign asked, IS YOUR CHURCH ATF APPROVED? When a Koresh supporter dragged a large wooden cross toward a checkpoint nearby, federal agents blocked her way. She planted the cross in muddy ground beside the road and disappeared in the crowd.

Later in March, a young Gulf War veteran joined a T-shirt Hill throng that ranged from several hundred to more than three thousand tourists in a day. Timothy McVeigh, a long-faced twenty-four-year-old with a buzzcut, was selling five-dollar bumper stickers reading, FEAR THE GOVT THAT FEARS YOUR GUN and A MAN WITH A GUN IS A CITIZEN, A MAN WITHOUT A GUN IS A SUBJECT. Hearing news reports about the siege, McVeigh had driven from Florida to support the Davidians. Sitting on the hood of his car, dressed in a checked flannel shirt and a camo baseball cap, he agreed to speak to a journalism student from Southern Methodist University.

"The ATF just wants a chance to play with their toys, paid for by government money," McVeigh said in a calm voice. "The government is afraid of the guns people have. I believe we are slowly turning into a socialist government. The government is continually growing bigger and more powerful, and the people need to prepare to defend themselves against government control." He said the US military should never be deployed against American citizens. "Waco is only the beginning," he predicted. "People should watch the government here, and heed the signs."

After a couple of days on T-shirt Hill, McVeigh packed up his gear and set off on a road trip that would take him to forty states in the next twenty months, leading him back to Florida and finally, two years later, to Oklahoma.

17

....

Signals and Noise

Dick Schwein arrived in Waco on March 16. Schwein, who ran the
FBI's field office in El Paso, was assigned to assist Special Agent in
Charge Jamar. A hard-nosed twenty-year FBI veteran, he thought it
was time to quit babysitting the Davidians and start enforcing the
law.

"There's no use trying to talk to these bastards," Schwein said.
"We've got to just go in there and cut their balls off."

He told Jamar about Operation Nifty Package, a 1989 Delta Force
action against Panamanian dictator Manuel Noriega. After Noriega
holed up in the Vatican embassy in Panama City, claiming diplomatic
immunity, Army Rangers had set up loudspeakers and blasted deafening noise at the embassy for three days and nights until the dictator staggered out and surrendered. One American diplomat called
Nifty Package "a low moment in US Army history—silly, reproachable, undignified." Schwein called it a victory. At his urging, FBI and
ATF agents got to work building stanchions for loudspeakers outside
Mount Carmel.

The government speakers began blasting noise loud enough to
shiver the compound's thin walls: acid rock, bawling babies, bag-
pipes, sirens, dentists' drills, the squeals of animals being slaughtered,
and "These Boots Are Made for Walkin'." Nancy Sinatra's hit single

was meant to suggest escape. The rest was supposed to make the Davidians so miserable they would give up. While the FBI declined to specify the volume level of its playlist, which included a trumpet blaring reveille each day at dawn, there is no doubt it approached or exceeded 100 decibels, comparable to a jackhammer or rock concert. Extended exposure to noise above 100 decibels can damage human hearing, particularly in children.

"I was embarrassed for the FBI and personally enraged," Noesner lamented. Jamar and the other commanders overruled him.

Several of the hotter-tempered Davidians wanted to shoot at the speakers. Koresh wouldn't allow it. Babylon's assault on their senses was part of God's plan, he said. As much fun as it might be to blast away at the speakers, they would turn the other cheek. "For now, anyway," Koresh said.

The Davidians packed their ears with cotton as the noise blared round the clock. Finally, Koresh had heard enough. "Two can play at this game," he said.

He had some of the men lug his band's sound equipment from the chapel to the front of the building, where they hooked amps to a gas-powered generator. They dragged an upright piano to the double front doors to block any incoming bullets, then flung the doors open. "We began a kind of duel of the amps," drummer Thibodeau remembered, "blasting our music through our own loudspeakers."

That night's duel featured "My Sharona" and "Madman in Waco" on one side, earsplitting screams and Nancy Sinatra on the other. Koresh's band was so loud that federal agents hundreds of yards away had to shout to be heard through a high-decibel cacophony that carried past T-shirt Hill and Satellite City and over the cattle ranches miles away.

◇◇◇◇

"Good evening, this is Dan Rather." Rather led the *CBS Evening News* on March 17 with a report on the standoff at Waco. "That heavily armed cult in central Texas is showing no signs of surrender. Indeed, it shows all signs of defiance." That evening the negotiators challenged Steve Schneider to "take responsibility" and bring some of the Davidians out on his own. Their suggestion went nowhere. The affable Schneider was a loyal follower who had long since cast his lot with Koresh. Still, as if to please his interrogators, he had asked around—"Who wants to go out?"—and found no takers.

When he took the phone the next day, shouting to be heard over the racket in the background, Schneider asked about magazines. "Do you have a *People*? I heard he was on *People* magazine." True enough, Koresh was on *People*'s cover and was obsessed with seeing it. "It's a curiosity thing," Schneider claimed. "David couldn't care less."

The negotiators stalled. Magazines might serve as bargaining chips; perhaps they could convince Koresh to release more children in exchange for them. And they couldn't predict how he would react to seeing *People*'s cover line: "The Evil Messiah—David Koresh claimed 19 wives, had sex with children, armed his followers, and led them to tragedy."

Schneider said he couldn't believe they were haggling over *People*, *Time*, and *Newsweek*. "Something so minor as a magazine becomes one of the greatest issues involved in this event!"

"Steve, I've looked at those magazines," said negotiator John Hyler, a Vietnam veteran they knew as John 3. "They portray David as a lunatic. A child abuser." With Noesner looking over his shoulder, Hyler tried another tack: "How about adultery—do you subscribe to that?"

"I do not. No way," Schneider said. He blamed ex-Davidian Marc Breault for talk like that. "He's the one who got this whole thing going." It was Breault, writing letters, phoning and emailing the press and Justice Department from Australia, who had turned the authorities against them. "He worked hard to get every agency of the government involved," Schneider said. "God will deal with him."

Hyler pressed the issue. The magazines "said David has multiple wives. He's having sex with twelve-year-olds."

"Some of this is true," Schneider admitted. He denied that Koresh abused children—at least physically. He said he'd seen Koresh give Cyrus a paddling when the boy was a toddler. According to him, the spanking consisted of five mild swats with a wooden spoon. "Then Cyrus turned around, hugged his dad, and they kissed each other on the cheek." Davidian mom Robyn Bunds was a different story, Schneider said. "She beat her own little boy till his bottom was bleeding. And she now blames David for that."

But Hyler wasn't talking about spankings. He said, "Your child, Mayanah, was fathered by David."

"Who's saying these kind of things?"

"Is it true?"

"It is not true."

"It's not true that 'Judy Schneider-Koresh'—"

Schneider interrupted. "Tell you what. Send in *Newsweek* and *Time*. Let us take a look, and I'll give you more answers than you might even be ready for. How's that?"

Hyler persisted. "What about sex with twelve-year-olds? You and I know that's not right, Steve."

"It isn't right. And it's not happening."

"A fourteen-year-old—"

"Fourteen?" Schneider took a breath. "What can I say? It's true."

"A fourteen-year-old is not a consenting adult."

"The person was. That person *was*. I wasn't even here! This was Rachel."

"It's rape. It's child rape. You know it and I know it."

"The parents consented."

"Steve, if you had a fourteen-year-old daughter, would you consent to David having sex with her?"

"Let me ask you—have you ever had more than one girlfriend?"

"I've never raped a child."

With Noesner listening, passing him notes, Hyler upped the ante. Knowing that Judy was one of what the negotiators called Koresh's concubines, he asked, "Have you had sex with your wife?"

"Pardon?"

"Have you had sex with your wife?"

"I most certainly have."

"David has, too," Hyler said.

"*Now listen to me*," Schneider sputtered. "Twenty-two years I've been with her. She's the only one in the world I ever had sex with. Isn't that awesome?"

For the moment, the negotiators had done what they hoped to do. They had pricked Schneider's pride, if he had any left. "Steve, I'm not arguing with you," Hyler said. "I'm just telling you what's perceived in the press."

"It's okay." Schneider said he wasn't surprised the FBI couldn't understand the Davidians. "You've got this 'cult' mentality. You've talked to psychologists and theologians that are supposed to be versed in these things, but they don't know what they're talking about."

"Steve, I'll interrupt you right there. I'll settle with the God I believe in when I die, but I will not hide behind a bunch of innocent children, you know? I'll not hide behind little children."

"You have no ears to hear," Schneider said. He hung up.

Later that day, Noesner's negotiators arranged for a tank to deliver copies of *People*, *Time*, and *Newsweek* to the compound along with documents Wayne Martin had requested: the ATF's search warrant and a copy of the National Firearms Act specifying fines for weapons violations. There was also a joint letter from Jamar and Sheriff Harwell, the one law officer the Davidians trusted, promising that once Koresh surrendered he "could meet regularly with his followers while in jail awaiting trial."

It turned out the FBI had nothing to fear from Koresh's reaction to journalists' calling him an evil messiah, polygamist, and pedophile. As Schneider put it, "it's no big deal. They put the same kind of material in the newspaper." Whatever the stories said, Koresh liked seeing his picture in magazines.

Later on the eighteenth, Jamar surprised the negotiators. He authorized the Hostage Rescue Team to advance with tanks and armored construction vehicles that destroyed four fuel-storage tanks, dragged away a bus, and smashed up the Davidians' parked cars, bicycles, and motorcycles—including Koresh's Harley. The assault was "done recklessly," Noesner recalled, "with no effort to minimize damage. Some of my negotiators began to speculate that this was done deliberately, to undercut the negotiation process."

Clive Doyle watched from a window. "The tanks knocked down our fuel tanks," he said, "soaking the whole area in diesel and gasoline."

Koresh told a negotiator that one of the tanks had been full of "ninety-two-octane super unleaded. We had our fingers in our ears," expecting an explosion. "We thought, '*Oh no, we're all going to be fried if somebody lights a match.*'" He warned that the tanks doing the damage "aren't fireproof." If one of them kicked off a stray spark, "those guys in there would have been popping like popcorn."

◇◇◇◇

Noesner described his strategy as "Trickle, flow, gush." If he and his team could convince even a few Davidians to leave, more might follow until the rest came out all at once. Despite the tactical teams' aggression, his negotiators had secured the release of twenty-one children and six adults including Kathy Schroeder. Through another day and night of talks they arranged for a new group to leave Mount Carmel on March 21, the third Sunday of the siege.

How many would be coming out? Schneider said there might be thirty, maybe even forty. Koresh spent the night of March 20 meeting with the ninety or so Davidians who remained inside. The bullet wound in his side had been acting up again. "The back hole," he said of the exit wound, "is worse than the front hole." He was treating it with hydrogen peroxide as he lay in his room upstairs, counseling the faithful about the FBI's offer. Noesner convinced Jamar to have the loudspeakers temporarily shut off in hopes of aiding the process. In these soul-searching meetings, Koresh told Davidians they were free to go but equally free to stay if God told them to. "He's almost had to push people out," Schneider reported. "He can't force them." What Schneider didn't say was that many Davidians saw the choice to stay or leave as a test of faith. So did Koresh. In his view, their community would be stronger without those who chose to leave. He had already kicked Kathy Schroeder out for smoking. He had sent two men out along with her after he caught them dipping into his private stash of scotch. "In the situation we're in, we need the highest soberness," he said.

He defended his vices in a late-night talk with negotiators. "People say I get all the wives. 'David gets all the cigarettes, David gets all the booze, David is screwing all the women.'" But leadership was a burden. The Davidians he sent out were "weak people. They were problems." In hindsight, he'd told Schneider, they were better off without Catherine Matteson and Margaret Lawson, the elderly women he'd sent out with the tape of his radio speech. People their age "start to digress," Koresh said. He was winnowing chaff, keeping his core believers around him.

Just after midnight on March 21, Victorine Hollingsworth and nurse Annetta Richards walked out. Like the others, they were patted down and arrested.

Schneider had a request. Could the FBI send female agents to frisk the Davidian women who came out? "It's a modesty thing." Negotiator Hyler ran that up the chain of command and came back with good news. "We don't have a lot of women SWAT team members, but we've arranged to have one come in the Bradley," he said. "She's got short hair and she's dressed like the others, but she *is* a woman, okay? We don't have any pink helmets for them."

After a spartan breakfast, five more adults emerged. One was Sheila Martin, who had sent out three of her children, including disabled Jamie, two weeks before. "I was so torn," she remembers. Her husband and their four other kids were staying behind. "I wanted to stay, too, but I thought the littler ones needed me."

She knew that other Davidians who went out had been arrested, but she believed the negotiators' vow that she would be able to spend at least some of her time with Daniel, Kimberley, and Jamie.

Before leaving, Sheila spent a moment at the door with her husband, the Davidians' lawyer. "Whatever happens, happens," Wayne told her. "What we're seeing—it's what David's been teaching all along. The government's right outside our door. I'm not going to cooperate with them."

She watched her husband walk away, then went out to meet the tanks. The female agent frisked her. "They took my Bible for evidence," Sheila says. After a short tank ride past the crowds on T-shirt Hill, the feds drove her to Sheriff Harwell's office for hugs with her youngest kids. The FBI put four-year-old Kimmy Martin on speakerphone to her dad at Mount Carmel.

"Daddy has certainly been thinking about you," Wayne said. "Daddy wants you to pray to God every day, okay?"

Sheila spoke up. "They seem happy," she told Wayne. "They look like they're eating really well." Her ride in the tank had been "a little bumpy," she said.

Wayne sounded grim. "It could get bumpy down the road, too."

From the tank she'd seen "people with signs—they were protesting."

"I wish they knew more about the Seven Seals. I wish they knew that time is short, that God is angry, and God is in total control." There was static on the phone. He could barely hear her. "Sheila, are you there?"

"I'm here. I'm here. You take care, okay?"

Wayne said, "We may be out of touch for a while."

◇◇◇◇

Only seven Davidians came out that day—more a trickle than a gush. The negotiators were confident they were making headway, but the hard-liners advising Jamar were not convinced. One of them, Vietnam veteran Byron Sage, became the FBI's voice over the loudspeakers. His amplified voice told the holdouts to *come out now!*

Judy Schneider-Koresh complained about Sage. "He was screaming!" she told one of the negotiators. "David just sent out seven people—they were apprehensive already, but they go out—then he comes on like a tiger: 'I want thirty people out!'"

Her legal husband stayed calm. Steve Schneider told negotiator Hyler he knew why the Davidians had trouble getting their message across: "To the outside world, we appear so bizarre and weird. I don't blame anybody." He said the negotiators must be exhausted, too, and eager to go back to their families.

Hyler saw an opening. "Yeah, I've got a six-year-old that called me yesterday and said he didn't remember what I look like. But I'm committed to helping you get through this."

"Thank you."

"Where's David?"

"Asleep."

As Schneider's exchanges with other negotiators demonstrated, they all knew Judy was a proud member of the House of David. They knew Koresh treated Steve more like a servant than as the foremost of his Mighty Men. That gave Schneider plenty of reasons to resent his master. Could driving a wedge between them help end the crisis?

"Steve, a lot of those people respect you in there," Hyler said. "I think a lot of them would even follow you out because they think well of you."

Schneider wasn't buying it. "They came here to hear David, not me. I came to learn from the guy myself. I mean, look, I have spent my life with theologians and very highly educated human beings, and there's no one that's had the consistency of answers when it comes to sciences and religion and health and all the other subjects. It's quite phenomenal. The man's only got a ninth-grade education. But you know what? These people have come to hear him. That's what I'm telling you."

"Okay," Hyler said. "But several days ago David said this would all be over in a few days and everyone would be out of there, and it keeps going on and on."

Schneider said, "I don't know what else to do. Honestly."

"Keep working on them."

Noesner's team was satisfied with what he called "incremental success. But once again, it was as if the command was purposely derailing our momentum."

Three hours after Sheila Martin and the others brought the day's total of Davidians released and arrested to seven, military vehicles again set upon the cars and motorcycles inside the perimeter. One of the cars, said Noesner, "was a beautiful, completely restored red Chevy Ranchero. In case Koresh wasn't getting the point as he watched from the compound, they crushed the car flat as a pancake before dragging it off." To Noesner, tightening the noose made no sense. They had brought nine people out in the past three days despite Dick Schwein's sonic psy-ops. This new assault convinced Noesner that Jamar, Schwein, Rogers, and the other hard-liners were too careerist or macho to understand what he called Psychology 101: "If you want to train your dog to fetch a newspaper, you don't kick the dog when it brings you the paper."

◇◇◇◇

Around midnight on the twenty-first, Mount Carmel went silent. As the Department of Justice's report drily noted, "The loudspeaker system malfunctioned. The night ended quietly." The Davidians had a chance to sleep soundly before the speakers boomed back to life the next day. Then, at 10:00 p.m. on March 22, agents delivered a letter to the compound. In the letter, Jamar and Sheriff Harwell promised that Koresh could hold services with his followers in jail and deliver another speech on the Christian Broadcasting Network—provided he led everyone out the following day. Koresh threw the letter in the trash.

Livingstone Fagan walked out the next morning. The elfin Davidian had conferred with Koresh and Schneider, who agreed to send him out as an ambassador who could explain their religious views to the press and public. Fagan was the thirty-fifth Davidian to leave Mount Carmel since the raid. Black-suited agents kicked his feet out from under him, dropped him into a puddle, searched him, handcuffed him, and drove him to the McLennan County Jail.

The FBI had guaranteed that Fagan could phone Mount Carmel to tell his wife he was safe. When he got to the jail, his captors told him the phones weren't working.

Yvette Fagan had planned to follow her husband out. When he didn't call, she decided to stay.

She was among fewer than ninety Davidians left inside. Koresh insisted that they all get "three squares a day" even if meals consisted of trail mix or half an MRE. The MREs ranged from a palatable tuna casserole to potatoes au gratin, which they called "potatoes au rotten." Each person also got two eight-ounce ladles of water per day. When it rained, some of them washed their hair by sticking their heads out windows, defying the sharpshooters.

Soon the agents guarding the perimeter cracked down. Until the last week of March they had let Dave Jones go outside to feed the chickens. Others were allowed to lug buckets of excrement to a dumping ground behind the compound. Now the tactical teams began throwing flash-bangs at anyone who ventured outside. After that, Jones and the others emptied their waste in the dirt-floored storm shelter where Doyle had buried the four Davidians who died on the day of the raid. They sprayed the mucky earth with Lysol to cover the smell. For the next several days, while the Davidians worked out a feeding schedule with the FBI, the chickens went hungry.

18

....

Regime Change

Koresh resumed his harangues on the phone. "We were under investigation for firearms misuse," he said. "It may be true that we stepped over the borderline of certain regulations. But isn't this all a little bizarre?" His account of the raid never wavered. "I went to the doorway and here come the chuck wagons, lickety-split. I said, 'Let's talk. There's women and children here.'" As he often reminded the negotiators, he was "totally unarmed" at the time, though he could easily have gone out locked and loaded. Instead he'd tried to play peacemaker, and what did that get him? "Lo and behold they jump out and *blap*—that's a nine-millimeter. *Blap blap blap!*" He recalled the noise of the dogs' being shot, but said he suspected an ATF raider might have fired the first round by accident. "He's nervous. He's got his finger on the trigger a little too hard. *Bang*, and that causes them all to jump the gun."

The negotiators said they couldn't discuss the raid. "That was the ATF," was their line. "We're FBI." They were trained to keep Koresh focused on how the standoff would end, not how it started.

He said the end looked better for them than for him. "You're going to go home," he told negotiator John Cox. "You're going to be with your wife and kids. I am going to be without a wife—my wives, plural. And my children. All I'll have is my Father."

Cox said he had a God, too.

"Yeah, the guy in the White House," Koresh said, shifting to a lecture on pharaohs, popes, and presidents. He said he was willing to render unto Clinton by surrendering. "And it won't be that long. Don't think I'm planning on staying in here for a month or two." He said he understood that the government had rights of its own, including the right to enforce its laws. "They had a penal code in biblical times, too, you know. Crucifixion seemed cruel, but it sure kept the crime rate down." He doubted the FBI's commanders would let him live for long, not at a cost he'd heard on the radio was over $100,000 a day. But he had an idea of how to save the government a few dollars in the end: "When they give me the lethal injection, I'll say, 'Give me the cheap stuff.'"

◇◇◇◇

Judy Schneider-Koresh took a turn on the phone. "Who's this?" she asked. "Are you John Three or Two or One?"

"One."

"You're number one. That's good!"

"Just John One," Cox said. "I'm not the number one guy."

"I'm only kidding."

He had a message for her. "Your dad called from Wisconsin," John 1 said. "He's worried about you." The FBI had been fielding hundreds of Waco-related calls every day. Public affairs officers followed up on tips that sounded worthwhile and forwarded messages from Davidians' families to the negotiators.

John 1 wrote down her reply. "*Dearest Dad, thanks for calling. Remember what they did to Christ two thousand years ago. Same thing. You will be seeing David's—our!—side of the story soon. Don't worry, trust in God.*"

"How do you want it signed?" Cox asked.

"Sign it '*Poopykins #2*,'" she said, laughing. "He'll know what that means."

◇◇◇◇

Noesner's team brought in a female negotiator. Agent Linda Barry tried to talk Juliette Martinez into bringing her five children out.

Martinez was the Davidian whose burritos and grilled fish were highlights of the Mount Carmel menu before the raid. Her record of misdemeanor drug offenses had helped the government make its case that the Davidians were "involved in drugs." Koresh had helped her trade drugs for religion. Aside from Koresh's own children, the thirty-year-old Martinez's five kids, ranging from three to thirteen years old, were the largest group of children left inside. The FBI hoped to score a public relations coup by convincing her to bring them out.

Negotiator Barry said, "Woman to woman—as a mother, I would think you'd want to get your kids out."

Martinez was wary. "You'll put me in jail and take my children away once I fall into you guys' hands."

"It's not a matter of falling into anybody's hands. It's a matter of walking to the safety of the free world."

"There *is* no free world. You know what the kids say? They say, 'Why did these people come and mess up our life?' You people are mocking us through the loudspeakers, flipping us off—"

"Because we want you to come out."

"They flip us off and moon us because they want us to come out?" Martinez asked. She was sure the authorities would put some of her kids in foster care and send the youngest ones back to their father. "And he's a junkie."

Negotiators are free to deceive hostages and hostage takers if it helps get them to surrender. "I assure you," Barry said, "nothing bad is going to happen to your children."

Martinez said, "No, they'll just end up in a foster home some-where, abused and slapped around."

◇◇◇◇

After the call, Steve Schneider asked Martinez if she wanted to leave. She said no. The negotiators hectored Schneider, hoping to turn him away from Koresh. "Lead by example," they told him. "Stand up and be counted. Be a man."

Schneider spent almost every waking hour either talking to nego-tiators or canvassing the Davidians, asking who wanted to stay and who might be willing to leave. "I've asked everybody!" he told the negotiators. "In all honesty, I haven't been able to affect anyone. If I came out, I'd be the only one." Bleary and miserable, he tried napping with a towel around his head to block out the noise. The FBI had added laughter, deafening gongs, and distorted Gregorian chants to the loudspeakers' playlist. Schneider would wake and pad to the phone, which always seemed to be ringing. "David's our leader," he said. "Not me."

During one sleepless night, he mused about the house he and Judy once dreamed of building on twenty acres in Oahu. "You should see it—it's so beautiful there. But of course my world, my life, turned upside down when I ran into him." Like many of the others, the Wisconsin-born Schneider had been raised as a Seventh-day Adventist. In 1986, he was working on his PhD in comparative religion at the University of Hawaii when a friend introduced him to Koresh's teachings. He and Judy were quickly hooked and moved to Mount Carmel together. On the phone to the FBI seven years later, he stressed that he had no regrets. Thanks to Koresh, the Bible finally made sense to him. *Life* made sense. "And it sure got interesting!"

A new negotiator asked Schneider how he could stand by while his wife was "being screwed by this prophet, and he's screwing children."

"You're reading too many of those *Enquirer* and *Star* magazines," Schneider said.

John O'Neill, a former marine immediately dubbed "John 5," took a firmer approach than his predecessors. "We need ten people to come out tomorrow. That is a minimum." This was the new, harder line his superiors preferred.

Schneider was unmoved. "The more you threaten these people, the more they'll lay down on the floor and you can run tanks over them. That's become the attitude."

"Is that so?"

"Do you know what would work? Throw a match to the building. Then people would have to come out."

"We're not going to do something like that."

"Read Isaiah Thirty-three about people living in fire and walking through and surviving," Schneider said. "And then, before you ask me about adultery and fornication, why don't you investigate Jerry Falwell and Jimmy Swaggart?"

◇◇◇◇

Somebody was banging on the front doors. "Let me in!" It was early in the evening of March 24. A shirtless man bounced back and forth in the klieg lights trained on the compound, pounding the bullet-riddled doors with his fists. He had somehow gotten through the fence and eluded more than four hundred federal agents. "Let me in! God sent me!"

The man appeared to be unarmed. The snipers held their fire. The doors opened a crack. He disappeared inside.

He was young, with buzz-cut hair and bulging, darting eyes. Breathing hard, he told the Davidians he wanted to meet David Koresh. He wanted to learn about the Seven Seals.

Schneider picked up the phone. Negotiator Cox said, "*Who is that? We can't have this happening.*"

The bare-chested intruder took the phone. "Sir," he told Cox, "if you'd like all this to end—"

"*Who is this?*"

"Allow God to handle it."

"I don't want to talk to you if you won't give me your name," Cox said.

"Have a good day, then." The man hung up.

Cox called back and got Schneider. "Sounds like you've got a fruitcake on your hands."

Schneider laughed. "It's possible."

"Send this damn fool down the road. We think he rode a horse in there."

"Seriously?" In fact, there was no horse. That soon-debunked report was a sign of confusion on the agents' part.

Koresh took the phone. "Hello there, John."

"You need to put him out the front door," John 1 said. "He's a screamer and a hollerer. We'll pick him up in a Bradley."

"Well, we never met him before, but the thing of it is, he risked his life to hear our side of the story. Christ did some screaming in his day, you know."

"What's his name? Who is he?"

"He wants to hear about the Seals, that's who he is. We're cool with it."

"Well then, I guess I'll talk to you later," Cox said.

"Wait a minute—"

This time it was John 1 who hung up.

The FBI's tape recorder caught the voices of other members of the negotiating team. "They're toying with us," one said.

"Crazy bastard."

"Check up on him."

The intruder's name was Louis Anthony Alaniz. Twenty-four years old, he lived in a Houston trailer park with his mother, who called him "a religious fanatic." A friend described him as "an oddball, walking up the street snapping his fingers." Alaniz told the Davidians he'd been watching on TV and wanted to meet "the great David Koresh" in the flesh.

Koresh thought he might be an FBI spy, but liked him anyway. "If he's one of yours," Koresh told negotiator Cox in their next call, "he's the best one we've seen so far." In fact, he said, "You should send another bug in here—I wish you could hear some of this!"

Cox was unimpressed. "When I get off the phone with you, I have to go answer to somebody, and they're looking for one answer: When is he coming out of there?"

"It's his decision. We just met the guy."

The rest of that week, the fourth week of the siege, negotiators set deadlines for Alaniz to come out. Koresh and the Davidians ignored them.

◇◇◇◇

Dick Wren took the headset on March 25. The newest negotiator epitomized the new, harder line favored by the negotiators' bosses. The moment Schneider mentioned John Dolan, Wren said, "He's gone. John Dolan went out of his way to try to resolve this. To work with you. Unfortunately, you didn't cooperate with him. Now he's gone. I mean, the guy is going to have to repair his own career."

Schneider said he felt bad about that. "What do you want from us?"

"I'm talking about numbers, Steve." Jamar and the other commanders wanted a head count. How many Davidians would be coming out tomorrow? "Numbers. I am telling you what the front office says."

Schneider and the others had been listening to the government's daily press briefings on the radio. They knew that Kathy Schroeder wasn't reunited with her son the way she'd been promised. She was in jail, charged with conspiracy to commit murder. She might never see her little boy again. "You keep lying to us," Schneider said.

"Steve, what would you like us to do? Let you walk down the road, walk into town, and check into one of the local motels?"

"David says you better hope he doesn't open the Seven Seals. Because you will have to answer for all this."

"I'll take that chance."

Schneider was worn out. He put lawyer Wayne Martin on the phone. The new negotiator greeted Martin with apparent relief. "Hello, Wayne. Harvard Law!" Wren said. "You're an intelligent man. Tell me—who's controlling this whole thing?"

"What do you mean?"

"There are lives at stake here," Wren told him. "Come out. Offer the facts that you have to the appropriate court in the appropriate manner."

"I'd like to discuss that proposal with my lawyer," Martin said.

"Beg pardon?"

"I'm joking." Martin said he couldn't represent the Davidians from a speakerphone connected to the FBI. He would listen to any ideas the negotiators had "just as soon as you restore our phone lines." That way, he and his clients could exercise their First Amendment right to free speech. During the siege, Martin said, he had been "wondering where I lost my Constitutional rights." With hundreds of federal agents outside, lights blazing and speakers blowing crazy noise day and night, "It's hard to think straight. This isn't the way I normally practice law, as an inmate in a concentration camp."

⬦⬦⬦

At four o'clock that afternoon, the CEVs advanced again. They dragged motorcycles and go-karts away from the compound, mangling them. The Davidians stood beside windows, using mirrors to watch the action without showing themselves.

Koresh fumed. "No one else will be coming out," he told the negotiators.

Lead negotiator Noesner sensed that his influence was waning. With Rogers, Schwein, and other hard-liners arguing for quick, decisive action—an attack to flush the Davidians out of their fortress—Noesner was often the only senior official counseling patience. He thought his bosses were wrong to signal their intentions with a new show of force—the latest assault on the Davidians' precious vehicles—but thought he knew why they had done it. "Jamar was feeling the heat. The entire nation was watching, and the FBI was spending about $128,000 a day, a rate of expenditure that would add up to more than $5 million before all was said and done." Noesner was determined to keep Koresh and Schneider talking, offsetting the hard-liners' tactics with all the positive reinforcement his team could muster. He told his negotiators their job was to secure the safe release of as many Davidians as possible, and in his mind that meant all of them. Even after three and a half weeks on the scene, enduring Koresh's maddening moods and constant flak from his superiors, Noesner kept the faith. "Despite the anger and disappointment," he recalled, "despite the bad decisions coming down from our commanders, the entire negotiation team felt we needed to continue our efforts."

He had about three hours left on the job.

On the night of March 25, almost a month into the siege, the phone rang in Noesner's room in a budget motel on the shoulder of I-35. The caller was Rob Grace, his boss at the academy at Quantico. "I'm calling to thank you for your work," Grace said. "It's time for you to step down."

Noesner had been in Waco longer than FBI negotiators usually work high-stress assignments. Grace told him he'd heard from higher-ups at FBI headquarters in Washington, who wanted a new man on the job: Clint Van Zandt.

Noesner had worked with Van Zandt in the academy's Behavioral Science Unit. He suspected that Van Zandt, one of the Bureau's most vocal born-again Christians, would try debating scripture with Koresh and lose the debate. But there was no point in arguing with the Bureau's choice. His replacement was set to take over the next morning; the decision was final before he picked up the phone.

Waco wasn't Noesner's fight anymore. He flew home to Virginia and followed the siege on TV.

◇◇◇◇

A Gallup poll showed that 70 percent of Americans supported the FBI over Koresh and the Davidians. "I get it," says Thibodeau. "I got it even then. If I'd been on the outside, I would have been the first to say, 'These people are nuts, man! What are they doing, staying in there?' But I challenge any American family to think about what they would do if tanks pulled up outside their house. Would you send your kids out? A lot of Americans would fight to the end."

Koresh's hand was healing, but the wound by his tailbone kept bleeding. He was still treating it with garlic and hydrogen peroxide. "My work is finished," he said one night. "I don't need to hang around here. All I need to do is cock the pistol back, keep my thumb on the trigger and my mind on the Psalms."

Was he contemplating suicide?

Van Zandt told the negotiators that their commanders thought the crisis was "developing as in Guyana with Jim Jones." Park Dietz, the UCLA professor and FBI advisor who had diagnosed Koresh as a psychopath without meeting him, informed the Bureau that Koresh was "suicidal and may have made a suicide pact with other members." According to FBI records, "Cyanide poisoning was thought to be a major risk, and therefore cyanide antidote kits were made available on the scene. The Attorney General asked about the possibility of a mass suicide."

There was no cyanide at Mount Carmel. Koresh told the negotiators again and again that he was "no Jim Jones." He wasn't going to go all

Rambo on them, either, he said. He had no desire to commit suicide by FBI. He had too much to look forward to.

He was no Rambo, but he thought his life was getting more and more like a movie. Not a war movie like the ones he screened in the chapel, but an old-time Western with the good guys holding the fort. Only this time it would be God's cavalry riding to the rescue on chariots of fire. He wouldn't miss that show for the world. When it was over, he said, the world would finally recognize David Koresh as one of the great prophets, the Lamb who opened the Seven Seals. "Unfortunately, all the top prophets get killed."

19

Breakthrough

On March 25, two nights after Louis Alaniz arrived, another pilgrim slipped through the fence into the compound. The FBI didn't learn about him until the following day.

"For your records, a guy came in last night," Schneider told negotiator Tony Oldham. "Kind of hippie-looking."

The new arrival was a drifter with long ginger hair and a beard. He had hitchhiked to Waco. Koresh said he looked like "an overgrown leprechaun." Schneider put him on the phone with Oldham.

"What's your name?" the negotiator asked.

"Jesse Amen!" the man said.

"Where do you live?"

"I travel. I live in the wind."

"What is your date of birth?"

"It doesn't matter, man."

Jesse Amen said he was there to "bring peace." The negotiators knew his presence at Mount Carmel would make the FBI look foolish. During the week since Livingstone Fagan became the last Davidian to leave, they'd warned Koresh of "consequences" if he didn't send out ten or more people—and soon. Over that time the compound's population had *risen* by two.

◇◇◇◇

On March 28 they put attorney Dick DeGuerin on the phone. DeGuerin assured Koresh that he had "a valid legal defense." He offered to negotiate Koresh's surrender, defend him in court, and discuss book and movie offers on his behalf. Koresh listened, then brought up the Guitar Nebula. He said the nebula was made up of countless luminous angels moving in formation in the shape of a guitar. "Is it still coming?" he asked. The lawyer said he didn't know much about astronomy.

The next day, a 50,000-pound Bradley tank delivered DeGuerin to Mount Carmel. Wearing his trademark short-brimmed white Stetson and toting a shiny black briefcase, the smartly dressed lawyer clambered down to the gravel drive outside the front gate. As he walked, he said, he felt spent shell casings "crunching around my feet. They were everywhere: nine millimeters, forty-five calibers. Wayne Martin and Steve Schneider cracked open the door, which was barricaded by an upright piano and a bunch of cases of canned food."

DeGuerin stopped on the front step. His client, a lean figure with a hint of a smile on his unshaven face, stood just inside the door per FBI instructions. Standing across from each other on the threshold, they talked for two hours while the government, observing attorney-client privilege, left them alone. But the meeting was "frustrating," DeGuerin recalled. "For every issue I resolved, he would bring up a new one."

They met again the next day and twice more on March 31. "He asked interesting questions about what would happen if they surrendered," DeGuerin said. Koresh said he didn't want to be "jailed with no bubbas," referring to good old boys who didn't take kindly to purported child molesters. He said he was thinking of leading everyone out on April 2, two days hence. If not then, they would need to wait at least another week because Passover was coming up four days later. Passover meant far more than Christmas ("a pagan holiday," Koresh called it) or Easter ("a counterfeit Passover") to the Davidians, who saw themselves as inheritors of Old Testament traditions. Their

God was demanding, even vengeful, more likely to dispense fire and brimstone than Christmas presents or Easter eggs. Koresh denounced Santa Claus and the Easter Bunny as "false idols." He said there was nothing cute about religion. In his view, faith was serious and time was short.

While he spoke with his lawyer, the negotiators tried appealing to some of the women close to him. O'Neill, the negotiator known as John 5, pressed Judy Schneider-Koresh to act on her own. "You're a reasonable lady," he told her. "You sound like a gal that can come up with the right answers. How long do you plan to stay in there?"

"I'll come out tomorrow if God says so."

"I keep wondering—how did you go from being Steve's wife to being David's wife?"

"That's a long Bible story," she said. "I mean, Psalm Forty-five—"

"No. Without the religious end of things—"

"There is nothing without the religious end of things."

"So whose wife are you?"

"I'm God's wife."

"You've got to start thinking about this, young lady," O'Neill said. "Maybe you gals will all get together and say you've had enough, and come out."

Rachel Howell Koresh spoke with another negotiator, John 1. "We need milk. We need chicken feed," she said. Their hens had quit laying eggs. Dave Jones had been feeding rotting potatoes to the hens to keep them from starving.

John 1 told Rachel the FBI had a new policy. "It's not our responsibility to take care of the people inside."

"Oh John, I don't understand you. Your attitude has changed," she said. She put Judy's two-year-old on the line. "Here's Mayanah."

"Want some chicken food. And milk," the little girl said.

John 1 was taken aback, "Well, um, tell your mama I'll pass it on. And I love you, OK?"

"We need milk," Mayanah repeated.

"OK. You be a good girl. I'll pass it on. Bye-bye!"

Rachel got back on the line. "That was funny!"

The FBI agreed to send in nineteen pints of milk, roughly one for each child left inside, plus a bag of groceries. Cow's milk was all the Bureau could come up with, and Mount Carmel's mothers, despite their preference for goat milk, were happy to have it. The groceries included cheese and crackers, which the Davidians parsed out as delicacies.

That same day, the FBI asked the army to provide "emergency medical support for contingency operations in Waco."

◇◇◇◇

Religion professors Tabor and Arnold still hoped to get through to Koresh. Spurned by FBI officials, who couldn't tell them from the countless astrologers, psychics, and tipsters trying to play a part in negotiations, they appeared together on the radio talk show the Davidians listened to. The scholars suggested that the book of Revelation's "little season"—the time leading up to the Last Days—need not be interpreted literally. Such a "season" might last years, leaving time for the Davidians to come out, go through trials and even imprisonment, and give interviews sharing their message of salvation with millions of people. Professor Tabor emphasized that the Dead Sea Scrolls mentioned a "branch of David . . . one who was wounded," a line Koresh might take as a flattering reference to himself.

Koresh renewed his requests to speak to the scholars he'd heard on the radio. The negotiators stalled him. Van Zandt, their new leader, was no more inclined than Noesner had been to put Koresh on the phone with a pair of religious eggheads who seemed to like his "Bible babble."

◇◇◇◇

Drifter "Jesse Amen" said his mission was fulfilled.

"I came to bring peace," he'd told Koresh, and not a single shot had been fired since he'd arrived. Koresh later told the negotiators he knew the real reason Jesse chose to leave: "He found out we don't smoke pot." Jesse walked out on April 4—the first person to leave Mount Carmel in two weeks. If nothing else, Koresh said, his departure proved the Davidians weren't holding hostages.

Next, the negotiators tried making Koresh mad. For several days they used his given name. "Vernon Howell is a coward and a con man," one of them told Schneider. "Think about the children—he's scarring them for life."

"Damn you!" Koresh said. He seldom cursed, but he was "getting sick of this. If you care so much about the kids, why don't you turn off the music outside?" He said he knew what the FBI was thinking: "*We'll just kill these fuckers. Shit, let's get the women and children out. We'll put 'em in jail and put the kids with foster parents.*"

FBI records list "no relevant activity" for the next day. The full entry for the day after that reports, "no activity on April 6, except that at 8:00 pm Schneider called the negotiators to complain about the music and noise being broadcast over the loudspeakers. He said that if it was not turned off in honor of Passover, he might never speak to them again. The FBI continued broadcasting music throughout the night."

◇◇◇◇

The Davidians let the phone ring for two days and nights. On April 8 a new bedsheet hung from a window: FBI GOD SEES YOUR LIES HAB 3:14. Habbakuk 3:14 refers to "wretched victims devoured in secret." Koresh and his followers saw themselves as victims of a government determined to keep the rest of the world from witnessing what happened to them.

Attorney DeGuerin told reporters he was concerned about the tactical teams' using combat vehicles to drag cars, buses, motorcycles, trees, and scrub brush from the area in front of Mount Carmel. As the *New York Times* reported, "FBI officials have characterized these as 'defensive maneuvers' intended to provide a clear line of fire into the compound." DeGuerin and his colleague Jack Zimmerman, representing Steve Schneider, described the same maneuvers as "destroying evidence." Through it all they allowed their clients to keep talking to FBI negotiators, reasoning that a peaceful end to the siege was in everyone's interest. And as DeGuerin well knew, no gag order could silence Koresh when he wanted to talk.

On April 8, Schneider phoned the command post. "They turned the noise on again!" The loudspeakers went silent for hours at a time only to resume blasting music, mad laughter, and chain saws. Still, Schneider seemed to have his sense of humor back. "Ask the loud-speaker guys if they have any crickets or whippoorwills," he said.

More important, he had a message: a letter from Koresh to the FBI.

The next day was Good Friday. Davidians marked the holiday not as part of a Lenten observance but as the day Roman soldiers killed the original messiah. Between three and four that afternoon, the time Jesus was said to have died on the cross, Schneider came out the front door with his hands up. He had arranged a brief foray with the negotiators. He left Koresh's letter under a rock so the wind wouldn't blow it away. Then he placed seven small canisters of incense in the mud beside the driveway. Schneider lit them one by one to mark the hour of Jesus's death, sending orange smoke drifting over the compound.

Koresh's letter began, "*Who are you fighting against?*" He went on in God's voice. "*The law is mine, the truth is mine . . . I am your God and you will bow under my feet.*" He wrote of "*seven thunders*" expressing God's wrath and closed with a warning: "*Learn from David My seals or bear the consequences. I forewarn you the Lake Waco area of Old Mount Carmel will be terribly shaken. The lake will be emptied through the broken damn.*" He never could spell.

He signed the letter "Yahweh Koresh."

As Schneider understood it, Koresh was predicting an earthquake. But the FBI interpreted his letter as a terrorist threat. Two FBI specialists—psychiatrist Joseph Krofcheck and Clint Van Zandt, the new chief negotiator—analyzed it for Attorney General Reno. In their analysis, the letter proved that Koresh was "a functional, paranoid-type psychotic." They predicted that he was preparing a "snare" for Babylon, a reference to the book of Jeremiah. For Koresh to give up "the power and omnipotence" he enjoyed inside the compound, Krofcheck and Van Zandt wrote, would be like "asking a crack cocaine addict who gets a sexual-like high from crack to give up his habit cold turkey." Without citing any evidence, they went on to claim Koresh might be planning a "mass break-out, in which the

FBI would be faced with women carrying a baby in one arm while firing a weapon from the other."

On that same Good Friday, according to Justice Department documents, "the FBI began to finish plans for inserting nonlethal Orthochlorobenzalmalonononitrile (CS) tear gas into the compound." The gas, called CS for the names of its inventors, commonly used for riot control, was toxic enough to be banned in warfare. FBI officials met with Reno "to determine if the plan would be approved and, if so, to decide when it would occur."

◇◇◇◇

The Davidians joked that they were getting skinnier than their chickens. Judy Schneider-Koresh, shot in the hand during the raid six weeks before, pulled slivers of bone through the purple skin of her index finger. One negotiator told Steve to "get her out of there—we'll get her the medical attention she needs." Steve said he'd told her the same thing, but "Judy fears God more than her finger."

Over the better part of a week, the negotiators kept asking to speak to Koresh. He sent word that he wasn't interested. "He's praying," Schneider said. "He's asking his God what to do, and he's getting one word. Wait. Wait. Wait." Since the raid, Koresh's followers had felt they were part of a great drama racing toward its conclusion, just as their prophet promised: the beginning of the end of the world. Like him, they were willing to wait.

On April 10 the tanks rumbled into action, turning their sides toward the compound. The FBI described this as another "defensive maneuver," with the tanks providing cover for the agents unspooling a six-foot wall of razor wire around the compound.

Koresh ranted about the barbed-wire barricade. "We're a religious minority who never aggressed against anybody. We pay our taxes. And our own government attacks us." Soon a new bedsheet would appear under a window: FLAMES AWAIT.

Despite his fury Koresh took the phone for an overnight talk with John Denton, a Vietnam veteran known as John 4. The FBI's account of their five-and-a-half-hour conversation describes it as "a rambling, disjointed religious discourse." In fact, Koresh's rant gave way to hours of friendly conversation that found him asking John 4 about combat in Vietnam, music and cars, and even quoting Nancy Reagan.

In the wee hours of April 14, Koresh made a point of saying he never took money for preaching, "unlike lots of 'em." He lived communally with his followers, like Jesus. He had traveled the world to recruit followers, visiting Australia, England, and Hawaii as well as Israel, but "never stayed in fancy motels." He mused on biblical resonances to "our time right now." The Prodigal Son "wanted to boogie," he said. The stained glass, bells, and golden ornaments of Catholic services reminded him of the Whore of Babylon, a temptress he called the Harlot of Babylon. "And what does a harlot do? She puts on makeup. She sings a pretty song. She dances. Everything feminine is promoted and highly exaggerated." In that way, he said, mainstream religion was packaged like breakfast cereal. "Look at Cap'n Crunch and Count Chocula—they're selling highly refined, highly processed wheat and sugar to appease the eyes and the senses. It's the same with Coca-Cola and Pepsi. It's the same with TV. People are in bondage to these things."

John 4 said he wasn't wrong. "Come out," he said. "Tell the world what you're thinking."

"My God says to wait."

"Well, you can wait in the slammer."

That made Koresh laugh. He said he wished they could be talking someplace else. "Fishing. Just drinking a beer, fishing and talking." He knew it was too late for that. Still, he hoped to set the record straight. "I was offended when I was accused of having drugs here," he said. "We don't have no drug labs. That was just something they had to say to cover their rear ends because they illegally obtained those helicopters." He said he agreed with Nancy Reagan that Americans should "Say no to drugs."

Koresh said good night. "I appreciate you talking with me. I know I sound like a broken record sometimes. I know we've got to come out."

"Okay."

"But you keep aiming those big tanks at us. What can we do?"

"I'm not aiming those tanks," Denton said. "I'd be delighted if you come out with a freaking posy and stick it right in one of those gun barrels. Send those macho guys home, you know? Send them home."

"Okey-doke," Koresh said. "Shalom."

◇◇◇◇

On Wednesday, April 14, Koresh said he'd had a revelation. He dictated a one-page note for DeGuerin to relay to the press and public. His letter opened with a renewed prediction of an earthquake, then moved to the tidings he had shared with his followers.

"I am presently being permitted to document, in structured form, the decoded messages of the Seven Seals," Koresh wrote. "Upon the completion of this task, I will be freed of my 'waiting period.' I hope to finish this as soon as possible and to stand before man to answer any and all questions regarding my actions. This written Revelation of the Seven Seals will not be sold, but is to be available to all who wish to know the Truth . . . I have been praying so long for this opportunity; to put the Seals in written form . . . as soon as I am given over into the hands of man, I will be made a spectacle of, and people will not be concerned about the truth of God, but just the bizarrity of me . . . I want the people of this generation to be saved. I am working night and day to complete my final work of the writing out of 'these Seals' . . . Many scholars and religious leaders will wish to have copies for examination. I will keep a copy with me. As soon as I can see that people like Jim Tabor and Phil Arnold have a copy I will come out and then you can do your thing with this Beast. We are standing on the threshold of Great events!"

The next time the negotiators got Koresh on the phone, they heard Davidians cheering in the background.

20

....

Pending Judgment

On April 14, the same day that Koresh affixed a childish-looking signature to his letter, Attorney General Reno met with representatives of the FBI and US Army in Washington. Records of the meeting were stamped *Secret* and only later declassified; multiple documents make it possible to reconstruct in detail. Reno was joined by FBI director William Sessions, who hosted the meeting in his office, as well as Sessions's deputy director Floyd Clarke, Associate Attorney General Webb Hubbell, and three FBI agents, including Hostage Rescue Team commander Dick Rogers, architect of the Ruby Ridge debacle. Rogers had flown in from Waco to present the Bureau's plan to use tear gas on the Branch Davidians. The army was represented by Brigadier General Peter Schoomaker and Delta Force colonel William Boykin. The FBI had flown Schoomaker from his Texas base at Fort Hood to Waco, where he'd spent a day observing the siege, and then to Washington, where he and Colonel Boykin shook hands in Sessions's office with the army's chemical-weapons expert Dr. Harry Salem.

The first order of business was what a partially redacted account calls "an explanation by the scientist on the effects of CS on humans." Salem, a former pharmaceutical-industry specialist who had helped formulate the cold medicine NyQuil, explained that CS gas "presented very little physical threat to the Branch Davidian occupants."

Next, the FBI's Rogers "gave a brief summary of his plan using enlarged photographs of the compound." Rogers said negotiation had failed—it was time to force the Davidians to come out. According to a US Army memo, "Rogers stated to Attorney General Reno that his primary concern was for the safety of the FBI agents and other law enforcement officers." He said the FBI's use of tear gas would "not be an assault. The stated intent was to incrementally 'gas' the compound for up to 48 hours."

Reno asked Schoomaker and Boykin for their views. Per an army memo, "Our assessment was as follows: a) Some people would panic; 'Mothers may run off and leave infants'; b) Some would continue to function by using expedient techniques to overcome the effects, e.g., use of a wet cloth on the face; c) Even with protective masks, eventually the facility would become untenable (inhabitants would have to eat and drink at some point); d) In summary, we assessed that if the objective of the FBI was to make the building uninhabitable, then CS would accomplish that."

Reno asked how the gas would affect children. "At first the concept of 'gassing' people did not seem right to the AG," the army's memo states. "Dr. Salem gave the AG as much scientific information about the gas as she believed she could absorb . . . The AG questioned why the plan had to be done now." During a follow-up meeting the next day, Associate Attorney General Hubbell spent two hours on the phone with Byron Sage, one of the commanders in Waco. During their call, Hubbell "became convinced that the negotiators believed there was no further hope of getting them out through negotiation." Hubbell and Reno discussed the possibility that the Davidians would commit suicide. Hubbell "believed, based on the FBI's representation, that a mass suicide could occur at any time."

Reno asked again and again about the children inside Mount Carmel. According to the army's memo, "The FBI said Koresh was beating the babies. Attorney General Reno then asked for our assessment of the plan. We collectively made the following points: This was not a military operation and could not be assessed as such. We explained that the situation was not one that we had ever encountered and that the Rules of Engagement for the FBI were substantially different than for a military operation." Other points made by the army representatives concerned "the principles of surprise, speed, and violence." A speaker whose name was redacted told the FBI men, "We can't grade your paper." The speaker was likely Brigadier General Schoomaker, the ranking military officer in the room. As one participant recalled later, the army's position was simple: "We don't have a dog in this fight."

According to the memo, "The final issue discussed was timing. Attorney General Reno asked simply, 'Why now?' The FBI's response was: a) There is no reason to believe that Koresh has any intention of coming out voluntarily; b) There are indicators that children are suffering." There were further details, but the army's position was clear: the plan to use tear gas at Waco "was an FBI plan."

Attorney General Reno was not told that Koresh had just agreed to have lawyer DeGuerin represent him in court, an unlikely move for a man planning suicide. She was not informed that Koresh had promised to come out as soon as he finished writing about the Seven Seals—a promise DeGuerin had shared with the press, but which the FBI called a stalling tactic. She approved preparations for the FBI's plan, reserving the right to decide when tear gas might actually be deployed. After only a month in her new job, she was keeping her options open.

Did the FBI deceive Attorney General Reno?

"You could call it a sales pitch," says Noesner, who was following developments from a posting in the Middle East. He believes his agency "played on her background in child-abuse cases. They presented her with select facts. Is 'deceived' too strong a word? No."

◇◇◇◇

On the evening of April 14, chief negotiator Van Zandt phoned the compound. He asked for Koresh but got Snow Flea Sonobe.

"What Seal do you feel you're in?" Van Zandt asked.

"I can't really answer that," Sonobe said. "You could ask David."

Van Zandt asked him to relay a message to Koresh. "I have my own knowledge base, my own comprehension of scripture," Van

Zandt said. "I'd like to hear what he has to say and compare it against the beliefs I have. I've got my notebook here and my Bible open."

Another cold spell swept over central Texas. Davidians shivered in sleeping bags inside sleeping bags. Koresh worked through the night on his interpretation of the First Seal, which describes an archer mounted on a white horse. "David's more or less locked up in his room," Schneider told one of the negotiators. "He's got papers strewn all over."

"So after this manuscript's put together, you're definitely coming out?"

"Oh yeah. Positively!"

The next night, Koresh got on the phone with Van Zandt. "Hello, Clint," he said. Soon he was calling the FBI man "brother Clint."

A day after Sage told the associate attorney general there was "no hope" for further negotiations at Waco, Van Zandt assured Koresh that the negotiators "would like to see this resolved safely and securely for you, for all of your followers, and everyone out here." The new lead negotiator agreed with his colleagues' view of Koresh's project: they considered it a stalling tactic. Still, he told Koresh he hoped they could connect as "fellow Christians." Van Zandt prayed every day, he said. He'd taught Sunday school for years. Others might call Koresh's views "Bible babble," but Van Zandt knew Jacob's well from a hole in the ground. He said he was eager to hear what Koresh had to tell him. "I'm not here to cross Bible swords with you. This is more of a personal thing, almost, than professional."

Koresh said he'd be glad to have a "heart-to-heart" with brother Clint.

"Who do you feel yourself to be?" Van Zandt asked. "Are you a prophet? Are you the Christ? Who is David?"

"Well, that remains to be seen."

They recited Bible verses, often agreeing on their meaning. Koresh, as he often did, mixed homespun "fixin's" and "okey-dokes" with digressions on Old Testament prophets and the trials of John of Patmos, also known as John the Divine, who was said to have written the book of Revelation. Defining biblical truth as "the spirit of all the prophets that perfectly harmonizes their testimonies together," he said he'd never claimed to be Christ, only to be "part of the last miracle to be given to this world."

Van Zandt pressed him for details. "I've got a responsibility to be able to discern false prophets," he said.

"Exactly."

"I'm a very basic King James type of Christian."

"That's good," Koresh said.

They went back and forth for four hours, trading quotations from Isaiah, Matthew, Proverbs, Psalms, and Revelation, with Koresh correcting the FBI man when he misquoted a passage. "Turn to Psalms Eighty-Nine. I'll show you a prophecy in fulfillment," he said. "*I will sing of the mercies of the Lord forever—*"

Van Zandt cut him off with a question: How long would the world have to wait before Koresh came out to be judged by God and man?

"Every time I try to go through these Psalms, you interrupt. You love the Lord, Clint, right?"

"Absolutely."

"But I'm telling you, you don't know Him."

"Yes, I do."

"Do you want to know the Seven Seals or not?"

Van Zandt said the Seals could only be revealed by the Lamb of God. "If you feel you're the Christ, then say it. I have a personal relationship with the Lord, and I don't feel that relationship is with you."

"Well, let's just look at Psalms Two. Can we please do that? Is that all right?"

"No—"

"Please?"

"No. This is wrong, David. Spiritually wrong."

"Why? Let's just learn a prophecy—"

Van Zandt told him they were getting nowhere. "I wanted the opportunity to talk to you because I wanted the Lord to work through me." He'd wanted to give Koresh "the opportunity to experience a brother Christian who happens to be an FBI agent who would do anything that the Lord would have him do to resolve this and give glory to Christ. And I don't see a willingness, David, on your part."

"Did I not tell you I was writing out the Seven Seals?" Koresh asked. "Did I not tell you I'll be out as soon as I finish my work?"

Van Zandt said he could finish his work in prison.

Koresh said he had to complete his manuscript before allowing himself to be judged by God and man. He offered to send out a cassette tape addressing the biblical passages they'd discussed.

Van Zandt said that wasn't possible. "The decision is made that we're not picking up anything like that."

"Oh. Okay."

"That's not my decision."

"Okey-doke. Well, I'd better get back to my work, then. Bye-bye."

◇◇◇◇

Bob Ricks, the FBI's second-in-command at Waco, scoffed at Koresh's promises to lead his people out once his manuscript was finished. "What's next?" Ricks asked. "He's going to write his memoirs?" Special Agent in Charge Jamar told reporters, "We have intelligence that this is just one more stalling technique." There was no clear evidence to that effect, though the FBI had consulted psychologists and profilers who said Koresh would never come out voluntarily.

Other agents shared their bosses' skepticism. "The man is a master manipulator," negotiator Dick Wren told Schneider. "What Seal is he on now? I'll bet you he hasn't written ten words."

Koresh came to the phone to confirm that he'd finished his interpretation of the First Seal and was working on the Second. Wren could barely hear him over noise from the loudspeakers outside. "What is that, sledgehammers?"

Koresh laughed. "The generals are serenading us with their strange and unique sounds."

"David, what are we looking at in terms of time?" Wren asked. "Let's be truthful with one another."

"Okay, truthful. That's a word you want to use. Let's lay that word out like peanut butter on bread."

"Are you telling me that as soon as you reduce the Seven Seals to a written form, you're coming out of there? I want an answer."

Koresh had an answer. "I'm coming out."

"As soon as you're done? Or—"

"Yes. Yes! I never intended to die here. We can't stay in here forever." The moment he finished his manuscript, Koresh said, he would give it to his attorney, "and my attorney hands it over to—what's the theologians' names?" Schneider, standing nearby, reminded him. "—to Phillip Arnold and James Tabor. *Then* I can spend my time in jail and people can ask all the stupid questions they want. They're not going to ask me about the Seals. They're going to say, 'Do you molest young ladies? Have you eaten babies? Do you sacrifice people? Do you make automatic weapons? Do you have bombs?' They're going to be interested in sensationalism."

"I just want to make sure I have this right," the negotiator said. "You're coming out as soon as it's finished?"

"That's what I'm saying. You can lock, stock, and barrel it."

It was 3:30 in the morning on April 16. "You know what?" Wren said. "I'm going to let you get back to work. I'm eagerly awaiting this manuscript."

"It's gonna blow your socks off."

◇◇◇

The next day, Attorney General Reno reviewed forensic psychiatrist Park Dietz's final report on Koresh. Dietz called negotiations with the Davidians "hopeless." He concluded that Koresh "would not come out" and "would likely continue to sexually abuse the children inside."

The FBI concurred, claiming yet again that Koresh was "beating babies."

Religious pilgrim Louis Alaniz left Mount Carmel that day. Shirtless on the night he'd dodged his way through the perimeter, he emerged in a T-shirt emblazoned DAVID KORESH/GOD ROCKS. "David is the Lamb," Alaniz told the agents handcuffing him. The charge against him: "Interfering with duties of police." He said his only act of interference was "to warn the FBI not to attack." His exit left sixty adults and twenty-five children inside.

Koresh was filling spiral-bound notebooks, tearing out pages for Judy to type. She kept up the pace despite the wounded forefinger that stuck out sideways while she typed. Like her husband, Judy believed that Koresh was divinely inspired. To her he was leader, lover, messiah, and more. He was Mayanah's father. Nothing but salvation meant more to Judy than her two-year-old daughter by Koresh.

She told the negotiators she needed ink cartridges for their word processor, an eighties-vintage Casio that ran on D batteries. They had a manual typewriter, but using it would slow things down—she'd have to retype pages every time David changed a word. With the Casio, "I can change paragraphs and sentences in a minute."

With Jamar's permission, the FBI sent an agent to the same Kmart where Koresh and his posse had bought boots and ammo for their 1986 raid on George Roden. The agent came up empty. Kmart carried typewriter ribbons but no Casio supplies. One of the negotiators told Steve that his wife's request suggested they were stalling. "I think she misled us."

Judy asked, "Why is he at Kmart? Office Depot would have it."

Koresh worked through the night, writing longhand. "My right hand's kind of crampy. I've never written so much," he told John 1. But he was starting to see his way toward the finish line, thinking of how it would feel to join the outside world again. The Davidians had "some of those little tiny bottles of Tabasco sauce" to spice up their MREs, he said, but he couldn't wait to taste a pizza again. He dreamed of eating at Jackie's Café, "where they give you a basket of food you can't finish. Chicken, steak fingers and fries!"

Recalling his hours on the phone with chief negotiator Van Zandt, he told John 1, "Some people get offended when they realize they don't know the Bible as well as they thought." But things were looking up. His manuscript was beginning to ring with what he called the "passionate tonality" of the Bible. That was why he couldn't rush it. His new testament had to be complete down to the letter if it was to convince "so-called Christians" like Van Zandt, "people who are all mouth and no ears."

◇◇◇◇

On Sunday, April 18, Reno notified President Clinton that she had approved the FBI's plan to use tear gas at Mount Carmel. According to Justice Department records, Clinton "concurred with the decision of the Attorney General." She later recalled lying awake at night, thinking of Koresh, asking herself, "Oh my God, what if he blows the place up? What if he holds children up in the windows and threatens to shoot them?" She gave the FBI specific instructions: if any children were in danger at any time during the tear-gas operation, "Back off."

At 2:00 p.m. on the eighteenth, negotiator Henry Garcia told Schneider to expect "some activity" on the perimeter. Tanks and bulldozers would be removing "obstacles" in front of the building. Schneider warned that they should steer clear of Koresh's '68 Camaro. "Just leave his car alone. Don't mess with that."

Within minutes, combat vehicles began flattening fences, trees, bushes, motorcycles, and cars. A tank crushed one of the Davidians' cars in a spray of chrome and window glass. Another one rolled over Peter Gent's shallow grave. SWAT agents hooked a chain to Koresh's black Camaro and dragged it away.

Koresh grabbed the phone to protest. The FBI's account has him "angrily complaining that the cars were irreplaceable . . . Koresh threatened that the safety of the women and children were in jeopardy." It is true that he was spitting mad at first, but he soon calmed down. "Look, we've done everything we can to communicate," Koresh told negotiator Henry Garcia. "We've not been your everyday kind of cult. We've not been your everyday kind of terrorist." In his view the FBI had now gone "way beyond the scope of reason. They're not only destroying private property, they're removing evidence. These don't seem like moves that should be made by a government who says we're going to take this up in a court of law. They're not showing good faith, and I just suggest they shouldn't do it."

Garcia said, "I understand, and I will impart that."

"In all courtesies, please—please impart that. These commanders are fixing to ruin the safety of me and my children—the lives of my wives, my friends, my family."

"That's something that you brought on," Garcia said.

"No. Your generals have violated our Constitutional rights. Are you covering up for the ATF?"

"David, *you're* the one that's doing wrong."
"No. No. No. No. No. No. No. No. No."

◇◇◇◇

That afternoon, a SWAT team dropped a wooden box outside the razor wire. The FBI had found word-processor supplies at a Service Merchandise outlet; the box held Casio ink cartridges and pints of milk for the children. Greg Summers went out to retrieve it. Summers was the one who had fed and looked after the Davidians' dogs. He would recall walking past their remains, reduced to fur and bone by fifty days' exposure to weather, crows, and ants, and thinking that these were surely the world's last days.

Koresh's chapter on the First Seal began with a poem he titled "Eden to Eden," a paean to a pair of lovebirds. He and Judy worked on it through the night with typing help from Davidian Ruth Riddle. One stanza featured a sort of disclaimer about the poem's "he bird" and "she bird": "*'Twas not her womb of which he sought / And certainly not her youth . . . And now we see the final meaning / Of this rhyme and verse: / The pending judgment of the King / Who rules the universe.*"

While Koresh dictated, Steve Schneider manned the phone. He complained about helicopters buzzing the compound with black-suited men leaning out, "giving us the finger." Schneider said he'd had enough of pressure tactics. "They can take measures or do whatever they want. I think there's some Rambo types that would probably like to have fireworks."

Koresh worked into the early hours of Monday, April 19. He had finished his six-thousand-word treatise on the First Seal, proclaiming that he and his followers "will be revealed to the world as those who love Christ in truth and in righteousness." Now he was working on his interpretation of the brief Second Seal, which occupies a mere ten lines in Revelation. He was so tired he could barely see straight, he told Schneider, but said the work was worth any amount of effort. His thirty-three years on Earth had led to this moment. With history racing to a close, he had found the role he was born to play.

"I never visualized it like this," he told church elder Clive Doyle.

Koresh had pictured a smoother path to the Last Days, one that was "not so weird, but here we are." Hungry and cold, they were surrounded by Babylon's army, with spotlights blazing and crazy music blaring from loudspeakers, "but truth is going to win!"

He was working on the Second Seal when the music stopped.

21

....

"This Is Not an Assault"

A few minutes before 6:00 a.m. on April 19, the fifty-first day of the siege, David Thibodeau heard an owl hoot. It was almost dawn. Thibodeau, the drummer in Koresh's band, thought there was something off about the sound, and he was right. It wasn't an owl. FBI agents were "signaling one another." The next sound he heard was a low rumbling. The tanks were on the move.

The phone rang. He picked up. "I want to speak to Steve," a voice barked. Thibodeau handed the phone to Steve Schneider.

"Steve?" the caller said. "This is Byron Sage." Sage was the senior agent who had convinced Associate Attorney General Hubbell that there was no point in negotiating with the Davidians. "I need to advise you of something very important," he told Schneider. "We're in the process of placing tear gas into the building. This is not an assault."

Schneider said, "You're putting tear gas in our building?"

"Do not fire your weapons. If you fire—"

Schneider hung up the phone. "Get your gas masks," he told the others. "Now!"

Seconds later, two combat vehicles drove into the compound's front walls. The building shook as they sprayed bursts of CS gas into the compound. Davidians ran from white billows of gas as Sage's voice boomed from the speakers outside:

> Steve, David, individuals inside the Branch Davidian compound! We are in the process of placing tear gas into the building. This is not an assault. This is not an assault.

Koresh was shocked. After seven weeks of back and forth with negotiators who promised to work with him and never to lie, a surprise attack. But it made a sort of sense to him. He had worked all night on his chapter on the Second Seal, with its rider on a blood-red horse coming "to take peace from the earth, that they should kill one another."

He stayed calm. After the initial ATF raid, each adult had been issued a gas mask, "part of a job lot we bought at a gun show," Thibodeau recalled. "We never imagined we'd end up needing them for our own protection." Now the adults strapped on their masks. Some reached for weapons. They had rifles, shotguns, and handguns. During the first raid, some of them had opened fire after Koresh told them not to. Now he said it was time to fight back. One of the bugs the FBI had smuggled into the compound captured his voice: "We want to hold them off," he said.

"*Do not, under any circumstances, discharge your weapons,*" Sage announced through the speakers. "*If you fire, fire will be returned. Do not shoot.*"

Sage, a white-mustached veteran of twenty-three years in the FBI, followed the action on closed-circuit TV and through a front window of the undercover house across Double-EE Ranch Road, three hundred yards from the compound. At 6:04, one of the snipers stationed outside Mount Carmel radioed a code word: "compromise." That was the signal meaning Davidians were shooting at the tanks. Hostage Rescue Team commander Rogers, back in Waco after his meeting with the attorney general, requested confirmation. He got it three minutes later and relayed the word to all agents: "compromise." That signal gave them permission to shoot back.

"*Come out of the compound with your hands up,*" Sage announced.

"Come out of the building and walk up the driveway toward Double-EE Ranch Road. You will observe a large Red Cross flag at that location. Come out now and you will not be harmed."

At 6:09, another agent tapped his arm. "Turn off the mic, so they don't hear something we don't want them to hear," he said.

Sage clicked off his microphone. "What?"

"They're shooting at the tanks."

Sage said, "Those fucking idiots."

◇◇◇◇

The Davidians crowded around Koresh. Their masks worked well enough for grown-ups but were too large for kids' faces. Mothers in gas masks held wet towels or washcloths over their children's faces and led them to the cafeteria, away from the tanks.

"This is not an assault. You are under arrest. This standoff is over. Do not fire any weapons."

Davidian bullets kicked sparks off the tanks. "They're shooting fully automatic weapons," agent Jim McGee reported over his radio. He began "lobbing CS gas rounds back at them" using launchers borrowed from the army.

At 6:31 the Hostage Rescue Team radioed the command post: "The entire compound has been gassed."

Inside Mount Carmel, the phone rang nonstop. Finally, Schneider tore the cord from the wall and threw the phone out the front door.

Attorney General Reno watched from the Strategic Information and Operations Center (SIOC) at FBI Headquarters in Washington, a complex of rooms equipped with closed-circuit links and TV monitors showing CNN and other networks. She was surprised to see the tanks firing rockets at the compound. Reno had given the go-ahead for the "insertion" of tear gas, a plan in which combat vehicles would knock holes in the walls, spray the gas inside, and then withdraw, giving the Davidians time and space to escape. She had repeatedly told Sessions and other FBI officials that if children were likely to be hurt, the tanks and hundreds of FBI and ATF agents on the scene were to "Back off." But as Reno admitted later, she had not read to the end of the FBI's lengthy action plan, which noted situations in which extreme measures would be allowed. Rather than back off, the document permitted the FBI to escalate the attack if its tanks came under fire. "If during tear gas delivery operations subjects open fire with a weapon," it read, "then the FBI rules of engagement will apply and appropriate deadly force will be used."

While the FBI chose not to return gunfire, it was now authorized to launch so-called ferret rounds into the compound.

A ferret round is a rocket the size of a salt shaker. Fired from a grenade launcher, ferret rounds can penetrate plywood from ninety yards or a car windshield from thirty. A ferret round can kill if it strikes a person directly. Its plastic shell shatters on impact with a wall or other object, releasing its concentrated contents, which vaporize on contact with air. The FBI classified ferret rounds of CS gas "nonflammable" though they had been used in several operations that ended in fires, including a 1974 showdown with the Symbionese Liberation Army, the group that had kidnapped Patty Hearst. During that shootout an exploding tear gas round sparked a fire that killed six members of the group; five died in a crawl space under a house that burned down around them.

Davidian elder Clive Doyle saw ferret rounds flying through windows. "They'd whiz past your head till they hit something, then break and start hissing . . . The gas stung like battery acid." Doyle put on a leather jacket to protect his skin. In an effort to maintain some semblance of normalcy, he had been feeding the last malamute puppy left inside the compound before the tanks struck that morning. Now he shooed the pup out a back door. He grabbed an ATF riot helmet he'd found on a nighttime foray outside. He ran to the chapel.

Doyle passed the cafeteria, where women and children crowded near an open door. Their leader was in his element, full of fire and adrenaline. Koresh directed the women and kids to the vault, a concrete-walled storeroom behind the cafeteria. The twenty-by-twenty-one-foot space was lit by camping lanterns. Koresh said the women and kids would be safer there. Tanks would have a harder time with the vault's concrete walls than the plywood and Sheetrock of the compound's outer walls.

The women spread blankets and sleeping bags on the floor of

the vault and tried to calm the children. They were accustomed to roughing it, but the gas added nausea, pain, and panic. Many of the kids wailed; some vomited. Rachel hugged her three children, Cyrus, Star, and sixteen-month-old Bobbie Lane. Judy held a wet cloth to Mayanah's nose and mouth. Nikki Gent Little and seventeen-year-old Aisha Gyarfas, both pregnant by Koresh, comforted their toddlers. The FBI's loudspeakers didn't sound as deafening here in the vault, but they could still hear Sage's voice.

"Steve, David, we're attempting to contact you by telephone. If the lines have been cut, indicate with a flag out the front door . . . Let's get this resolved."

"Steve, David, an armed standoff is not going to help anyone." Sage waited, then returned to his script. *"Good morning. Those of you inside the Branch Davidian compound, we are in the process of inserting tear gas into the building. This is not an assault . . . If you intend to come out, place a flag out the front door and we will ensure that you have a safe exit."*

No one came out.

TV coverage showed a tank breaking through Mount Carmel's front doors. CNN's Bonnie Anderson reported, "Everyone was expecting the FBI would wait until David Koresh finished his manuscript." Anderson noted that Koresh had been "tipped off" before the ATF's February raid. "With everyone expecting federal agents to wait another week or two, this would be a prime time to go in. They would certainly have the element of surprise."

Forty-mile-an-hour winds dispersed white clouds of CS gas. The commanders had expected their supply of ferret rounds to last forty-eight hours, but after two hours of steady bombardment they were running out. They sent a call for ferret rounds to FBI field offices around the country; soon there were four dozen rounds on their way from the office in Houston, three hours away.

CNN interviewed Koresh's mother. Bonnie said she had no idea why the government would strike now. Her son had "promised not to do anything drastic. When he got through writing the Seven Seals, he would come out. I was really surprised, watching the TV this morning. It scares me."

◇◇◇◇

Koresh was annoyed at Schneider for tearing out the phone. He instructed several followers to spray-paint a message on a bedsheet and hang it from an upstairs window. As the sheet unfurled, negotiators thought it might be a white flag of surrender. Then they read the message:

WE WANT OUR PHONE FIXED.

Sage answered over the loudspeakers: "*Due to hostile fire being received by the tanks earlier today, we are not in a position to expose agents to hostile fire to replace the phone service to your compound. You are demanded—you are requested to exit the compound. Once again, this is not an assault.*"

As Sage recalled later, "Hours went by, and no one came out. I was absolutely astounded. We wondered if they weren't able to get out because they had barricaded the doors. So the decision was made to penetrate further, both to make sure that the tear gas was inserted all the way into the building and to open up exits to allow people to come out."

"Penetrate further" meant knocking down walls. The commanders ordered a tank that Justice Department records call Combat Engineering Vehicle 1 (CEV-1) to "enlarge the opening in the middle of the front side of the building, to provide a larger opening from which the Davidians could leave." Another tank, CEV-2, had broken down outside the compound. At 9:17, CEV-1 burst through Mount Carmel's steel double doors and kept going. Thibodeau watched the upright piano they'd used to barricade the doors "being shoved deep down the hallway by a tank."

Fifteen minutes later another tank broke through a rear wall near the gym and cafeteria. As one negotiator remembered, the commanders "speculated that the women and children were being physically blocked from leaving." Jamar "ordered the CEVs to begin smashing into the compound's walls, opening up holes large enough that those who wanted to leave could do so."

But no one came out.

During a news conference that morning, spokesman Ricks told the press that Koresh's cultists might try to hide or escape through "an underground tunneling system." He was referring to crawl spaces and a bus the Davidians had buried to use as a tornado shelter. The bus might have provided shelter to people fleeing the tanks and tear gas, but debris from the tanks' incursions blocked its doors. No one could hide there. "We believe there probably is crawl space underneath the compound, but gas will permeate those areas," Ricks announced. "We will continue to apply pressure. We will try to make their living environment as uncomfortable as possible."

At ten o'clock, four hours into the tear gas attack, Graeme Craddock ran outside to retrieve the telephone. He held it over his head as if to say, "See? We want to talk!"

At the same moment, Attorney General Reno was leaving her Washington office for a judicial conference in Baltimore. She had been told the standoff in Waco might last for two days before the gas forced all the Davidians out. With that timeline in mind, Reno went to Baltimore despite the FBI's escalation from mere "insertion" to ferret rounds, planning to be back at her desk by the time the fireworks ended.

At 10:30, Davidians in the compound's inner rooms were listening to news reports on the radio. Thibodeau thought their gas masks made them look like a bunch of aliens or insects. They couldn't see more than a few feet where the gas was thick, but south winds gusting to forty miles an hour dispersed much of the gas. Even so, it burned their faces and eyes when they lifted their masks to speak or test the air. Thibodeau recalls hearing a radio reporter say the Davidians were shooting at FBI agents. "That was no good. It sounded like we were making a suicidal last stand, like the Alamo. It felt like our own government was setting up a massacre." He found himself thinking of a line from Don McLean's song "American Pie." *This'll be the day that I die.*

A tank plowed through the east wall of the gym. The women and children in the vault heard a sound like thunder as the wall and part of the ceiling collapsed. Sage's amplified voice carried through clouds of dust and tear gas.

"This is not an assault. Do not fire any weapons. Submit to the

proper authorities. David, Steve, Wayne, all of you need to realize this is not going to end until all of you are out of that building."

No one came out.

Sage tried again. *"David, don't put your people through any more of this. You have said that those inside are free to leave. It's time for you to live up to that word, not only to send them out but to lead them out."*

At noon, Sage's booming voice took a harder line. *"David, you have had your fifteen minutes of fame. Vernon is no longer the messiah. Leave the building now."*

He tried appealing to second-in-command Schneider. *"Steven, you've indicated to us over and over and over again that you're willing and able and ready to leave that building. Now is the time. Do not rely on David Koresh . . . he is no longer able to make decisions. Vernon is finished. He's no longer the messiah."*

While Koresh's "wives" and children huddled with other mothers and kids in the vault, some of the men discussed setting the compound on fire.

There was so much noise that only a few exchanges can be heard in the FBI tapes. In one, Koresh asks Schneider about "two cans of Coleman fuel."

"Empty," Schneider says.

"All of it?"

"I think so."

Koresh had the presence of mind to tease a Davidian who'd grabbed someone else's mask. "You're not supposed to steal those gas masks, by the way," he said.

Snow Flea Sonobe would recall a Bible session in which Koresh predicted a Last Days battle with Babylon. He'd compared the struggle ahead to childbirth, an agony leading to a whole new life. "It feels like dying," Koresh had said, nodding to the mothers, who knew what he was talking about. "Well, *your* flesh is gonna go through that. You will get to the point where you see no way out. You know you're about to die. And then you're gonna trust God. Even if it's the last second before the tank hits you, you're gonna trust God."

Now Thibodeau ran to the chapel through hallways strewn with lumber and Sheetrock. He saw Clive Doyle, who had dodged a tank on his way to the chapel. As Doyle remembered, the tank "drove through the first floor to the entrance of the vault and sprayed CS gas pretty much at point-blank range."

There was no ventilation in the vault, where more than thirty women and children scooted as far from the tank as they could. The tank struck a wall, sending dust and chunks of mortar and concrete onto them. Babies howled. Mothers prayed. The tank withdrew.

22

....

Apocalypse

It was a heartbeat before noon—11:59:16 a.m., according to the FBI—when a sniper reported seeing smoke from the compound.

An FBI bug had caught a voice that sounded like Schneider's: "I want a fire around the back . . . let's keep that fire going."

Seconds later, church elder Doyle heard a voice: "Fire!"

Mount Carmel was a tinderbox on its best day. Since early March, when the FBI cut off their electricity, the Davidians had used candles and kerosene lamps to read their Bibles and find their way around. They had blocked windows with mattresses, bedsheets, and bales of hay. Once, when a negotiator asked if they had a fire extinguisher, Schneider said they did, "but I'm not sure it works." When the subject came up again, Judy Schneider-Koresh said they weren't afraid of fire. Hadn't God saved Shadrach, Meshach, and Abednego from Nebuchadnezzar's fiery furnace? David had told them the Last Days might feature a great fire that protected them while consuming their enemies.

Ten minutes after the first sniper's report, smoke rose from the front of the compound. The speakers thundered: *"Bring your children and leave the building. Fire is plainly visible."*

At 12:13 the FBI requested assistance from the fire department, but the commanders had not thought to restore the flow of water to Mount Carmel, a process that would take hours.

"We have a very large-scale fire breaking out," CNN's Mike Capps reported. "A roaring fire. I haven't seen any fire trucks." Fire engines arrived at 12:34, but SWAT agents stopped them at a checkpoint half a mile from the compound. Jamar sent an order to the checkpoint: "Keep them there." As Jamar explained later, he didn't want firefighters getting shot by the Davidians.

Orange flames billowed from windows in the tower. A plume of black smoke rose a hundred feet. Forty-mile-an-hour winds blew the smoke north toward Dallas. "We still do not see any firefighting equipment," Capps told CNN viewers. "Apparently the strategy is to let this thing burn."

"The building is going to be engulfed in fire very shortly," Byron Sage announced over the speakers. He and negotiator Dick Wren, watching on closed-circuit TV, kept waiting for someone to come out. They saw nothing but flames and a rising black mountain of smoke. *"Leave the building now,"* Sage pleaded. *"Leave the building and walk toward the Red Cross sign. You will not be fired on. Put your weapons down and leave the building."* He neglected to turn off his mic before another word came over the speakers. *"Shit."*

"We saw the fire blowing right through the compound," Sage said later, "through those holes we had punched in the building, not realizing that we had turned that building into a funnel for the fire to take hold."

"David, don't do this," he announced over the speakers. *"The smoke will not allow you to exit in an orderly fashion and you will be consumed . . . Lead your people out, David. Be a messiah, not a destroyer."*

Inside, acrid smoke filled the halls. The walls began to burn. Floors sagged. The vault behind the kitchen was intact, but piles of debris blocked the way out. In the chapel ten yards away, Doyle and Thibodeau crouched between pews. As the chapel filled with smoke, they saw Wayne Martin. The lawyer looked lost. "People gathered around, asking Wayne what we should do," Doyle recalls. He was close enough to hear Martin's reply, muffled by his gas mask.

"I think we should pray," the lawyer said.

The building burned around them, walls falling inward. *"God,"*

Doyle prayed, "*if you're going to do a miracle, hurry up. It's get-*
ting awful hot in here." He felt a "great heat in the ceiling, and the
smoke got so bad I couldn't see." Then the wind dispersed some of
the smoke, and Doyle had a view he would never forget: green grass
in April sunshine. One of the tanks had broken through a wall and
backed out, leaving an escape route.

"Do you think they'll shoot us if we go out?" he asked Thibodeau.

Thibodeau didn't answer. "My hair was on fire," he recalls. Neither
man believed Sage's promises of safety over the loudspeakers that
had tormented them. "But at this point I'm willing to jump out and
hope the FBI won't shoot me."

Doyle remembers "heat and black smoke. People screaming. The
skin's burning off my hands. I looked over my shoulder and saw
Wayne."

The Davidians' lawyer leaned against the chapel wall. Martin had
blamed himself for his son Jamie's disability. He had blamed his ten-
dency to gain weight on his own lack of faith. Now he could see the
same patch of grass the others saw, but made no move to follow them.
"Wayne just slid down the wall and sat there," says Doyle, whose last
view of the compound's burning interior was of Wayne Martin sitting
with his back to a wall "like he was waiting for something."

"Wayne could have followed us out," Thibodeau says. Instead,
with a wife and three kids waiting for him on the outside, with four
more children somewhere among the flames, Martin chose to stay
put. He would die for his faith.

Thibodeau ran a few steps and flung himself through the hole in
the wall. Doyle followed, his clothes burning. "My jacket was melting all over me." He landed in the grass, rolled sideways, scrambled
to his feet, and stumbled straight into the six-foot wall of razor wire
circling the compound.

With the skin on his hands bubbling, Doyle barely felt the wire's
barbs. He remembers disentangling himself and hobbling to a spot
where a black-suited agent shoved him to his knees. "Don't make any
moves," the agent barked, "or I'll blow your fucking head off!"

Doyle tried to hold still. He thought, "*I still seem to be alive. This*
would be a bad time to get shot."

"You're gonna remember this day!" the agent said.

Doyle thought, "*At least that is a true statement.*"

Other agents marched the fifty-two-year-old churchman to the front of the compound and put him facedown in the gravel drive. They used zip ties to cuff his charred hands behind his back. Then Doyle felt something moist on his cheek. The puppy he'd shooed out that morning had found him and was licking his face.

◇◇◇◇

Heather Jones was watching TV with other Davidian children at the Methodist Home in Waco, where social workers looked after them. Nine-year-old Heather liked seeing Mount Carmel on the screen. "I felt a little better because I could see my home on TV. Then I saw flames!" Coverage of the conflagration confused and frightened the children. Social workers told them Koresh and his people had started the fire. "They told us our parents killed theirselves. I hid under a coffee table and cried and cried and cried."

At the same moment, Sheila Martin was at a Salvation Army half-way house with several other Davidians the government chose not to prosecute but considered material witnesses. Someone said Mount Carmel was being attacked. Thinking of Wayne and their four kids who had stayed inside with him, Sheila hurried to the TV room, hoping to see them walking out. "I thought, '*It's over. I'll get to see them soon.*'" She and Annetta Richards, the nurse who had stitched up Koresh's wounds, joined several other Davidian women in prayer. "We were just hoping and hoping and hoping."

◇◇◇◇

As the fire spread, one of the largest government forces ever gathered on American soil did little but watch and wait. One tally put the total at sixteen tanks and combat-engineering vehicles, 672 federal agents, 131 Texas Department of Public Safety officers, 31 Texas Rangers, 35 local police officers, 15 members of the army, and 13 from the Texas National Guard. None of them dared rush in to try to save the eighty-five people inside. They had reason to believe the Davidians might shoot them.

Misty Ferguson hurried to one of the compound's windows. Her mother, Rita Riddle, had left the compound with the last group in March, but seventeen-year-old Misty chose to stay. Looking down from a second-floor window, she saw that the tanks had pushed the razor-wire barricade up against the building. There was nowhere to jump. She turned from the window and ran into the inferno. She felt her gas mask melting to her face. Then the floor collapsed. Landing on the first floor, she crawled to safety as the fire burned her hands. She would lose all ten of her fingers.

Marjorie Thomas was still in the tower. A London-born Davidian who had celebrated her thirtieth birthday during the siege with an MRE and candles, she was sweating under five layers of shirts and sweaters to protect her from the gas, so it took a few seconds to notice that her clothes were on fire. "I heard people moving and screaming. I made my way towards the light" of a second-story window. "I don't like heights, but I thought, '*I can stay inside and die, or I can jump.*' I put my hands over my head and leaped out."

Like a diver, she turned in midair on the way down. She landed on her back, got to her feet, and then, frantic, disoriented, and eager to rejoin the others, ran back into the compound.

An FBI agent chased her. "I found her inside, lying facedown," agent McGee recalled. "I grabbed her and said, 'Where are the kids?' Things were burning all around us. I asked her again, 'Where are the kids?' She wouldn't give me an answer."

Thomas was in shock, with third-degree burns over half her body. Agents zip-tied her wrists, shouting, "Where are the kids? We want to find the kids!" That was their mission, passed from Washington to the agents on the scene. The attorney general wanted to save the kids.

Doyle, facedown in the gravel with his hands cuffed behind him, heard the same refrain. "*Where are the kids?*"

"You probably know, from your listening devices," he said.

The agents brought another Davidian, Misty's aunt Ruth Riddle, to the front of the compound and forced her to the ground. A thirty-year-old Canadian, Riddle had spent the night helping Judy type up Koresh's work on the Seals. At the last moment she'd grabbed a disk from the Casio word processor—the only copy of Koresh's manuscript—and stuck it in her pocket before leaping from a window. The landing shattered her ankle. Now a black-clad agent was shouting about the kids while another demanded that Riddle tell them her name. "When Ruth didn't answer right away," says Doyle, "an agent grabbed her by the hair and started jerking her head back and forth." He heard another Hostage Rescue Team member say, "You better quit that—they're getting this on camera."

Looking back at the compound, he saw "nothing but fire." Doyle knew that Wayne Martin and many others who had stayed inside by choice or misfortune were almost certainly dead by now, but his teen-aged daughter, Shari, was still in there somewhere. He prayed she'd be the next one out.

◇◇◇◇

Eighteen-year-old Shari Doyle was on the second floor when she saw Koresh and Schneider hurry past. While they went to see about the fire, she made her way through the smoke to find Sita Sonobe and about ten others in the cafeteria kitchen, adjacent to the vault. Inside the vault, women waited with their children per Koresh's instructions, praying to be delivered from their suffering.

During the siege, Shari Doyle had told her father she'd rather die quickly than slowly. Like the others, she was accustomed to being around guns. She knew Neil Vaega had shot Perry Jones and Peter Hipsman in what the Davidians called mercy killings. If the day came when Babylon attacked and there was no escape, she'd told her dad, "Don't let me suffer. Put me out of my misery." But now her father was nowhere to be seen. Shari huddled with the others in the kitchen while flames closed in on them, while the mothers and children in the vault a few feet away fought for breath.

◇◇◇◇

"*It's 12:25,*" Sage announced through the speakers. "*The compound looks to be totally engulfed in flame. We've been broadcasting continuously for quite some time, trying to get at least a few people to come out and respond at least to the volume of the voice. At this point in time it's going to be very doubtful if there's many people left alive inside that compound.*" He appealed to those who could still hear his voice: "*Anyone remaining in the compound, exit to a position of safety as soon as possible. Leave your hands in the air and surrender to the agents. Exit the compound to a position of safety.*"

While Sage spoke, agents reported hearing "systematic gunfire" from the compound. The Davidians were shooting again, but not at the tanks. They were shooting each other. The burning kitchen was now the site of a dozen murder-suicides. In a frenzy of shooting, one or more of them killed several others, usually with a single bullet to the head, before turning the gun on him- or herself. The primary shooter may well have been Neil Vaega, the man Koresh had sent to put Perry Jones and Peter Hipsman out of their misery on the day of the ATF raid. Investigators would find it impossible to determine precisely what happened between 12:15 and 12:30 due to fires that would level the compound, reaching what some accounts call "cremation temperatures," but it is clear that Shari Doyle died of a single shot to the head. So did Sita Sonobe and others including Vaega, who may have saved his last bullet for himself.

In the vault, Judy and Rachel and a dozen other women swathed the children in wet towels to protect them from the gas. Eighteen-year-old Michele was there with her three daughters by Koresh: Serenity and twin sisters Chica and Little One. Nikki Gent and Aisha Gyarfas, both pregnant, tended to Nikki's two toddlers, three-year-old Dayland and year-old Page, and Aisha's two-year-old daughter, Startle, all fathered by Koresh. With the door blocked by debris and flames, smoke filling the dark, airless space, there was no escape.

No one in the vault survived. Rachel suffocated, buried alive by debris along with Cyrus, Star, and Bobbie Lane. Judy and Mayanah died the same way. Several Davidian women and children died of blunt-force trauma from falling masonry as tanks bore down on the vault. Others endured "mercy killings" or suicide in their last chaotic moments. Seventeen-year-old Aisha Gyarfas, who would be found with a fatal gunshot to the chest, and Nikki Gent, shot in the head, died while giving birth. Pregnant women suffering sudden trauma sometimes go into spontaneous labor. The body tries to save a life. During their death agonies, both women gave birth to infants who did not survive.

In the starkest example of what the Davidians must have considered mercy, one of them stabbed three-year-old Dayland Gent to death.

◇◇◇◇

The FBI knew about the vault but saw it as Koresh's version of Hitler's bunker. The commanders thought he might be hiding there. As FBI spokesman Bob Ricks told the press that day, "intelligence sources" had described "a room inside the compound, surrounded by cinder blocks." According to Ricks, "It was believed that Koresh and his chief lieutenants avoided the gas by staying inside that room." He was pleased to report that "a tank was finally able to penetrate the room." At that point he thought the tank might flush Koresh from his hideout, rather than spraying tear gas on women and children and sending the walls tumbling down on them.

But Koresh was never in the vault. At the first sign of smoke, he and Schneider had hurried past Shari Doyle to see about the fire.

Sometime between noon and 12:30, Koresh and his right-hand man made their way through the smoke to a first-floor room. One of them, probably Koresh, had a pistol. Schneider had never fired a gun before, but he understood what David expected of him.

There were no witnesses to what happened next. It is possible that Koresh was prepared to shoot himself as Mount Carmel burned down around him, but it seems that when the moment came, he let Schneider do the deed. The vast majority of gunshot suicides shoot themselves in the temple or the mouth. Koresh's autopsy would show that he died of a single shot to the forehead. In the likeliest scenario, Koresh held still while Schneider put the pistol barrel to his forehead and pulled the trigger.

The bullet went through Koresh's forehead, through the brain that had seen the world ending in flames, and exited through the back of his skull. Koresh fell over in a heap.

Schneider had one more decision to make. He could still save himself. He must have hoped Judy was still alive. He could try to find her. He could run. It wasn't too late to jump through a window. But Steve Schneider was his master's apostle to the end. He put the gun in his mouth and pulled the trigger.

◇◇◇◇

At 12:30, Sage sent a last announcement over the speakers: "*Come out.*"

With that, he clicked off his microphone. "I was in a daze," he recalled. Sage walked up the drive toward the compound. As he approached, "I felt the heat radiating on my face from two hundred yards away. The building was collapsing in on itself. I'll never forget the stench and the heat."

The fire trucks waiting at the nearest checkpoint were finally released at 12:41. By then there was no nobody to save. All that was left of one mother and child who had sheltered in the vault was her wrist and hand, still tightly squeezed around the remains of her toddler's hand.

ATF agents celebrated, cutting down the Davidian flag and hoisting the blue and gold ATF flag in its place. For hours, stray rounds of ammunition "cooked off," exploding in the smoking ruins.

One of the negotiators walked the perimeter, then made his way back to the command post, where another FBI man greeted him. "Welcome back," the agent said. "How was the barbecue?"

23

....

Out of the Ashes

Seventy-six Davidians died between noon and 1:00 p.m. That made April 19, 1993, the deadliest day in FBI history. No domestic government action had led to so many American deaths since US Cavalry troops killed more than two hundred Lakota Sioux at Wounded Knee, South Dakota, in 1890. Along with the six Davidians and four ATF agents killed on the day of the raid, the death toll of the event known as Waco had reached eighty-six.

At a press briefing that afternoon, FBI spokesman Bob Ricks called the incident a repeat of the mass dying at Jonestown. "David Koresh, we believe, gave the order to commit suicide," Ricks announced, "and they all willingly followed." In the government's scenario, many of the women and children who died in the vault had committed suicide by tank. Ricks added that unnamed officials "had received reports" that the Davidian children "had been injected with some kind of poison to ease their pain." Those reports, if they existed, were false.

That afternoon, President Bill Clinton issued a statement: "I am deeply saddened by the loss of life in Waco today. My thoughts and prayers are with the families of David Koresh's victims." Clinton promised to say more the next day.

At 5:30 Eastern time, Attorney General Reno held a press conference in Washington. "Today was not meant to be D-Day," she told reporters. Instead, the FBI's use of tear gas had been intended as "a step in trying to bring about a peaceful resolution by exerting further pressure to shrink the perimeter." Asked why she gave the go-ahead rather than waiting, she said, "We had information that babies were being beaten. I specifically asked, 'You really mean babies?'" The FBI's answer, she said, was "Yes, he's slapping babies around."

Reno went through with a scheduled appearance on CNN's *Larry King Live* that night. "The buck stops with me," she told King, explaining again that she had relied on the FBI's advice. "Based on what we know now, it was obviously wrong." On the same program, Special Agent in Charge Jamar announced that the FBI had "incontrovertible evidence" Koresh had been lying about his manuscript on the Seven Seals—he had never started writing it "and had no plans to do so." As Jamar must have known, that claim wasn't just controvertible; it was also false. Even if he had not yet been told of the disk Ruth Riddle stuck in her pocket, holding Koresh's chapters on the first two Seals, Jamar had been privy to his negotiators' recent nights of haggling with Koresh over the manuscript. He was the supervisor who'd allowed agents to deliver a box of replacement ink cartridges—so that Judy Schneider-Koresh and Ruth Riddle could keep taking down Koresh's dictation—the night before the tear gas attack.

A new struggle was underway, one that would last far longer than the fifty-one-day siege. It had to do with questions that would still be debated thirty years later. Were the Davidians a cult? Was Koresh crazy? Were the government's actions a necessary response to religious fanaticism or a massacre? Above all, what did Waco *mean*?

Protesters planted seventy-six crosses outside the White House gates. A mile away, activists unfurled a banner outside FBI Headquarters on Pennsylvania Avenue: WACO MASSACRE: NEVER AGAIN. A young mother holding her daughter's hand waved a placard: PLEASE DON'T GAS OR BURN ANY MORE CHILDREN.

A Texas A&M University professor found dozens of jokes taped to her office door. Sylvia Grider taught a class that focused on "sick humor" as a safety valve people use to fend off anxiety. Many of the new wisecracks her students stuck to her door were "in terribly bad taste," which was precisely the point. In Grider's view, bad taste was "a way to express our deepest concerns and fears."

Why did Koresh do it? He wanted to be the toast of the town.
What was he wearing? A charcoal suit and a smoking jacket.
What did the FBI say? "Anybody bring marshmallows?"
How do you pick up a Branch Davidian? With a Dustbuster.

Texas Department of Public Safety spokesman Mike Cox, who collected Waco jokes as a distraction from his duties, added several new ones.

What does Waco stand for? We All Cremated Ourselves.
When Attacked, Cook Out.
We Are Cruelly Overdone.
Want a Christian Omelet?
Did you hear about the ice-cream flavor called Mount Carmel?
    You have to melt it to get the nuts out.

On April 20, President Clinton greeted the press in the White House Rose Garden. "The Federal Bureau of Investigation made every reasonable effort to bring this perilous situation to an end without bloodshed," he declared. "No provocative actions were taken for more than seven weeks by federal agents." Asked if he had supported Attorney General Reno's decision, Clinton said yes. Like Reno, he had believed the FBI's assurances that once combat vehicles fired CS gas into the Davidians' compound, "the tear gas would permit them to come outside." Asked about Reno's job security, the president insisted he was "frankly surprised—*surprised* would be a mild word—to see that anyone would suggest that the attorney general should resign because some religious fanatics murdered themselves."

Clinton said he'd shared many Americans' sorrow and alarm at seeing the compound burning on TV. "I was sick. I felt terrible. And my immediate concern was whether the children had gotten out, whether they were escaping, or whether they were inside trying to burn themselves up."

Clive Doyle watched the president on TV from a hospital bed in Dallas. One of nine Davidians to escape the fire, church elder Doyle had hazy memories of a bumpy, excruciating ride in a tank the day before. With his throat burning from smoke, blackened skin peeling off his hands and feet, Doyle was in agony until a medic gave him a shot of morphine. After that, "things got a bit surreal." A medevac helicopter flew him to Dallas's Parkland Hospital, where President Kennedy had died thirty years before. Federal agents met Doyle in the burn unit, where they cuffed one of his charred, bleeding ankles to his hospital bed. His heart leaped when a nurse told him there was another survivor, "a girl about sixteen, burned pretty bad," being flown in from Waco. He prayed it was Shari, his daughter, but the new patient turned out to be Misty Ferguson, who had third-degree burns on more than half her body.

Despite news reports that there were no more survivors, Doyle held out hope that his daughter was still alive. In his morphine haze, watching replays of the fire on TV, he remembered something Koresh liked to say: "The Lord's always fixing to surprise you."

That evening, an ABC News special titled *Waco: The Decision to Die* blamed the loss of life on "the power of this madman and his skills at manipulation and mind control—powerful skills, frightening skills." *Time* magazine began preparing a second cover story on Koresh. This one would show him laughing amid flames over a line from Revelation describing the Fourth Seal's pale rider: "*His name was Death, and Hell followed with him.*"

Other outlets took a more measured view of the event. The *Austin American-Statesman*'s April 20 front-page story referred to "Monday's mass suicide," and quoted "cult experts" comparing Koresh and Mount Carmel to Jim Jones and Jonestown, but the *American-Statesman* also ran photos of protesters waving signs outside the Texas State Capitol (ARREST THE GESTAPO CULT ATF, one read) and quoted Gary Johnson, a Libertarian Party presidential candidate and future governor of New Mexico. "What will the feds do next?" Johnson wondered. "Who will be their next target?"

Congress wanted to ask Reno what she knew, and when. Newt Gingrich, the Republican Speaker of the House, told reporters that the attorney general had phoned him after the fire. "I can tell you, from the tone of her voice, the degree of pain in her voice, she was shattered. I think what happened is that the people below her miscalculated." Gingrich promised that the House of Representatives would investigate the chain of events that had led to disaster. "Americans were killed, and they deserve a hearing."

FBI director William Sessions and ATF director Stephen Higgins vowed to cooperate with the arson investigators and Texas Rangers poring over Mount Carmel's still-smoking ruins. Within days, however, the investigators began to doubt what federal agents were telling them. The ATF had kept three cameras trained on the compound from the undercover house across Double-EE Ranch Road, but now ATF agents reported that two of the cameras had malfunctioned. A third camera somehow disappeared from a locked evidence room in the days after the fire. It was never recovered.

The compound's front doors lay flat after the rest of the compound burned down. Those bullet-pocked steel doors were key pieces of evidence. Koresh had told negotiators that the holes in the doors would prove there had been far more incoming rounds than bullets fired the other way on February 28—evidence that ATF raiders had been the aggressors. "*They* were shooting at *us*," he said. Now, during the initial investigation of a cordoned-off crime scene, the right-hand door, twenty square feet in size and weighing more than a hundred pounds, disappeared. It has never been found. Like the ATF's broken and missing cameras, the lost door would feature in conspiracy theories revolving around Waco.

Reno made a return appearance on *Larry King Live* two weeks after the fire. "I made the best judgment I could, based on the information available," she said.

The host asked about opinion polls showing that most Americans supported her. "Even though you said on this program it was a mistake—'Maybe we shouldn't have done what we did'—your popularity has grown immensely," King said. "How do you explain that?"

"I think people understand that you make the best judgment you can," Reno said. "You can't forecast the future and you certainly can't forecast a David Koresh."

A CNN caller had a question for Reno: "When you said after the Waco incident that you want to prevent this from happening again, does that mean gun control?"

"We want to consult with experts in terms of cult behavior," she said. "The president has supported a ban on assault weapons that are not used for sporting purposes." That reply lent credence to many gun owners' suspicions that the government would use Waco as an excuse to pass new restrictions on firearms. While admitting that the ATF and FBI may have been "overzealous" at Waco, Reno and other Clinton administration officials saw the siege partly as a case of law enforcement officers' being outgunned by armed citizens. Within a year, Congress would enact new, stricter regulations on rifles of the sort the Davidians had used, semiautomatic "assault weapons." In the year before the new laws took effect, the price of semiautomatics jumped again.

◇◇◇◇

Bonnie Haldeman buried her son in Tyler, Texas, on May 27, 1993.

There wasn't much left of him. After the fire, Koresh's body measured three and a half feet from shattered skull to charred leg bones. Burned beyond recognition, his remains were identified by dental records. The coroner attributed his death to "Massive craniocerebral trauma due to gunshot wound of mid-forehead."

Koresh had told his mother that if and when he died, he wanted to be buried with an Israeli flag. After all, it was Israel, the Holy Land of the original King David, where he'd received the vision that gave him what he called "a complete understanding" of the universe and his role in it.

After days of searching, Bonnie phoned Rabbi Lawrence Finkelstein at Tyler's Ahavath Achim Synagogue. The rabbi said he'd recently heard from a motorist who had found an Israeli flag in the weeds by the interstate. The man brought it to Finkelstein, who had the blue and white flag cleaned, pressed, and folded. He gave it to Bonnie, who draped it over Koresh's casket during a brief service at the cemetery.

Sheila Martin and Clive Doyle still hoped to be reunited with their loved ones and their leader, in this life or the next. Livingstone Fagan predicted Koresh would soon rise from the dead "as a sign to the world." Doyle, suffering through skin transplants, relished the thought of seeing Koresh strolling up the drive to Mount Carmel again "just when the FBI thought they'd got rid of him." If that ever happened, the reborn prophet would walk past an elaborate memorial someone had placed in the grass just outside the perimeter fence: a small wooden cross adorned with colorful ribbons, a Dr Pepper bottle holding a chrysanthemum, Koresh's 1988 mug shot, and a hand-lettered sign reading, THEY WILL NOT FIND DAVID'S BONES! HE IS ALIVE!

Other followers took up the cause in their own ways. Timothy McVeigh had spent the middle of April at his friend Terry Nichols's family farm in Michigan, planning a second trip to Waco to support Koresh and the Davidians. "There should be ten thousand people shouting at the FBI, 'Go home! Go home!'" he said. Former sergeant McVeigh had been flat on his back in Nichols's garage at noon on April 19. He was changing the oil in his Chevy Spectrum, a drab gray subcompact he called "The Road Warrior," prepping the car for the twenty-hour drive to Texas, when he heard a shout: "Tim, get in here! It's on fire!" He ran inside to join the others watching the fire on TV. As Mount Carmel burned, McVeigh muttered, "What has America become?"

That moment was a turning point in McVeigh's life and the nation's near future. According to the authors of the McVeigh biography *American Terrorist*, Lou Michel and Dan Herbeck, "He no longer had any reason to go to Waco, but now he was beginning to think something else would have to be done."

McVeigh made the rounds at gun shows, wearing a T-shirt emblazoned FBI—FEDERAL BUREAU OF INCINERATION. He told his sister the US government was "laughing at people in the patriot and gun communities" and used her word processor to type out a manifesto of his own. In "Constitutional Defenders," as he called it, McVeigh claimed that Americans had a right, even a duty, to resist government tyranny. "We members of the citizen's militias do not bear our arms to overthrow the Constitution, but to overthrow those who

PERVERT the Constitution," he wrote. "Many of our members are veterans who still hold true to their sworn oath to defend the Constitution against ALL enemies, foreign and DOMESTIC." Calling for a second American revolution, he asked, "Who will come to the rescue of those innocent women and children at WACO?!? Surely not the local sheriff or the state police! Nor the Army—whom are used overseas to 'restore democracy' while at home are used to DESTROY it." McVeigh saw the inferno at Waco as the spark that would set off a war between latter-day patriots and "the power-hungry stormtroopers of the federal government."

He wasn't alone.

24

....

Forensics

The news from Waco spurred the rapid growth of America's home-grown militias. As a commander of a group calling itself the Texas Constitutional Militia told reporters, "Waco was the second shot heard 'round the world," after Ruby Ridge the year before. "It woke us up to a very corrupt beast." But while Ruby Ridge had worried and angered thousands of gun owners including Koresh, Waco spurred tens of thousands more to take action. The Texas Constitutional Militia, founded on April 19, 1994—the first anniversary of the fire at Waco—boasted more than two thousand members a year later. These patriots, as they called themselves, saw the siege as proof that the government had declared war on them. Before Waco, the number of armed militia groups scattered around the country numbered in the dozens; by 1995, according to the Southern Poverty Law Center, there were 441.

The Department of Justice's 342-page *Report to the Deputy Attorney General on the Events at Waco, Texas*, issued in October 1993, dodged so many key questions that both the *New York Times* and *Soldier of Fortune* dismissed it as "The Waco Whitewash." The report's shortcomings left room for everyone from skeptics to psychics to claim the FBI had deliberately started the fire, a version of events that galvanized an Austin teenager named Alex Jones. Jones,

who would go on to a career as America's most popular conspiracy theorist, followed the murder trial of eleven surviving Davidians,
including Clive Doyle, Livingstone Fagan, and Ruth Riddle, with rapt
attention. These surviving Davidians, including some who had not
fired a shot or even been present at Mount Carmel on the day of the
initial ATF raid, were charged with conspiracy to murder the four
ATF agents who died that day: Conway LeBleu, Todd McKeehan,
Rob Williams, and Steve Willis. The defendants were also charged
with attempted murder of federal officers, aiding and abetting murder of federal officers, and weapons violations. Their trial opened on
January 10, 1994, at the federal courthouse in San Antonio, a drum-
shaped building that once held Texas's largest movie screen. Judge
Walter Scott Smith, a ruddy-faced pillar of Texas's legal establish-
ment, presided. Local lawyers said that boded ill for the Davidians.
Judge Smith was known for favoring prosecutors.

"The government is not on trial," Smith declared as proceedings
began. The prosecution team featured government attorneys flown in
from Washington, while most of the Davidians' lawyers were public
defenders, including one who sold his watch and his Mustang to pay
bills during the trial. Over six weeks of proceedings, Judge Smith
chose not to inform the jury that the state's constitution guaranteed
Texans the right to "resist lawmen when those lawmen use excessive
force." Smith allowed testimony that the Davidians had "butchered
and tortured" ATF agents. He instructed the jurors—four men and
eight women, including a nun who admitted she had "negative feelings about cults"—to ignore protesters waving antigovernment signs
on the jury's daily route to the courthouse. One courthouse reporter
joked that the defense's only hope would have been "a jury of twelve
Anabaptist members of the NRA."

As evidence of the defendants' plan to murder federal agents, prosecutors showed the jury more than three hundred guns and grenades
and thousands of rounds of ammunition recovered from the compound. When defense attorneys declared that the weapons and ammo
were for resale or firearms training, prosecutor Bill Johnston scoffed.
"Firearms training—yeah, every church does that," he said. "Let's get
the Methodists and Knights of Columbus together and go out and

shoot some machine guns!" He described the Davidians as "sniveling cowards" and called their court-appointed lawyers "hyenas."

The defendants admitted they had illegally turned semiautomatic rifles into automatics. Koresh had said as much himself. In the end, the jury agreed to convict the Davidians of several weapons violations. But in the jury room, according to forewoman Sarah Bain, "We spoke about the fact that the wrong people were on trial. It should have been the ones that planned the raid and orchestrated it and insisted on carrying out this plan who should have been on trial."

On February 27, 1994, a day before the anniversary of the ATF raid, the jury found all eleven defendants not guilty of conspiracy to murder federal agents. They found all eleven not guilty of aiding and abetting the murder of federal agents. They convicted seven Davidians of aiding and abetting voluntary manslaughter; found five guilty of carrying a firearm during the commission of a violent crime; and convicted two of other weapons offenses. Church elder Doyle was acquitted on all charges. As forewoman Bain saw it, their verdicts vindicated the Davidians. The jury urged Judge Smith to emphasize "leniency" in sentencing the ones convicted of what the jury considered "lesser charges."

That evening the Davidians' lawyers uncorked several bottles of champagne at San Antonio's Fairmount Hotel, toasting the verdicts. Foreign-born defendants like Fagan might simply be deported, they predicted, while the Americans might well be sentenced to time served, allowing them to go free after the year they had spent behind bars.

Their sentencing hearing came in June. In a nearly silent courtroom, Judge Smith said he was displeased at what he viewed as the Davidians' lack of remorse. "Not one single defendant apologized or expressed any real sorrow for the dead or injured agents." His mention of sorrow discounted a pre-sentencing statement by Ruth Riddle, who had called the siege "a tragedy, from my point of view and I'm sure from the agents' and their surviving families' point of view." The judge went on to surprise the press, the gallery, and the jurors by declaring that the jury had made a crucial error. In convicting most of the defendants of carrying guns in the commission of a crime, Smith declared, the jury made it necessarily true that they had conspired to murder federal agents. Ignoring the jury's plea for lenience, he would sentence the guilty on that basis.

Smith sentenced the Davidians to terms ranging from five years in prison for Ruth Riddle to forty years for Fagan and five others, the maximum possible punishment. With good behavior, those sentenced to forty years could hope to be released in 2028. He also fined the defendants $2,000 to $10,000 each, hefty sums for Davidians, and ordered them to collectively pay precisely $1,131,687 in restitution to the FBI and ATF.

Jury forewoman Bain burst into tears. "The federal government was absolutely out of control" at Mount Carmel, she told reporters outside the courtroom. Smith's sentences were "entirely too severe." Alternate juror Mary Pardo said Judge Smith had tricked Bain and the others. "They said there *wasn't* a conspiracy to murder agents. Today the judge said there was, and sentenced as if there was. He ignored the jury!"

Bain sent a letter to the US Senate's Judiciary Committee. "Under the guise of concern for the children and 'hostages,' the FBI terrorized the residents of Mt. Carmel," she wrote. "And supposedly, because the FBI was still concerned for the children, they began inserting canisters of CS gas." The judge's harsh sentences "were in direct opposition to the jury's intention." Bain demanded that the Senate investigate the advisors she believed had bamboozled Attorney General Reno and the "glaring atrocities" perpetrated at Waco by the FBI and ATF.

Her letter was logged, filed, and forgotten. According to Delaware senator Joe Biden, the Judiciary Committee's chairman at the time, "The record from Waco does not evidence any improper motive or intent on the part of law enforcement." Biden declined to hold hearings on the matter. "The ATF had a legitimate and very important reason to be at Waco," he said.

Several Davidians appealed their sentences. Livingstone Fagan chose not to appeal, refusing to recognize the court's jurisdiction, saying only God could judge him. Jaime Castillo's appeal would eventually reach the US Supreme Court, but until then Castillo, Fagan, and the others would spend six years in various federal prisons. Fagan, the elfin Afro-Brit who lost his wife and mother in the fire, considered strip searches "degrading" and would spend years in solitary confinement for fighting with guards who took off his clothes. At Leavenworth Penitentiary in Kansas, he said, guards stripped him, beat him senseless, and sprayed him with a firehose. Fagan accused some of the guards of abuse he would not describe except to say he was looking forward to "the vengeance that is to come."

Dick Reavis, who covered the Davidians' trial for the *Texas Observer*, saw Judge Smith's sentences as overkill. The *Observer* killed his story. "It seemed like an apologia for the militias and the rest of the far right," editor Lou Dubose explained to Reavis. "It seemed to imply a false dilemma: that a choice has to be made between the goons on the right and the jack-booted ATF cowboys." As for the tear gas attack on April 19, "I agree that the assault on Koresh's compound was criminal and amounted to mass murder," Dubose said. Still, he spiked the story for fear of inciting "white separatists."

◇◇◇◇

During his days in the army, sergeant Tim McVeigh had been irked at the sight of Black soldiers sporting BLACK POWER T-shirts. He had a WHITE POWER shirt printed up and was reprimanded for wearing it. McVeigh saw combat in Iraq during Operation Desert Storm in 1991, serving as a gunner in a Bradley tank, killing at least two enemy soldiers and earning a Bronze Star. He also took it upon himself to hand out MREs to hungry Iraqi civilians. Honorably discharged later that year, he gambled on sports, wrote antigovernment letters to newspapers, and quit his membership in the National Rifle Association, which in his view was "weak on gun rights." After the fire at Waco, he spent two years on the gun-show circuit, planning revenge on the government that once paid his salary, a regime he believed had murdered Koresh and the Davidians after it couldn't disarm them.

McVeigh hoped to foment an uprising. In 1995 he and his friend Nichols chose a federal outpost in the heartland, the Murrah Federal

Building in Oklahoma City, as the target for an attention-getting spectacle. To remind the world of his casus belli, McVeigh chose the second anniversary of the fire at Waco for his attack.

On April 19, 1995, he parked a rented Ryder truck in front of the nine-story Murrah Building in Oklahoma City. His Chevy Spectrum had proved too small to hold the two tons of fuel oil and ammonium-nitrate fertilizer he and Nichols had used to make a bomb. A few minutes before nine that morning, McVeigh lit a three-foot fuse and hurried away from the truck. At 9:02 it exploded, destroying the front of the building. The blast was powerful enough to register on seismographs more than a hundred miles away. It flipped parked cars, damaged more than three hundred nearby buildings, killed 168 people, and wounded more than 800. Nineteen of the dead were children who had just arrived at a second-floor day care center. Like many of the mothers and children in the vault at Mount Carmel, they died of suffocation and blunt-force trauma as the building fell in around them.

McVeigh would claim he didn't know there were children in the building. But if his recklessness took innocent lives, he said, he believed his cause was worth it.

McVeigh expected his bold strike to bring new members to the militia movement. Instead, "Oklahoma City" now stood for home-grown terror that killed the wrong people. "The optics were lousy," a sympathizer said. "It looked bad, killing kids."

The Michigan Militia, known as the Wolverines, was one of many that suffered after the bombing. Founded in 1994 in the aftermath of Waco, it soon became the largest in the country, claiming ten thousand members. McVeigh and Nichols had attended Michigan Militia meetings. Then, in the wake of the Oklahoma City bombing, the patriot movement retreated, with the number of active militia groups falling from more than four hundred in 1995 to fewer than forty a decade later. Michigan's organization disbanded before reemerging in April 2020, when members of a reconstituted Michigan Militia, now an association of more than a dozen local groups, carried long guns into the Capitol Building at Lansing. Paul Klinkenberger, former commander of Genesee County Volunteer Militia, was among them.

"One of dozens of Second Amendment actions militia members had held there," he calls their action that day. "The rest of them got hardly any media." In his view, such actions are meant not to intimidate but "to stand our ground for what's right—lawfully." Four members of the state's militias were charged with joining a 2020 plot to kidnap Governor Gretchen Whitmer, a scheme orchestrated by FBI agents. The charges came to nothing in April 2022, when a Michigan jury sided with defense attorneys who called it a case of entrapment—a new instance of government overreach. The jury acquitted two defendants and deadlocked on charges against two others who would later be convicted—a temporary victory for the militants that went almost unnoticed outside Michigan. It didn't take a conspiratorial bent to acknowledge that the alleged plot got far more press attention than the news that it had been an FBI operation. "We don't expect justice," Klinkenberger says. "We do hope the result brings more people to the cause. In some ways the Governor Whitmer business was just like what happened at Waco. Big media jumped all over it at first, but then the follow-up's on page five. Many people think of government as their representative and media as their friend. We don't."

◇◇◇◇

After their shared debacle at Mount Carmel, the FBI and ATF reformed their approaches to what they classified as "Waco-like situations." The ATF produced a five-hundred-page report admitting that "sufficient thought was not given" to what the February 28 raiders should do if they "met with either an organized ambush or scattered pockets of resistance." ATF director Stephen Higgins, who had approved the raid, offered a fanciful rationale for it: if his agents had arrested Koresh outside the Davidians' compound, he said, "they might have begun to execute people until we freed Koresh." Higgins resigned in October 1993. Jeffrey Jamar and other FBI commanders who had overseen the siege stayed in their posts for a year or two before quietly taking early retirement.

Gary Noesner, the Waco negotiator who had been replaced for what his superiors saw as his overly patient approach, was brought back from the Middle East and promoted following the FBI's internal review.

Noesner helped formulate new rules for handling armed standoffs. In 1996 he helped lead an FBI negotiating team in Montana, where a militia group named the Montana Freemen held off federal agents for more than two months. The Freemen, members of what they called the Christian Patriot movement, rejected the authority of a godless US government and holed up at a farm in Jordan, Montana, surrounded by federal agents. Like Koresh and the Davidians, they saw the siege as one battle in a holy war.

During the standoff, FBI director Louis Freeh phoned the negotiators on the scene. "Gary, are you on the phone?" Freeh asked.

"I am," Noesner said.

"I want you to know your director is in no hurry to end this," the director said.

After eighty-one days, the Freemen surrendered.

Noesner thought the FBI was making progress. He was proud of his fellow agents for holding their gunfire on April 19, 1993. Not one government bullet had been spent during the tear gas attack and subsequent fire. At the same time, he believed his bosses had tricked Reno into approving the attack by playing on her sympathy for children in peril.

In 1999, Attorney General Reno learned of another deception.

After the disaster at Waco, FBI officials assured her that federal agents had used only nonflammable ferret rounds to launch tear gas into the compound. Then, more than six years later, the *Dallas Morning News* reported that tanks had launched at least two rockets equipped with explosive charges—so-called pyrotechnic ferret rounds that could start a fire. FBI agents had logged them into evidence but had labeled them "silencers."

Again, critics called for Reno to resign or be fired. Angry and embarrassed, she appointed former Missouri senator John Danforth to answer what both Reno and Danforth referred to as the "dark questions" of Waco.

After a yearlong inquiry, special counsel Danforth absolved the government of blame for the fire and loss of life at Mount Carmel. "The investigation revealed that a few government lawyers and an FBI agent did conceal from the public, Congress, and the courts that an FBI agent fired three pyrotechnic tear gas rounds," Danforth admitted. He went on to assure the press and public that those rounds "did not cause the fire." As unlikely as it seemed to doubters, he was almost certainly correct on that count. The pyrotechnics had been launched more than three hours before the fire began. Danforth went on: "Although the government did nothing evil on April 19, 1993, the failure of some of its employees to fully and openly disclose to the American people the use of pyrotechnic devices undermined public confidence in government and caused real damage to our country."

Danforth's conclusions satisfied Reno and President Clinton. Others weren't so sure. Six years after an attack that was "not an assault," many Americans had lost confidence in a government that gassed American citizens and religious pilgrims from other countries, ran over them, and then covered up crucial facts. Rather than shed light on Waco's dark questions, the Danforth report left gray areas.

How did the fire begin? Did at least some Davidians plan to commit suicide? Why did the FBI send word-processing supplies into the compound—along with pints of milk for the children—only hours before launching a final tear gas attack? Why didn't the FBI give Koresh and his followers more than a minute's notice? Why did the commanders claim Koresh never started writing his treatise on the Seven Seals?

Danforth's report did more than keep the story in the news. After six years and several investigations, it left open questions both pro- and antigovernment forces could exploit, turning Waco into a dispute ready-made for the twenty-first century, one that turned not only on politics, religion, police power, and citizens' rights, but on the very meaning of facts.

One gray area concerned the fate of Peter Gent, the Davidians' Australian handyman. He was Nikki Gent's twin, which made him one of Koresh's many unofficial brothers-in-law. Federal officials and Davidians agree on many aspects of the account David Thibodeau told about his friend Pete: Gent was scraping rust off the inside of Mount Carmel's empty water tower on February 28, 1993, standing on a ladder amid scaffolding and plywood planks. In the moments after the shooting started, he climbed the ladder and stuck his head and upper body through the hatch at the top of the tower—the highest point on the property. Moments later he was dead, shot by an ATF bullet.

In the Davidians' account, Gent poked his head out to see what was going on and was gunned down from a helicopter. "He was unarmed," Thibodeau insists. Many who sympathize with the Davidians consider Gent's death a state-sponsored homicide. In films, videos, books, pamphlets, and Reddit threads, they point to the fact that he was killed by a hollow-point bullet of a sort that ATF agents used. (US soldiers are not allowed to fire hollow-point bullets, which often fragment on contact with a flesh-and-blood target, causing more tissue damage than full-metal-jacket rounds. Police and other domestic law enforcement agents use them for a simple reason: they tend to stay inside a target's body, decreasing the chance that a bullet goes through the target and hits your partner or a bystander.) Despite the government's denials, the Davidians said, Gent must have been shot from a helicopter because the hatch atop the tower was the compound's highest point. As proof, such accounts cite his autopsy, which describes an entry wound in Gent's upper chest and a hollow-point bullet that stopped inside his body, "inches from his heel." Clearly, a bullet entering a man's chest and coming to rest near his heel could only come from above—in this case from a helicopter.

But to credit such a plausible account is to misread the evidence. In fact, Gent's autopsy describes a bullet recovered from a spot "53 inches above the heel." Not inside his heel but four and a half feet away, near his right lung.

What happened is this. In the first moments of the raid, Gent heard helicopters, gunfire, or both. He climbed ladders inside the water tower and emerged through the hatch to see what was happening. Below him, black-suited ATF agents were piling out of cattle trailers, climbing ladders to the compound's roof, shooting and being shot. The dogs lay dead in their pen under the flagpole. At that moment, Gent, who was not unarmed, leaned out of the hatch and bravely— rightly or wrongly but bravely—began firing at the attackers, calling attention to himself. ATF agent Lowell Sprague, kneeling behind a van parked in front of the compound, recalls seeing "a silhouette" at the top of the water tower. A man with a rifle. Sprague fired a pair of two-round bursts from his MP5 submachine gun. It was an unlikely shot, complicated by the fact that Sprague was eighty-nine yards from Gent and seventy feet below. "I didn't know where to hold," he says, meaning where to aim. "My point of aim was the middle of his torso."

The bullet that killed Gent entered his chest and lodged near his lung. There is no doubt that it came from below.

To the government, Peter Gent was a domestic terrorist. To the Davidians and those who see them as victims of government terror—including Thibodeau, who still claims his friend was unarmed—he was a martyr. To Gent's parents, who flew from Australia to Texas during the siege only to claim the bodies of Peter and his sister, he was a twenty-four-year-old son who deserved a decent burial.

25

....

Weaponizing Waco

On a sunny Wednesday in 2000, several hundred visitors parked cars, trucks, vans, and RVs on the gravel drive and in the grass at Mount Carmel. Davidian survivors and their families mixed with tourists, curious neighbors, TV and newspaper reporters, and a half dozen militia members decked out in camouflage uniforms and black berets. They had come for the dedication of a church on the seventh anniversary of the fire.

The government bulldozed the compound's ruins after the fire. This new church, built on the spot where the Davidians' chapel inside the compound had stood, owed its existence to Alex Jones. In the seven years since he became fascinated by the Waco story as a high schooler, Jones had dropped out of Austin Community College and gone on to host a public-access TV program as well as a talk show on Austin's KJFK radio, railing against the Clinton administration, mainstream media, and "left-wing lies." Thanks to the young, gravel-throated Jones, a local newspaper named KJFK the city's "Best Radio Station for Paranoid Insomniacs."

In 1999 he announced a fund drive to build a new church at Mount Carmel, a memorial to the Davidians he said the government had murdered there. That autumn, despite his show's high ratings, KJFK canceled it for what the *American-Statesman* described as the host's "obsession with the Waco siege and rebuilding the Branch Davidian church at Mount Carmel, which had become a personal crusade."

Getting fired barely slowed him down. Given his anti-authority image, it may have given Jones a boost. He registered the domain infowars.com and began hosting shows from his house. By 2000 he had a nationwide audience. "I've got more listeners than ever," he crowed. His plan to build the Davidians a church—the "Phoenix Project," he called it—made national news. *Tonight Show* host Jay Leno offered some advice to the volunteers working on the site of a compound that had burned down in half an hour. "Use concrete this time," Leno joked.

Alex Jones was now twenty-six, with a receding brown pompadour and an eye for the nearest microphone. On April 19, 2000, he hurried toward a TV news crew outside the new church. "What happened here was wrong!" he bellowed. "They murdered all the children." It was "proven," Jones said, that the FBI had "machine-gunned men, women, and children as they tried to exit" the burning compound. What was more, it was "proven" that Timothy McVeigh was not responsible for the Oklahoma City bombing on Waco's second anniversary. Bill Clinton was. The destruction of the Murrah Federal Building "was an inside job—a false-flag operation" coordinated by Bill and Hillary Clinton. Asked about the victims of the Oklahoma bombing, Jones said he felt "horribly sad" for the office workers and preschoolers who died that day. "I'm sad that the FBI and NSA had to blow that building up and kill all those people."

Just before noon, visitors began filing into the church, a tidy white building beside the Davidians' long-neglected swimming pool. Koresh's mother, who had driven down from Tyler for the dedication, told a TV crew she missed her grandchildren: "Cyrus and Star and Serenity and Chica and Hollywood—all of them." Bonnie took a seat in a row of folding chairs while Jones and church elder Clive Doyle stood up front, under a chandelier. Jones, acting as host and emcee, got things rolling by commanding the podium. Shaking his fist, he said, "Victory is ours! Against the communists and socialists and the bankers that run the whole filthy show!"

When Doyle's turn came, he read the names of the dead in alphabetical order. "Shari Doyle . . . Yvette Fagan . . . Nicole Gent . . ." A replica of the Liberty Bell rang once for each Davidian who died in the siege and the fire. "Michele Jones . . . David Koresh . . . Wayne Martin . . . Steve Schneider." Fighting tears, Doyle read eighty-two names, including "Little One Jones" and those of ten others who weren't yet five years old when they died.

Later, Alex Jones held court on the driveway. He was taping a low-budget documentary titled *America Wake Up or Waco*. "Right on this spot," he said, "the tanks drove directly in and pumped CS gas, a banned form of chemical weapon, point-blank range into children's faces. No matter what propaganda you want to believe, those babies did not deserve to be murdered by black-ski-mask thugs." He went on to call Janet Reno "the butcher of Waco—Hermann Göring in drag." Attorney General Reno and the Clintons were globalist plotters, he said, determined to disarm freedom-loving Americans on behalf of what would soon be known as "the deep state." Between plugs for infowars.com, Jones proclaimed what he described as the lesson of Mount Carmel: "If they can surround a group of people, murder them, and then the general population says, 'Well, they got what was coming to 'em,' and they never met them or had any idea of what really happened, then it can happen to any of us. And I say, *Never again! No more Wacos in America!*"

The Davidian survivors weren't sure what to make of their energetic champion. "At least he believed our side of the story," Doyle recalls. "He raised the money for our new church. We were grateful for that."

"Yeah, but he got us tangled up with some crazy theories," says Thibodeau. "Alex Jones put us on the road to Trumpland."

◇◇◇◇

Five days after the new church's dedication, a unanimous Supreme Court overruled Judge Smith's harsh prison sentences for five Davidian defendants. Before long those five would be free. Livingstone Fagan, who wasn't party to their appeal, would spend another seven years being shuttled from one federal penitentiary to another before he was finally released and deported to England, still claiming that Koresh would soon rise from the dead.

Doyle and several other survivors stayed in Waco. They gathered for Bible studies in the new church, which became one of the area's top tourist attractions. Thibodeau became a popular speaker at militia gatherings in the South and Southeast, including one in the Florida Everglades, where he told his story to "several hundred men and women dressed in military fatigues," equipped with rifles and walkie-talkies. "These guys mean business," Thibodeau thought. While most Americans accepted the mainstream view of Koresh and the Davidians as a suicide cult, these people looked up to him and the other Davidians as heroes. "The patriot community and its militant extremists adopted us," he says. "They were turning 'Waco' into a war cry."

In February 2001 former White House aide Linda Tripp—best known for wiretapping her friend Monica Lewinsky's accounts of Lewinsky's dalliance with President Clinton—told CNN that First Lady Hillary Clinton had been behind the final attack on Mount Carmel. In her account, Hillary Clinton told deputy White House counsel Vincent Foster, Tripp's boss, to order the tear gas operation. Why? Political infighter Roger Stone provided the answer. "Hillary Clinton gave the go order," Stone declared. "She wanted Waco off the front pages so she could do Hillarycare," a precursor of the medical-insurance program later known as Obamacare.

Vince Foster's death was a puzzle piece in the theories of Stone and Alex Jones. A forty-eight-year-old lawyer from Hope, Arkansas, who suffered from clinical depression and loathed his White House job, Foster had written a suicide note that read, "I was not meant for the job or the spotlight of public life in Washington." After Foster drove to a public park in Virginia, sat on a park bench, and shot himself in the mouth, Jones claimed it was "proven" that his suicide was actually murder, a secret hit ordered by the Clintons and their cronies. "And it all goes back to Waco!"

Next came 2001's attack on the World Trade Center. Jones said 9/11 proved he'd been right all along. Like evangelists from Saul of Tarsus to John of Patmos to Koresh, Jones was expert at weaving disparate threads into a vivid narrative that supported his worldview. Like the Oklahoma City bombing, the Trade Center's destruction was "obviously" an inside job, he said. "Government demolition." His theories found an eager audience of more than two million as InfoWars became one of the most profitable sites on the internet. Jones became a multimillionaire on annual sales of over $135 million in nutritional supplements, gold, body armor, and other products while spreading his views on Waco to millions of Americans.

"It's strange, talking to people who believe him," says Clive Doyle. "Some of them, if you don't agree with them, they say the FBI put a chip in my head when I was in the hospital, and I've been taking orders from the government ever since. I've tried telling them there were no 'flame-throwing tanks.' The tanks shot tear gas. But they don't believe me. If you don't go along with the militias and white supremacists, who attach themselves to us for their own ends, they say, 'You're one of *them*.' Some people don't want to hear what a real survivor has to say."

◇◇◇◇

Negotiator Noesner retired from the Bureau in 2003. Today he calls Waco "a self-inflicted wound for the FBI. It contributed to a broad antigovernment sentiment that's out there today. Right-wing militias grew after Waco. They lost ground after Oklahoma City, but then came Obama, a Black president, and that rubbed a lot of people wrong."

The Davidians were diverse, with nearly as many believers of color as whites. "The militias ignored that," says Michael German, an FBI colleague of Noesner's who worked undercover with several militia groups in the 1990s. After Waco, "the skinheads said, in effect, 'We should stop shaving our heads and wearing Nazi regalia.' They adopted libertarian talking points and began penetrating antiabortion groups, anti-immigration and gun-rights groups, allying themselves with a violent vanguard." The Illuminati, Trilateral Commission, and deep state served as shadowy symbols of evil to the militias he infiltrated, "but Waco worked better. With Waco, you can go to YouTube and see women and children incinerated, the government using military tools and training against Americans. There was hardly one militia member I met who *didn't* mention Waco as his awakening."

Catrina Doxsee of the Center for Strategic and International Studies in Washington echoes German's view of the siege and its meaning to modern-day militias. "Ruby Ridge came first, but there were neo-Nazis at Ruby Ridge. Randy Weaver was an avowed white supremacist," she says. "Waco was more relatable. *The government is willing to kill children to take away your guns*—that became the narrative." The election of Obama, the Tea Party movement, and the rise of Donald Trump all kindled belief in a cabal of secret power brokers working against "real" Americans, she says. "Now you've got militias blending with QAnon—people who see Democrats as child-abusing predators." According to Doxsee, 2021 saw the most right-wing terror attacks in recent history, "starting with January sixth."

On January 6, 2021, between two thousand and three thousand Trump supporters stormed the US Capitol, hoping to keep Joe Biden from being certified as president. They beat, pepper-sprayed, and tased Capitol Police officers, urinated and defecated in Democrats' offices, and chanted "Hang Mike Pence" after Vice President Pence refused to declare that Trump was still president. One of the rioters, a gun-rights activist known as Monkey King, slipped through police lines that day and returned to his home in Virginia, where he hosted a meeting of the Three Percenters, an antigovernment militia who took their name from the mistaken idea that only 3 percent of American colonists fought against England in the Revolutionary War (the true figure is closer to 20 percent). Fi "Monkey King" Duong told an undercover agent he was ready to barricade himself in his house "in a similar manner to the standoff in Waco, Texas, of David Koresh." He had an AK-47 and knew how to make Molotov cocktails. His standoff with police, he said, would be "Waco 2.0."

Daryl Johnson wasn't surprised by the events of January 6. A flinty-eyed Virginian, Johnson joined the Department of Homeland Security in 2004 and became the department's leading expert on domestic extremism—a big fish in what was then a small but dangerous pond. "We had *hundreds* of analysts working on Islamic terror," he recalls. As for domestic threats, "I was pretty much it." In 2009 he filed a ten-page report, "Right-Wing Extremism: Current Economic and Political Climate Fueling Resurgence in Radicalization and Recruitment," warning that Obama's election, the Great Recession of 2008, and other factors were fueling a new militia movement. His paper sounds prescient in retrospect, including its portrayal of military veterans returning from Afghanistan and Iraq being radicalized online by what he called "antisocial media." But Republicans denounced it. Televangelist Pat Robertson called Johnson's paper "an outrage" and told his viewers to phone Washington and complain. Homeland Security Secretary Janet Napolitano went on *Fox & Friends* to apologize for Johnson's report. Soon he was demoted. He left the government a year later.

Today Johnson runs a consulting firm, DT Analytics. He takes pains to point out that the vast majority of veterans have nothing to do with extremist groups, but notes that with more than 2.5 million Afghanistan and Iraq vets scattered across the country, "Even if it's a tenth of one percent, that's *thousands*." Militia membership "may have plateaued after the Capitol insurrection, but the movement is still growing. The militias are *succeeding*. An event like Russia's invasion of Ukraine adds only fuel to the fire because they think, 'Here comes World War III.'"

Johnson sees Ruby Ridge and Waco as the movement's Lexington and Concord, but considers Ruby Ridge no more than an opening act. "The modern-day militia movement owes its existence to Waco," he says. "Waco resonates in the hearts and minds of today's militias. And the movement evolves. Now they're taking the fight to school boards and county councils, mainstreaming ideas that would have seemed fringe a few years ago. There are now close to eight hundred state delegates all over the country promoting those ideas."

By one tally there were 875 state legislators serving in 2021–22 who had joined right-wing extremist Facebook groups. They represented all fifty states and more than 10 percent of state legislators in the country. One was Arizona state senator Wendy Rogers, a member of the Oath Keepers who condemned "the LGBTBQ movement" and "communist" Anti-Defamation League. Rogers closed a speech by urging "fellow patriots" to bide their time. "When we do take back our

God-given rights," she said, "we will bring these criminals to justice. I've said we need to build more gallows. It will make an example of these traitors who've betrayed our country. We have a nation to save and a gospel to preach."

◇◇◇◇

After the uprising of January 6, 2021, local and federal agents arrested Monkey King and almost a thousand other Capitol rioters. A significant minority of them—about 20 percent—were military veterans. Many were tried, convicted, and sentenced to jail terms far lighter than those the convicted Davidians served. They represented a few of the millions of angry Americans Gary Noesner calls "the tip of the spear."

Long after his failed efforts at Waco, the former lead negotiator winces when he hears both sides twist the facts.

"Calling Waco a massacre isn't fair," Noesner says. "Why? Because life is not black and white. The real story isn't 'Big bad government murders the Branch Davidians.' And it's not 'Those kooks got what they deserved.' Those ideas are both wrong." Yet both ideas are promoted by zealots seeking to turn Waco to their own purposes. After thirty years, partisans from both ends of the political spectrum were still stirring Mount Carmel's ashes.

◇◇◇◇

In addition to memorials, investigations, reforms, volunteer armies, dark humor, conspiracy theories, and a 2018 TV miniseries, the events at Waco in 1993 spawned a scholarly dispute. Little noticed outside the pages of *Nova Religio: The Journal of Alternative and Emergent Religions*, the debate pitted four American professors against a lone Englishman who joined the fray after a visit to Mount Carmel in 2003. The Americans had a personal stake in the matter. They included James Tabor and Phillip Arnold, the religion professors Koresh respected so much that he planned to send his manuscript to them ("As soon as I can see that people like Jim Tabor and Phil Arnold have a copy I will come out"), and two Texas-based scholars who shared their belief that the disaster's main cause was the FBI's failure to understand the

Davidians' religion. Kenneth Newport, an Oxford-educated Angli-
can priest and professor of theology at Liverpool Hope University,
called their view naïve.

Newport's fascination with the fusion of religion and violence at
Waco led him to Mount Carmel for tenth-anniversary services at the
church Alex Jones built. While there, he encountered a "militia chap"
in camouflage vest and combat boots, muttering darkly about Janet
Reno. Newport pored over tape transcripts, investigation reports,
autopsies, and other documents. Following the American professors'
work at academic conferences and on YouTube, he found them referring to Koresh familiarly as "David." Tabor had joked that the FBI
"thought the Seven Seals were aquatic mammals." Newport agreed
with Tabor and the others on many points, but tilted with them in
Nova Religio on the subject's most pivotal question: Who started
the fire?

The American professors' position was that the government, seeing Koresh and his followers as a cult, forced them to defend themselves and may well have killed them by triggering the fire, whether
purposely or carelessly. The high winds of April 19, the pyrotechnic
rounds fired that morning, the stability of kerosene lanterns, and the
tanks' paths all factor in this scenario, which relies on what Newport
calls an unlikely chain of events.

"It is impossible to know what happened in every detail," he says,
sitting in his book-lined office in Liverpool. "But it's pretty obvious
that the Davidians set fire to the place. Intentionally. Why? Because
Koresh told them to." Like the American scholars, Newport is convinced the Davidians' beliefs are at the heart of the matter, but he
draws a different conclusion. "You have to put yourself in their place.
Their apocalyptic dreams are coming true. They're very excited.
Koresh was always talking about a war against Babylon—now here
it is."

He cites evidence including conversations recorded by the listening devices the FBI smuggled into Mount Carmel. In one, recorded
on April 18, the day before the fire, Steve Schneider tells another
follower he's just had a thrilling meeting "with David." Asked if he'd
learned what Koresh had in mind, Schneider says, "It may be scary.

You always wanted to be a charcoal briquette." A tape from the following day caught Schneider telling the others to spread fuel. One Davidian asked him to clarify, saying, "We only light it if they come in, right?"

Says Newport, "Lois Roden was Koresh's tutor, and she claimed Mount Carmel was the New Jerusalem. She preached that it had to be 'cleansed by fire' as a gateway to the Kingdom of God. Baptism by fire was a prerequisite." He notes that a Swedish team of arson investigators unaffiliated with the FBI or ATF found charred remnants of the Coleman lanterns the Davidians had used. The lanterns had been slashed with knives to let the fuel out. "That would seem to clinch the case," Newport says. "It doesn't *prove* the Davidians set fire to Mount Carmel, but that is the most coherent framework."

Twenty years after his first visit, Newport remains enthralled by the many uses of what happened at Mount Carmel in 1993, from Thibodeau's sincere belief that Peter Gent was unarmed to Alex Jones's conspiracies to claims that Koresh and his followers were insurrectionists.

"How can people believe things that are so barmy? That is part of the story of Waco, and I doubt we've heard the last of it."

Survivors

Today's Mount Carmel is a chapel on a grassy floodplain near the corner of Elk Road and Double-EE Ranch Road. The gravel drive leads past a row of red and green crepe myrtles. Survivors planted eighty-two of the trees in 1994, one for each Davidian who died during the siege. Today there are eighty-one: the current pastor, Charles Pace, chopped down the tree dedicated to David Koresh.

One Sunday not long ago, a breeze rustled the crepe myrtles' leaves. Dog-day cicadas chirred. Black Angus cattle grazed on the neighbors' ranch across the fence. The church Alex Jones built, sporting a fresh coat of paint, looked as clean and white as on the day it first opened its doors. After almost a quarter century, it was still one of the top tourist attractions in McLennan County. The only sign of decay was the Davidians' rock-lined swimming pool, now half full of rainwater. Nearby, a placard identified a hole in the ground as the entrance TO THE VAULT AREA WHERE MOTHERS & CHILDREN WERE GASSED TO DEATH. This was not a true fact—the vault had been at ground level, not underground, and about ten yards away, and the mothers and children inside had burned to death, died of smoke inhalation, or been buried as the compound collapsed around them. But the empty space in the earth suited the mood of the place.

Inside the chapel, ceiling fans stirred the heat. A whiteboard cited a verse from Psalm 77: "*I have considered the days of old, the years of ancient times. I call to remembrance my song in the night . . . Hath God forgotten to be gracious? Hath he in anger shut up his tender mercies?*" The board held a map of the Old City of Jerusalem. Today's Davidians—there are a couple dozen in Waco, several thousand scattered around Texas and the rest of the world—still believe they are God's chosen few. Many consider Koresh a false prophet, perhaps the antichrist. Others expect him to rise again in time for the Last Days.

Pastor Pace and his wife, Alexa, greeted visitors. He had a shaved head and a neatly trimmed beard. Her T-shirt read PRAY TO END ABORTION. Pastor Pace had split off from the sect in the 1980s. "I saw through their delusions," he says in a hoarse voice. He returned to lead Waco's diminished flock in 2006. Now seventy-two, he gets around in a wheelchair and has a stainless-steel right leg, the result of a tractor accident that mangled his right foot.

The church's walls hold photos of Davidian leaders: Victor Houteff, Ben and Lois Roden, Koresh. Despite his doubts about his predecessor, Pace knows it's Koresh most visitors want to hear about. Posters show Koresh's 1988 mug shot and aerial views of the compound before and after the fire. A memory book holds snapshots of the Davidians who died here in the ATF raid and the fire fifty-one days later. Those too young to be photographed are remembered with cards showing their names and nationalities. Two of the cards read, "Trauma born baby, American."

The Paces rely on donations. They also sell merchandise: GOD ROCKED FROM WACO T-shirts and postcards showing Koresh playing guitar, Trump flags and shirts emblazoned MR TRUMP YOU ARE MY PRESIDENT 2020–2024. Another shirt reads, PATRIOTS, REMEMBER THE ALAMO? AND FORGET NOT WACO! Posters show Bill and Hillary Clinton with their fingers to their lips—*Shh!*—and Koresh wielding a rifle over a line directed at President Joe Biden: SLEEPY JOE, WAKE UP OR WACO! COME GET IT!

Pastor Pace works day and night to maintain the church and the grounds, host Sabbath services, and run a website that blames deep-state conspirators for the siege and fire of '93, a subsequent cover-up that led to the murder of Vince Foster, and more.

"Koresh may have been a false prophet, but he was onto something," Pace said that day. Partially blind, he had a gray left eye that wandered while his blue right eye fixed a listener in an iron gaze. "That's why the Clintons couldn't let him live. He knew too much about the human trafficking, pedophilia, and gun- and cocaine-running the Clintons and Bushes were guilty of." The Davidians had built their swimming pool, he believed, "to reclaim a desecrated spot" after Koresh found evidence of a sex-slavery ring based in the cellar, though Koresh never mentioned such a thing.

"This is all proven," said Pace. The website he built for the church, wacothebranchdavidianpropheciesfulfilled.info, featured a Star of David logo, posts including "Why the Deep State Massacred David Koresh and his Followers," references to Republicans and "Demonic-rats," and the QAnon hashtag WWG1 WGA ("Where we go one, we go all"). President George H. W. Bush, he said, "was a pedophile and homosexual. As head of the CIA, Bush built tunnels under the White House. They found fifteen hundred dead children in those tunnels, dead from torture and sexual abuse. When they found out, Donald and Melania Trump cried for hours. And Donald Trump did the right thing: he had Bush arrested for his crimes. George Bush did not die of natural causes in 2018. They executed him for treason. This will all come out in the near future."

Like Koresh, Pastor Pace knew his Bible well enough to recite much of it from memory. "Prophecy is real," he said. "I trust in prophecy. That's what has kept me sane, so to speak." He was tender with his adult sons, who helped with chores and still found an occasional spent bullet in the acres of grass around the church. Pace said they knew their father might sound unhinged to some, but he was not a hypocrite. He was a believer. He had chopped down the bush dedicated to Koresh "because God told me to." He thanked God for the militia members who came to Mount Carmel from all over the country. "The Holy Spirit leads them here. The Proud Boys were here, about thirty of them. They say Waco is the Alamo of the modern patriot movement. I told them, 'If David Koresh were here today, he'd be one of you.'" Later, Proud Boys chairman Enrique Tarrio would encourage his followers to "remember Waco."

◇◇◇◇

Shaun Bunds was another recent visitor. For him, Mount Carmel was more than the site of a long-ago siege and flash fire. He was born there.

He guarded his privacy but spoke briefly to a Swedish film crew in footage the public has not seen. Born in 1988 and named Wisdom by his father—Koresh—he was the toddler who got such a rough spanking that his bottom bled—the likely source of the "He's beating babies" reports that convinced Attorney General Reno to approve the tear gas attack. His mother, Robyn, was a proud member of the House of David. (Steve Schneider insisted it was Robyn who spanked the boy until he bled.) Robyn and Wisdom left the compound for good when he was two years old, after she learned that Koresh was also sleeping with her mother, the boy's grandmother. She renamed her son Shaun. Now he was almost as old as Koresh ever got, with black bangs hanging over sharp features and eyes as lively as his father's. His legal surname was Bunds, though he sometimes referred to himself as Shaun Howell or Koresh.

"My mother was very young when she had me—nineteen years old," he said. "She was forced into it. My father stripped all her clothes off. I was born because eventually she gave in."

Growing up in California, he learned what he could about his father. "I don't want to portray him as evil. I think he was very, very conflicted. He desired deeply." As for the Davidians who followed Koresh, he said, "Those people all had something missing from their lives that was exploited by him."

In the end, Shaun found himself drawn to his heritage as well as repulsed by it. With dark humor, he founded an electronics start-up he called Wake Co.

◇◇◇◇

Several survivors who stayed in town still meet for Bible studies or Sunday supper at a restaurant. They seldom visit Mount Carmel for fear of getting into fights with Pastor Pace, who considers them apostates. On the same day Pace showed sightseers around the chapel and railed

against the deep state, church elder Clive Doyle met David Thibodeau, once Koresh's favorite drummer, and other friends at the Golden
Corral in Waco. Doyle, eighty years old with close-cropped gray hair,
greeted Thibodeau with a wave. Doyle's leathery hands still bore scars
from the burns he endured in 1993. Thibodeau, fifty-two, was no longer the scrawny musician he had been the day Doyle followed him
through a hole a tank had made in a wall so they could escape the fire.
Graying at the temples and much heavier than he was in those days, he
joked about his size, calling himself "the poster boy for COVID risk."
After living through the deadliest day in US law enforcement history,
he didn't want to fall victim to the latest variant of COVID-19.

At the Golden Corral, they put tableware on trays and lined up for
their meals, just as they had in Mount Carmel's cafeteria three decades
before. The mood was festive. Compared to the beans, bananas, and
popcorn that constituted much of the menu at the compound, to say
nothing of the MREs that got them through the siege, the Golden
Corral's fare was a cornucopia: fried chicken, fried shrimp, corn on
the cob, pizza, macaroni and cheese, carrot cake, cinnamon apples,
and dessert kebabs of chocolate-dipped Rice Krispies Treats.

They traded war stories. Doyle, still with a slight Australian accent
after half a century in Texas, spoke of how reporters interrupted him
at a 1995 memorial service with news of the Oklahoma City bombing. "They were blaming us! I told them we don't condone any sort
of violence. But we've become a magnet for conspiracies. One fellow
had a surveillance tape of two shadowy figures walking by the Murrah Building in Oklahoma—'David Koresh and Steve Schneider!' he
said. Some others showed me a picture they swore was David resur-
rected. I said, 'But that's a Black guy.' They said, 'Yeah, because he
was *burned*.'"

"To those people, we're a wing of the Alex Jones movement,"
Doyle's friend Ron Goins said.

"Do you want to know how Alex Jones interviews people?" Doyle
asked. "He'll give you a sentence to say, and if you do it just right,
he'll use it. If not, he says it himself."

They stayed in touch via a Facebook group, Branch Davidian Survivors Waco, a forum for family news and photos that had blocked

"the crazies" who sometimes tried to take it over. Looking back to the siege, as they often did, the survivors agreed about most things. They said they always got along with law enforcement officers, particularly Sheriff Jack Harwell, until the day cattle trucks full of ATF agents came roaring up the drive. Koresh told them to keep cool—he'd handle it. Then the shooting began. The black-suited agents may have started the gunfight by shooting the dogs. Whoever fired the first shot, bullets were soon coming through the walls and front doors. Perry Jones was gutshot, screaming bloody murder while Koresh ducked inside. Then they were besieged: fenced in, blasted by spotlights and maddening noise. But they adjusted. "It's funny what you can get used to," Doyle said.

They remembered that Koresh liked Gary Noesner, the FBI's first lead negotiator, despite his digs at Noesner over the phone. Things went downhill after Noesner got replaced by Bible-thumper Clint Van Zandt, who thought he could out-scripture David. They remembered reading their Bibles by lantern light. They prayed Koresh would finish his manuscript on the Seven Seals and lead them out. No one gave any thought to defying Koresh. They said they'd followed him not because they feared him but because they feared God. Koresh was the Lamb, chosen to lead them through suffering, perhaps even fire, to God's kingdom.

They swore they'd had nothing to do with setting the fire. "If there was a plan to do that, we weren't part of it," Thibodeau said. "I wouldn't put it past some of our people to throw a Molotov cocktail. But to me the smoking gun—pardon the pun—is how the FBI claimed for years they used 'no pyrotechnic devices.' Then they admitted they had them stored away in evidence, marked as 'silencers.'" In the absence of proof one way or the other, he preferred to believe the feds caused the fire. "It suits their style."

Doyle nodded agreement. "Were we a suicide cult? No way."

Both believed Janet Reno had been "played" by her advisors, but they differed on other issues. When Doyle said militia members calling him a "patriot" gave him the creeps, Thibodeau rolled his eyes. "I've got to stick up for the militias. The Bundys in Oregon? You go, Bundys," he said, referring to a family of ranchers who held off federal agents in 2014 with help from armed militias. "If the government's going to destroy churches, kill people, roll over them, and then lie about it, people have a right to fight back. I'm *glad* they formed militias after what happened to us. When those guys got between the Bundys and the feds, that was power to the people."

The talk turned to the rioters who overran the US Capitol in 2021. "That was different," said Thibodeau. "Those were Trump supporters. To them I'd say, 'Don't use Waco as an excuse to do crazy violent shit.' And as for their savior, Donald Trump? *He's* your savior? And people think *we* followed the wrong guy!"

They spent a silent moment remembering friends and family they lost in 1993. After thirty years, Doyle said, he seldom went a day without thinking of his daughter. He consoled himself with the thought that Shari was "eighteen forever."

Thibodeau's phone played the whistling theme from *The Good, the Bad, and the Ugly*. He checked a message, sent a text, and recalled a recent message from "a tipster. They come out of the woodwork. Someone called me to say David was reincarnated: 'David's alive! He's in Florida, and he needs you to send him money for a bus back to Waco.'"

Doyle nodded. "I got that one, too. I said, 'If David's come back from the dead, he should be able to make it back from Florida.'"

◇◇◇◇

Sheila Martin sent regrets to her friends at the Golden Corral. She worked long hours at a day care center in Waco. At seventy-two, the Davidian mother of seven was perhaps the most devout of the survivors, reading her Bible every day, listening to cassette tapes of Koresh's sermons. She said she wasn't political, "but not vaccinated, either." Few Davidians wanted a shot from the government.

She recalled her horror at seeing the fire on TV. Her heart sank when a newscaster read the names of survivors. Her husband, Wayne, and four children who stayed inside with him were not among them. "I thanked God for the ones who made it out," she said. She went on to single-parent her three surviving children until her disabled son, Jamie, died in 1998. At fifteen he was still the size of a three-year-old.

She recalled how Koresh would cradle Jamie in his arms. Davidians believe in resurrection of the body; Sheila expected to meet "my Jamie" again in the next life, and hoped he would be healed. "He might be an adult when I see him again. He might stand up and come to me."

Recent news of pandemics and war struck her as ominous. "It's still coming," she said of the apocalypse, with its earthquakes and blood-red skies. "Not as soon as we thought, but it's coming, just like David said it would." Thinking of her husband, who chose to die for his faith, she sometimes imagined she could feel the heat and flames he felt as Mount Carmel burned down around him. Smiling, she gave thanks for their two grown children and for the twenty years she and Wayne had together. "Life is sadness and joy." She and the other survivors had their share of sorrows, but their story wasn't over.

"That's the good thing," she said. "God isn't finished with us yet."

Epilogues

Attorney General JANET RENO's approval ratings spiked after she took responsibility for the tear gas attack of April 19, 1993. She denied that the FBI had deceived her by emphasizing Koresh's "beating babies." After George W. Bush won the presidency in 2000, Reno ran for governor of Florida, but lost the Democratic primary in a narrow, disputed vote.

In the end she regretted her decision to approve the use of tear gas at Waco. "Knowing what I do, I would not do it again," she told NPR. In a 2004 interview for the Clinton Presidential History Project at the University of Virginia's Miller Center of Public Affairs, she recalled conversations with President Clinton. "I explained to him that Koresh seemed to be a being of his own making," she said. "I will never know what the right answer was." She wondered if things might have been different had she not left the FBI's Strategic Information and Operations Center at 10:00 a.m. for a speaking engagement that day. "I don't know what would have happened if I had been at the command center watching them tear down those walls," she said, though she had stayed long enough to see the first combat vehicles break through Mount Carmel's exterior. "I think I would have ordered them back and been criticized for not letting them do their job."

Reno died in Miami in 2016.

In a speech at Hofstra University in 2005, BILL CLINTON called the decision to use tear gas at Waco one of the worst moments of his presidency. "I will always regret that," Clinton said. "We should have waited them out. Janet Reno was new on the job. She got enormous pressure from the FBI to go ahead and go in there . . . she thought it was right. It was a mistake and I'm responsible. And that's not one of those you get an A for effort on."

TIMOTHY MCVEIGH was apprehended less than two hours after the 1995 Oklahoma City bombing, when an Oklahoma state trooper pulled him over for driving without a license plate. McVeigh was wearing a T-shirt reading, SIC SEMPER TYRANNIS. He later referred to the children he'd killed as "collateral damage," saying he couldn't delay the bombing because the date—the second anniversary of the fire at Waco—"was too important." According to a psychiatrist who evaluated him, he then "went into a tirade about all the children killed at Waco."

McVeigh continued to support what he called the patriot movement. Sentenced to death in 1999, he said he had no fear of dying. "If there is a hell, then I'll be in good company with a lot of fighter pilots who also had to bomb innocents to win the war." He was executed by lethal injection at the federal penitentiary in Terre Haute, Indiana, on June 11, 2001.

AMO RODEN, George Roden's common-law wife, who made breakfast during his shootout with Koresh, moved back to Mount Carmel in August 1993 and stayed there until 2000, when she lost a legal battle with Charles Pace and was forced off the property. Like Pace, she believes the government covered up crimes at Waco. Her website, amoroden.com, claims, "Our world is grim reality papered over with a tissue of lies."

President JOE BIDEN nominated David Chipman to head the ATF in May 2021. A twenty-five-year ATF veteran who worked with gun-control groups, Chipman had exaggerated by claiming the Davidians "shot down" two government helicopters at Waco, rather than damaging them enough to make them land. The National Rifle Association and other gun-rights groups lined up against him. His critics cited a photo of "David 'Waco' Chipman" in the ruins of Mount Carmel in 1993. Their claim was false. In fact, the photo showed an FBI agent, not Chipman of the ATF.

Facing mounting opposition, Biden withdrew the nomination and named Deputy Director Marvin Richardson as the ATF's acting director. Richardson, a thirty-two-year agency veteran and one of the ATF's few Black senior officials, had been part of the raid on Mount Carmel on February 28, 1993. "Do I feel that my leadership misled me? Sure I do," Richardson said of the raid. Still he laid the blame at the Davidians' door. "The people that pulled the trigger were in that compound."

When Biden nominated former federal prosecutor Steve Dettelbach to head the ATF in April 2022, one of the first social media commenters asked, "Was this guy at Waco too?" He wasn't.

DAVID THIBODEAU splits his time between Waco and his native Bangor, Maine. He and FBI man Noesner had what he called "an unlikely friendship," appearing together in *Waco*, a fictionalized 2018 Paramount Network miniseries starring Michael Shannon as Noesner and Rory Culkin as Thibodeau. At the end of the last episode, Noesner and Thibodeau shared the screen with the actors who played them.

Now fifty-three, Thibodeau is "looking forward to doing some drumming again soon."

CLIVE DOYLE turned eighty-one in 2022. His hands still scarred by the burns he suffered in 1993, Doyle lived in Waco with his friend Ron Goins, stayed in touch with other Davidians and former Davidians, and often served as their spokesman. Asked how he should be identified to today's readers, he said, "Survivor."

Doyle died of pancreatic cancer on June 8, 2022. His last message, posted on Facebook, said that he hoped to see his friends and family again "in the Kingdom."

SHEILA MARTIN turned seventy-five in 2022. She lost her husband and four of their seven children in the fire at Mount Carmel, and son Jamie five years later. Still she feels "blessed," she says, to have lived to raise two children, Daniel and Kimberley. She has worked at a Christian day care center in Waco since 2002.

HEATHER JONES, the last child to leave Mount Carmel during the siege, had nightmares for weeks after the fire that killed her father and her aunts Rachel and Michele. "I'd be on the property again, with David driving up in a monster truck. He'd stop, get out, come toward me—and I'd wake up."

Now thirty-nine, the mother of three daughters, she lives in Waco. "I'm not religious," she says. "You don't need a church to know right from wrong, and going into a church makes me feel like I'm nine again. I have to get away." She keeps in touch with family, friends, and other survivors, but still has panic attacks she attributes to her time at Mount Carmel. "A couple days a week I won't want to take a shower or leave the house. I keep waiting for it to get easier, but it doesn't."

After fourteen years in American prisons, LIVINGSTONE FAGAN was released and deported in 2007. He returned to Nottingham, England, where he had heard Koresh give a mesmerizing speech in 1988. Now sixty-three, Fagan still serves as an ambassador for Koresh and the Davidians' beliefs on Facebook.

BONNIE HALDEMAN went on to become a pediatric nurse at Mother Frances Hospital in Tyler, Texas. When people heard she was David Koresh's mother, they were "mostly sympathetic." On January 30, 2009, Bonnie drove twenty minutes to Chandler to take her sister, Beverly, who had a history of mental illness, to a doctor's appointment. Beverly stabbed her to death. Bonnie was sixty-four.

GARY NOESNER, lead negotiator during the only time any Davidians came out of Mount Carmel, has spent thirty years fending off charges that he and the FBI were wrong to bombard the Davidians with lights and loud music and then go in with tear gas. "That wasn't me!" He considers Koresh "a narcissist and sociopath. His every thought was, 'What's best for me?'"

Did Koresh brainwash his followers? "I think that comes down to terminology," he says. "I don't view 'brainwashed' as a psychological diagnostic category, but as a general description of someone who isn't thinking clearly due to being overloaded with bogus information. I'd characterize Koresh's followers as having an almost hypnotic belief in anything he told them. Is that being brainwashed? Are followers of the QAnon conspiracy brainwashed, naïve, stupid, or purposefully manipulated by others? The definition seems less important to me than the absolute, unquestioning loyalty, worship, and adherence to the instructions of the harmful narcissist in question. Donald Trump and his most ardent followers are a clear example, in my view. One could say they've been brainwashed. I see it as psychological manipulation at its worst. If Koresh said God wants you to do this or that, they did it. If Trump says something similar, his followers do it."

Noesner retired from the FBI in 2003. He became an executive for Control Risks, a firm that aids clients "managing overseas kidnap incidents." In 2022 he consulted on a sequel to Paramount TV's 2018 miniseries and a Netflix documentary about Waco, both scheduled for 2023.

CLINT VAN ZANDT, Noesner's replacement as lead negotiator at Waco, headed the FBI's so-called Silence of the Lambs Behavioral Science Unit and led the profiling team that helped capture Unabomber Ted Kaczynski in 1996. Looking back on his time at Waco, Van Zandt said watching the CEVs insert tear gas on April 19, 1993, was "akin to sitting on the bow of the *Titanic* and watching the iceberg approach."

ATF agent JIM CAVANAUGH, the first Waco negotiator, shed tears during testimony for the House of Representatives' inquiry. Recalling the chaos of the February 28 raid, he said, "I had a radio mic in one ear with an agent pleading for his life and I had a guy on the phone who thought he was God." He no longer thought of Koresh as his "buddy," the term he often used when they talked on the phone. In 2009 Cavanaugh called Koresh "a two-bit thug from the country in Texas. He was raping little kids . . . He was going to fulfill his destiny. We just interrupted it." He retired in 2010 after thirty-three years in the ATF.

One visitor to the April 2000 dedication of the new church at Mount Carmel went almost unnoticed. The broad-shouldered fellow was ROBERT RODRIGUEZ—Robert Gonzalez to the Davidians. The undercover agent had received the ATF's Distinguished Service Medal for his work at Waco. In 1995, after being diagnosed with post-traumatic stress disorder, he sued the United States, the ATF, and several of his superiors for defamation, claiming they made him a scapegoat for the Waco debacle. His lawsuit was settled out of court, with Rodriguez receiving a reported $2.3 million. At the dedication, he said he didn't want to cause any trouble. "I just came to pay my respects."

SARAH BAIN, jury forewoman in the 1994 trial of eleven Davidians, spoke at a memorial service at Mount Carmel on April 19, 1998, the fifth anniversary of the fire. After the verdict, she said, "We sat back and said, 'Well, the Branch Davidians have now been held accountable for the deaths of the four ATF agents. We can rest assured that the ATF will have to someday be made accountable for the deaths of the six Branch Davidians who died on that exact same day.' We took some consolation in that. We're still waiting." Bain called for "a trial for the ATF officers" in charge of the February 28 raid and "some accountability for the FBI for their activities on April 19—for their activities during the entire fifty-one days." She is still waiting.

ALEX JONES built InfoWars into an empire worth well over $100 million by claiming that events ranging from Waco in 1993 to the 1995 Oklahoma City bombing, the 2001 destruction of the World Trade Center, the 2012 shootings of twenty children and six staff members at Sandy Hook Elementary School in Newtown, Connecticut, and the January 6, 2021, riot at the US Capitol, which he supported, were "inside jobs," false-flag operations. In April 2022, after losing a multimillion-dollar lawsuit against Sandy Hook parents, whom Jones called "crisis actors" conspiring in "a hoax," InfoWars filed for bankruptcy.

The INCIDENT AT WACO remains the deadliest action by federal forces on American soil since the massacre at Wounded Knee in 1890. In 2007 the Native American activist, actor, and musician Russell Means released a song called "Waco, the White Man's Wounded Knee." Means, who had joined American Indian Movement leaders in a seventy-one-day standoff against federal agents at Wounded Knee in 1973, saw the Davidians as kindred spirits. According to his song, "Soldiers burning babies is nothing new. It happened to us, now it's happening to you."

AMERICAN MILITIAS celebrated the 2022 acquittal of Daniel Harris and Brandon Caserta, members of a group called the Wolverine Watchmen charged with plotting to kidnap Michigan governor Gretchen Whitmer. The case fueled conspiracy theories, with the conservative website the Trumpet tying it to the Capitol riot of January 6, 2021: "It is not a stretch to think that the FBI could have orchestrated the violence on that day." According to Republican candidate Garrett Soldano, a chiropractor hoping to unseat Whitmer in November 2022, "The FBI conceived a plot to kidnap Gretchen Whitmer and preyed on Michiganders."

In August 2022, a Michigan jury convicted two other extremists of planning to kidnap Whitmer. Their goal, said prosecutor Nils Kessler, was to "set off a second American Civil War and the second American Revolution." That same month a candidate for Florida's House of Representatives announced a plan to give Floridians "permission to shoot FBI, IRS, ATF and all other feds ON SIGHT! Let freedom ring!"

By then Oath Keepers founder Stewart Rhodes had warned federal agents not to "Waco" modern militants.

Others echoed Three Percenters cofounder Mike Vanderboegh: "Waco can happen at any given time. But the outcome will be different this time."

Appendix

ATF AGENTS KILLED ON
FEBRUARY 28, 1993
Conway LeBleu, 30, New Orleans
    field office
Todd McKeehan, 28, New Orleans
    field office
Robert Williams, 26, New Orleans
    field office
Steve Willis, 32, Houston field office

BRANCH DAVIDIANS WHO DIED
ON FEBRUARY 28, 1993
Winston Blake, 28, UK
Peter Gent, 24, Australia
Peter Hipsman, 28, US
Perry Jones, 64, US
Michael Schroeder, 29, US
Jaydean Wendell, 34, US

CHILDREN RELEASED
DURING THE SIEGE
February 28:
Nehara Fagan, 4, UK
Renae Fagan, 6, UK
Angelica Sonobe, age 6, US
Crystal Sonobe, 3, US

March 1:
Chrissy Mabb, 8, US
Jacob Mabb, 9, US
Scott Mabb, 11, US
Jamie Martin, 10, US
Bryan Schroeder, 2, US
Joshua Sylvia, 7, US
Jaunessa Wendell, 8, US
Landon Wendell, 4, US
Patron Wendell, 5 months, US
Tamara Wendell, 5, US

March 2:
Daniel Martin, 6, US
Kimberley Martin, 4, US
Natalie Nobrega, 10, UK
Joanne Vaega, 7, New Zealand

March 3:
Heather Jones, 9, US
Kevin Jones, 11, US
Mark Jones, 12, US

BRANCH DAVIDIANS WHO
SURVIVED THE FIRE ON
APRIL 19, 1993

Renos Avraam, 32, UK
Jaime Castillo, 24, US
Graeme Craddock, 31, Australia
Clive Doyle, 52, Australia
Misty Ferguson, 17, US
Derek Lovelock, 37, UK
Ruth Riddle, 30, Canada
David Thibodeau, 24, US
Marjorie Thomas, 30, UK

BRANCH DAVIDIANS WHO
DIED ON APRIL 19, 1993

Chanel Andrade, 1, US
Jennifer Andrade, 19, US
Katherine Andrade, 24, US
George Bennett, 35, US
Susan Benta, 31, UK
Mary Jean Borst, 49, US
Pablo Cohen, 28, Israel
Abedowalo Davies, 30, UK
Shari Doyle, 18, US
Beverly Elliot, 31, UK
Doris Fagan, 60, UK
Yvette Fagan, 30, UK
Lisa Marie Farris, 24, US
Raymond Friesen, 76, Canada
Dayland Gent, 3, US
Paige Gent, 1, US
Aisha Gyarfas, 17, Australia
    (and her stillborn child)
Sandra Hardial, 27, UK
Diana Henry, 28, UK
Paulina Henry, 24, UK
Phillip Henry, 22, UK
Stephen Henry, 26, UK
Vanessa Henry, 19, UK
Zilla Henry, 55, UK
Novelette Hipsman, 36, Canada
Floyd Houtman, 61, US
Sherri Jewell, 43, US
Chica Jones, 1, US
David Jones, 38, US
Little One Jones, 1, US

Michele Jones, 18, US
Serenity Jones, 4, US
Bobbie Lane Koresh, 2, US
Cyrus Koresh, 8, US
David Koresh, 33, US
Rachel Howell Koresh, 23, US
Star Koresh, 6, US
Jeffery Little, 32, US
Nicole Gent Little, 24, Australia
    (and her stillborn child)
Livingstone Malcolm, 26, UK
Anita Martin, 18, US
Diane Martin, 41, UK
Lisa Martin, 13, US
Sheila Martin, 15, US
Wayne Martin, 42, US
Wayne Martin Jr., 20, US
Abigail Martinez, 11, US
Audrey Martinez, 13, US
Crystal Martinez, 3, US
Isaiah Martinez, 4, US
Joseph Martinez, 8, US
Juliette Martinez, 30, US
John-Mark McBean, 27, UK
Bernadette Monbelly, 31, UK
Melissa Morrison, 6, UK
Rosemary Morrison, 29, UK
Sonia Murray, 29, US
Theresa Nobrega, 48, UK
James Riddle, 32, US
Rebecca Saipaia, 24, Philippines
Mayanah Schneider, 2, US
Steve Schneider, 43, US
Judy Schneider-Koresh, 41, US
Clifford Sellors, 33, UK
Floracita Sonobe, 34, Philippines
Scott Sonobe, 35, US
Greg Summers, 28, US
Startle Summers, 1, US
Hollywood Sylvia, 1, US
Lorraine Sylvia, 40, US
Rachel Sylvia, 12, US
Margarida Vaega, 47, New Zealand
Neal Vaega, 37, New Zealand
Mark Wendell, 40, US

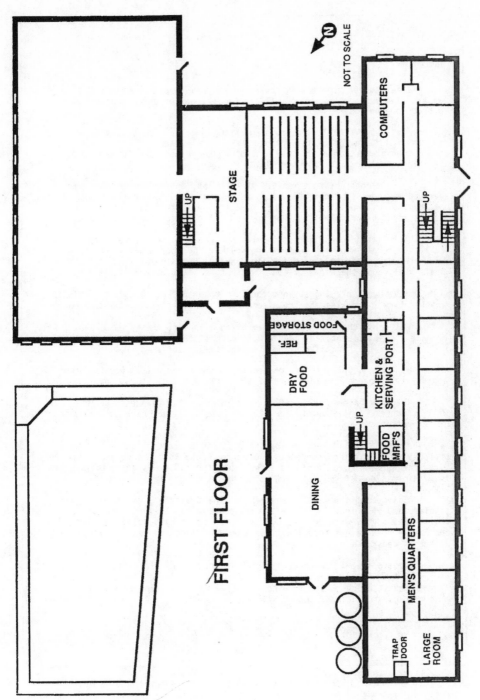

A diagram of Mount Carmel's first floor. The vault was the area marked "Dry food" and "Ref." The stage occupied the front of the chapel, with the gym behind the stage and the outdoor pool at lower left. (ATF)

April 14, 1993

Hello Dick,

As far as our progress is concerned, here is where we stand: I have related two messages, from God, to the F.B.I.; one of which concerns present danger to people here in Waco.

I was shown a fault line running throughout the Lake Waco area. An angel is standing in charge of this event. Many people, here in Waco, know that we are a good people, and yet, they have shown the same resentful spirit of indifference to our "warnings of love."

I am presently being permitted to document, in structured form, the decoded messages of the Seven Seals. Upon the completion of this task, I will be freed of my "waiting period." I hope to finish this as soon as possible and to stand before man to answer any and all questions regarding my actions.

This written Revelation of the Seven Seals will not be sold, but is to be available to all who wish to know the Truth. The Four Angels of Revelation 7 are here, now ready to punish foolish mankind; but, the writing of these Seals will cause the winds of God's wrath to be held back a little longer.

I have been praying so long for this opportunity; to put the Seals in written form. Speaking the Truth seems to have very little effect on man.

I was shown that as soon as I am given over into the hands of man, I will be made a spectacle of, and people will not be concerned about the truth of God, but just the bizarrity of me - the flesh (person).

I want the people of this generation to be saved. I am working night and day to complete my final work of the writing out of "these Seals."

I thank my Father, He has finally granted me the chance to do this. It will bring New Light and hope for many and they will not have to deal with me the person.

The earthquake in Waco is something not to be taken lightly. It will probably be "the thing" needed to shake some sense into the people. Remember, Dick, the warning came first and I fear that the F.B.I. is going to suppress this information. It may be left up to you.

I will demand the first manuscript of the Seals be given to you. Many scholars and religious leaders will wish to have copies for examination. I will keep a copy with me. As soon as I can see that people, like Jim Tabor and Phil Arnold have a copy I will come out and then you can do your thing with this Beast.

I hope to keep in touch with you by letter, so please give your address.

We are standing on the threshold of Great events! The Seven Seals, in written form are the most sacred information ever!

David Koresh

David Koresh

Koresh's April 14 letter to lawyer Dick DeGuerin (Department of Justice)

Notes on Sources

Waco Rising combines new reporting—interviews and private correspondence with Davidian survivors and others involved in the story, including FBI sources, current and former ATF agents, and academic specialists—with archival and multimedia research to shed new light on an event that remains vivid and controversial after thirty years.

My days in archives at Baylor University and Texas State University were so fascinating I often lost track of time. What I learned reinforced my regard for a short stack of books I often turned to: David Thibodeau's *Waco: A Survivor's Story* (New York: Hachette Books, 2018), an update of his *A Place Called Waco* (New York: PublicAffairs, 1999), written with Leon Whiteson and Aviva Layton; Gary Noesner's *Stalling for Time* (New York: Random House, 2010); Clive Doyle's *A Journey to Waco* (Lanham, MD: Rowman & Littlefield Publishers, 2012), written with Catherine Wessinger and Matthew D. Wittmer; and Dick Reavis's *The Ashes of Waco* (New York: Simon & Schuster, 1995). The Justice Department's 342-page *Report to the Deputy Attorney General on the Events at Waco, Texas, February 28 to April 19, 1993* (US Department of Justice, October 8, 1993) proved flawed but invaluable. I also relied on Bonnie Haldeman's *Memories of the Branch Davidians* (Waco: Baylor University Press, 2007); Sheila Martin's *When They Were Mine* (Waco: Baylor University Press, 2009); *Armageddon in Waco: Critical Perspectives on the Branch Davidian Conflict*, ed. Stuart Wright (Chicago: University of Chicago Press, 1995); and to a lesser degree Marc Breault and Martin King's *Inside the Cult* (New York: Signet, 1993).

Lou Michel and Dan Herbeck's *American Terrorist* was my go-to reference for material on Timothy McVeigh. Lee Hancock's important work for the *Dallas Morning News* and her archived papers would be a boon to any researcher.

Most crucial were those who shared their time, expertise, and memories with me: survivors Doyle, Martin, Thibodeau, and Heather Jones; Gary Noesner; Baylor's Bill Pitts and Liverpool Hope University's Kenneth Newport; and others thanked in the acknowledgments.

A note on tenses: if a source spoke to me during my work on the book, I put her or his quote in the present tense. Otherwise I use past tense.

PROLOGUE

Sunrise was not until 6:56 a.m. in Waco on April 19, 1993. FBI recordings and the Department of Justice's October 1993 report detail the government's minute-by-minute actions that morning. Branch Davidian survivors recalled Koresh's surprise (and their own) at the tear gas attack that was "not an assault."

1. WANDERING BONEHEAD

Sources for Bonnie Clark Haldeman's life and her son Vernon's youth include her memoir, *Memories of the Branch Davidians*, books by onetime Davidians, including Marc Breault and David Thibodeau, archives at Baylor and Texas State Universities, and Koresh's revealing recollections during 117 phone conversations with negotiators during the siege, covering more than sixty hours. He spent much of that time expounding what the negotiators called "Bible babble," but sometimes offered first-person accounts of his youth and his views that provided key details in this book. Several details ("A lot of prostitutes hung around . . .") come from Reavis's *The Ashes of Waco*. The *Washington Post* reported Vernon Howell's 1983 expulsion from the Tyler, Texas, congregation on May 9, 1993.

2. A NEW RELIGION

My account of Branch Davidian history owes a debt to Bill Pitts of Baylor, who has spent decades studying the Texas-based sect. (Any mistakes are my own.) I also relied on James Tabor, professor of Christian Origins and Ancient Judaism at the University of North Carolina at Charlotte, who shared a recording of his "scholars' summit" with professors Philip Arnold, Catherine Wessinger, and Stuart Wright. Boston University's Nancy Ammerman helped me understand the Davidians' view of their place in religious history and how the government misunderstood it. Reavis's *The Ashes of Waco* provided helpful background. A Seventh-day Adventist blog (godsloveandlaw.com) contributed details on Florence Houteff. I found back issues of Lois Roden's newsletter *SHEkinah* (Clive Doyle, editor; Charles Pace, art director) in the priceless Texas Collection at Baylor. Lois Roden cradled a dove in her hand for the photo accompanying an October 27, 1980, *Dallas Times Herald* story on her. Pastor Pace shared details of Davidian history during my visits to Mount Carmel. Texas judge Bill Logue's comments on the Davidians come from the Texas Collection's Robert F. Darden III collection at Baylor, which also holds George Roden's recorded rantings and Amo Bishop Roden's recollections. Clive Doyle described George's apparent symptoms of Tourette's syndrome, which matched Koresh's descriptions in his talks with negotiators. Rebekah Ann Crowe's 2004 Baylor master's thesis, "Because God Said I Was!," included helpful details. The *Waco Tribune-Herald* covered the 1988 trial that followed the raid. Crowe's thesis added details of George Roden's relationship with Dale Adair and the day he killed Adair. Clive Doyle and Sheila Martin shared memories of the Davidians' exile in Palestine, Texas. Doyle's *A Journey to Waco* provided details of life at Palestine and Mount Carmel before and after Vernon Howell arrived.

3. SLEEPING WITH A PROPHETESS

Reavis depicted Vernon Howell's ascendance at Mount Carmel. The *Waco Tribune-Herald*'s Mark England and Darlene McCormick brought a different view in their "Sinful Messiah" series, which debuted on February 27, 1993—the day before the ATF raid, which it helped trigger. Koresh added many details during his talks with FBI negotiators. David Thibodeau helped me understand Koresh as a guitarist as well as a guru. Jaime Castillo's quote ("If Satan can inspire musicians . . .") comes from one of the letters he wrote from prison to Waco researcher Carol Moore, part of the Witliff Collections at Texas State University. George Roden's claims to be the Davidians' prophet and his charges against "pervert and rapist" Vernon Howell can be found in the Texas Collection at Baylor. Koresh recalled his first impressions of Rachel Jones and his "vision" in Israel during phone calls with FBI negotiators. The last days of Jim Jones and his Peoples Temple in Guyana were widely reported, including in Jeff Guinn's *The Road to Jonestown*. Bonnie Haldeman described the Davidians' time in Palestine, Texas, in her *Memories of the Branch Davidians*. Sheila Martin did the same in her talks with me. I found the flyer Vernon Howell handed out to Seventh-day Adventists at the Superdome in 1985 in the Texas Collection at Baylor. Marc Breault was the

Davidian who described Vernon Howell's "dead of night" encounter with Michele Jones. I relied on Breault and Martin King's sensationalistic *Inside the Cult* for several details of life at Mount Carmel before Breault split with Koresh only if they corresponded with others' accounts. Castillo's comments about Michele Jones's maturity ("Not all girls between twelve and thirteen . . .") are from a letter he wrote to Moore. Koresh recalled George Roden's daring him to a "miracle-off" during a talk with an FBI negotiator.

4. MADMAN IN WACO

Sheila Martin told me about her husband, Wayne, and their lives together, an account supplemented by her memoir, *When They Were Mine*. That book and Bonnie Haldeman's *Memories of the Branch Davidians* contributed memories of the Davidians' sojourn in Palestine, Texas. Judge Logue's characterization of Martin can be found in the Texas Collection at Baylor. Amo Roden's comment on Anna Hughes ("Her hair was still there . . .") can also be found there. Bill Pitts helped me understand this period in Branch Davidian history, as did Reavis's *The Ashes of Waco* and James Tabor and Eugene Gallagher's *Why Waco?* (Berkeley: University of California Press, 1995). Rebekah Ann Crowe's 2004 Baylor master's thesis provided details of the shopping trip Vernon Howell and his crew made before raiding Mount Carmel. Koresh vividly described the shootout with George Roden during his talks with negotiators. Amo Roden's report on that morning came from the Robert F. Darden Collection in the Texas Collection at Baylor. Reavis's and Bonnie Haldeman's books held other details on the shootout, which the *Tribune-Herald* covered on November 4, 1987, and its later "Sinful Messiah" series. Crowe's thesis added to the *Waco Tribune-Herald*'s extensive contemporary coverage of the 1988 trial of Vernon Howell and his raiding team. Both sources reported on Howell and his loyalists' reacquiring Mount Carmel. George Roden's rants against "Vermin" Howell and his followers occupy many pages in the Texas Collection's Darden Collection at Baylor. Koresh's rendition of his song "Madman in Waco" can be heard on YouTube. David Thibodeau and Kristin Hunsaker shared a Messiah Productions business card with me. Judge Logue describes his late-night call about George Roden's fate in his papers in the Texas Collection at Baylor.

5. PLANET KORESH

McLennan County records specify the dimensions of Mount Carmel in 1988. *Waco: A Survivor's Story* carries compelling descriptions of life there after Thibodeau arrived. He shared many other recollections in conversations with me. *Memories of the Branch Davidians* and *Waco: A Survivor's Story* describe Livingstone Fagan's hearing Vernon Howell in England. Fagan has often explicated his faith on his Facebook page. Rita Riddle's comment ("I learned more with him in one night . . .") is from "Post-Involvement Attitudes of Voluntary Defectors from Controversial New Religious Movements," by Stuart Wright, in the *Journal for the Scientific Study of Religion* (June 1994). Koresh's many misspellings are noted in Eastern Mennonite University professor Jayne Seminare Docherty's intriguing *Learning Lessons from Waco* (Syracuse, NY: Syracuse University Press, 2001). Sheila Martin, Doyle, and Thibodeau spoke with me in Waco and by phone and text. The biblical verse including "*I saw a mighty angel*" is from Revelation 5:1–2. Koresh often spoke of his Christlike role with Doyle and others, including FBI negotiators. Koresh quote to Martin Smith ("If the Bible is true . . .") was reported in David Maxwell's 1993 "Report of Investigation" for the Texas Department of Public Safety. Martin and Doyle recalled instances of Koresh's testing his followers during conversations with me. Doyle mentioned Koresh's taking girls' toy dolls in *A Journey to Waco*. Reavis's *The Ashes of Waco*, *Why Waco?*, and numerous other sources describe Koresh's encounters with gun dealer Henry McMahon. Koresh talked expertly about night-vision scopes and their prices during talks with negotiators. Thibodeau described Koresh's Camaro and some of his favorite movies. Robyn Bunds is the former Davidian who quoted Koresh on "training films." Reavis, Doyle, and Breault recalled his fascination with Madonna; Breault's *Inside the Cult* quotes him quoting God on that subject. Jeannine Bunds told *Newsweek* (May 16, 1993) that Koresh "wouldn't do it unless you wanted it." Thibodeau quotes the House of David member who spoke of "Koresh's loins." Breault described Rachel's giving other women advice on how to "bathe and perfume" themselves in *Inside the Cult*, which Heather Jones's description corroborated. Davidian Gladys Ottman told *Maclean's* magazine (May 3, 1993) about Bible studies in which he discussed "deviant" sex. Descriptions of the House of David come from multiple Davidian sources, as does Koresh's talk of "hating" various racial groups. Martin, Haldeman, Breault, Thibodeau, and others recalled the sexually charged atmosphere at Mount Carmel. Charles Pace forwarded me an email from the former Davidian whose mother told her "what it means to be born a girl." Martin recalled Koresh's urging the others to hear what Breault said about scripture. Breault's campaign to discredit Koresh is told from different angles in *Inside the Cult*, *Waco: A Survivor's Story*, and FBI records recounted in the Department of Justice's 1993 report.

6. THE SINFUL MESSIAH

Haldeman and Martin offered similar estimates of operating expenses at Mount Carmel. Thibodeau recalled the bill of fare there in *Waco: A Survivor's Story* and conversations with me. Steve Schneider described daily life there in talks with negotiators. Martin remembered Koresh's treatment of her son Jamie in our conversations. She described his reaction to Marc Breault's letters in *When They Were Mine* and our conversations. Koresh spoke with negotiators about his views on holidays and UFOs. Doyle and Heather Jones shared memories of shooting guns in our talks; she also described troubling interactions with Koresh in our talks and in YouTube interviews with Catherine Wessinger of Loyola University at Los Angeles, who was pivotal in preserving Doyle's, Bonnie Haldeman's, and Martin's accounts in their memoirs. Reavis and Professor Wessinger examined the *Tribune-Herald*'s preparations for the "Sinful Messiah" series in "The Branch Davidians and the Waco Media 1993–2003," published by the Center for Studies on New Religions on June 7, 2004. Tabor and Gallagher and the *Tribune-Herald* portrayed Special Agent Davy Aguilera's investigation of Koresh and the Davidians, which Aguilera testified about during the House of Representatives' Waco investigation. *Spin* magazine reported Koresh's talk with musician Eddie Goins in its November 6, 2015, issue. The affidavit Aguilera prepared can be seen at Constitution.org. John R. Hall of the University of California at Davis provided background details and directions to other sources in "Public Narratives and the Apocalyptic Sect," his contribution to *Armageddon in Waco*. The Department of Justice's 1993 report noted Breault's contacts with FBI representatives; Breault brought a different perspective in *Inside the Cult*. Doyle discussed Breault's warning that the Davidians would commit suicide during Passover 1992 in *A Journey to Waco*. Koresh told negotiators about his reaction: "We're still here." Nancy Ammerman, professor of sociology of religion at Boston University, helped me understand the government's apparent befuddlement at the Davidians' beliefs. Reavis, Doyle, and the *Tribune-Herald*'s "Sinful Messiah" series provided helpful aspects of the ATF's undercover operation.

7. DEADLINE PRESSURE

The *Tribune-Herald*'s "Sinful Messiah" series opened on February 27, 1993. The *Tribune-Herald*'s preparation of the series was outlined in its February 24, 2018, retrospective, "Lost in the Chaos." The Green Berets' participation in training ATF agents for the next day's raid was discussed in the House of

Representatives' hearings and more colorfully in *Soldier of Fortune* (May 1994). My research on Operation Trojan Horse, aka Showtime, included army memos recording the ATF's requests for helicopters and Bradley tanks ("Fighting Vehicles" in the memos), noting that the army and Army Reserve National Guard "will be reimbursed for all use." Reavis described federal agents pouring into Waco in preparation for the raid. Thibodeau's and Doyle's books contributed details to my account of the run-up to the raid, as did David T. Hardy's self-published *This Is Not an Assault* (Bloomington, IN: Xlibris, 2001). The tip-off to Dave Jones ("You better get out of here . . .") was reported in the *Washington Post*, August 28, 1993. The Davidians' memoirs and Robert Rodriguez's testimony to the House of Representatives' investigation informed my account of the moments before the ATF raid. TV cameraman Jim Peeler recalled his colleague Mulloney's encounter with ATF agents in Pamela Colloff's oral history "The Fire That Time" (*Texas Monthly*, April 2008), a key source of compelling quotes and details.

8. SHOWTIME

Doyle and Thibodeau recalled Koresh's telling his followers not to "do anything stupid." Reavis reported Special Agent Ballesteros's experience on February 28, which Ballesteros corroborated in testimony during the 1994 trial of eleven Davidians. ATF agent Tim Gabourie testified at the trial that he had shot one of the dogs for "barking offensively." Doyle described the dogs' shooting in *A Journey to Waco*. *Texas Monthly* reported that Ballesteros aimed a shotgun at Koresh. The *New York Times* (March 28, 1993) reported a bullet's "whizzing past" the ATF's Philip Chojnacki. Reavis reported Graeme Craddock's reaching for guns and ammunition. The fact that Agent LeBleu died clutching his shotgun was reported by Associated Press on January 24, 1994. Reavis contributed details to my account of the ATF raid. The October 17, 1995, PBS program *Frontline* was also helpful. Former ATF agent Chuck Hustmyre described the raid in a long 2003 post at Crimelibrary.org, and confirmed details in correspondence with me. Current and former ATF agents provided invaluable details about the raid and its aftermath. Wayne Martin and Koresh's 911 phone exchanges with Lieutenant Larry Lynch were recorded and can be heard in government archives and the Texas Collection at Baylor.

9. CEASE-FIRE

Reavis and Haldeman recalled Koresh's phone call ("Hello, Mama . . .") to his mother that day. The exits of Davidian children were carefully documented by the FBI. Koresh described being shot by ATF agents ("It's like a 250-pound man kicking you . . .") during talks with negotiators. Reavis added details. Doyle and Thibodeau recalled Perry Jones's wounding and Neal Vaega's shooting Jones and Peter Hipsman. Davidian survivors recalled Annetta Richards's dressing Koresh's wounds. Tabor and Gallagher recounted Koresh's conversation with KRLD's Charlie Serafin in *Why Waco?* The *Tribune-Herald* and other sources reported the FAA's no-fly zone over Mount Carmel. The Department of Justice's 1993 report detailed the February 28 release of Angelica and Crystal Sonobe and Renae and Nahara Fagan. The *Houston Chronicle* reported Vic Feazell's comments ("The feds are preparing to kill them . . .") on March 2, 1993.

10. DAVID AND GOLIATH

The *New York Times* quoted an ATF agent at Mount Carmel ("Inexcusable . . .") and noted ATF agent Cavanaugh's role in the February 28 raid on March 28, 1993. Tabor detailed the FBI's "complex hostage barricade rescue situation" classification and the Davidians' view of the US government as "Babylonian" in "Religious Discourse and Failed Negotiations," his contribution to *Armageddon at Waco.* Former assistant attorney general Edward Dennis's assessment ("Koresh made no threats . . .") comes from his *Evaluation of the Handling of the Branch Davidian Stand-off in Waco, Texas* (Washington, DC: US Government Printing Office, 1996). Gary Noesner described his joining the FBI effort and FBI practices in Waco in his *Stalling for Time.* His exchanges with Koresh are recorded in the Bureau's tapes of their phone conversations. The Seven Seals are the subject of Revelation 6:1–17 and 8:1–6. Numerous sources, including the *Dallas Morning News* (April 19, 2018), note that most hostage situations end in six to eight hours. The ATF's March 1, 1993, press conference can be seen on YouTube. The *New York Times* reported that the raid was the costliest and deadliest in the agency's history. The *Washington Post* quoted local pastor Bob Ratley ("Why didn't they get him . . .") on March 2, 1993. The Department of Justice's 1993 report detailed the timeline of that day's events. The Davidians reported Koresh's blood pressure in their talks with negotiators. The FBI taped Koresh's talks with agent Henry Garcia and other negotiators. Thibodeau recalled the Davidians' celebration that night in *Waco: A Survivor's Story.*

11. WAIT

Doyle, Reavis, and Thibodeau recalled preparations for Koresh's message on the Christian Broadcasting Network. The Department of Justice's 1993 report lists the times and dates when children were released, matching the

survivors' accounts. Koresh's exchanges with Henry Garcia and other negotiators were recorded by the FBI. Catherine Matteson recounted her talk
with Koresh ("I made this tape . . .") and taking his tape with her in the April
2008 issue of *Texas Monthly*, where the FBI's Byron Sage claimed Koresh
had been "milking" the moment. Reavis noted Koresh's calling his plan for
an exit "good TV." Ted Koppel's *Nightline* program on events of the day
aired on March 2, 1993. Koresh's "Radio Sermon 1993" from the Christian
Broadcasting Network can be heard on YouTube. Texas Department of Public Safety spokesman Mike Cox's papers, featuring Cox's memories of the
siege and his collection of Waco jokes, are in the Texas Collection at Baylor,
as is the KDFW news director's exultant "I finally beat Oprah . . ."

12. A GATHERING STORM

Much of this chapter, including Koresh's exchanges with Agent Cavanaugh,
consists of recorded conversations between Davidians and Noesner's negotiating team. Steve Schneider identified Mark Jones as the child who took
out $1,000 in an April 14 talk with negotiators. Doyle recalled burying four
fellow Davidians in *A Journey to Waco*. Kevin Jones's departure was logged
by the FBI and appears in the Department of Justice's 1993 report. Heather
Jones's leaving Mount Carmel was recorded by the FBI; she elaborated in a
conversation with me.

13. HARD BARGAINS

Jamar's description of President Clinton's interest was reported by the *Dallas Morning News* on March 5, 1993. Reavis described the roles Governor
Ann Richards and ATF deputy director Hartnett played; the *Austin Chronicle* explored Richards's involvement in "What Did Ann Know?" (November
12, 1999). Noesner's *Stalling for Time* tells of the delivery of a first-aid kit
without mentioning that the kit was bugged. Reavis and many other sources
describe the mixed results the FBI got from its listening devices; Byron Sage
spoke of them in a *Vice* video posted April 1, 2021. Davidian survivors
described daily life during the siege in their memoirs and conversations
with me. Koresh called himself "pro-woman" in a talk with negotiators.
Michael Schroeder's February 28 shooting by ATF agents was examined by
the *Chicago Tribune* (March 11, 1993), *Washington Post* (March 13, 1993),
Los Angeles Times (March 14, 1993), and *Tampa Tribune* (February 27,
2003) and discussed during Kathy Schroeder's talks with negotiators. Doyle
described the Davidians' relationship with Sheriff Jack Harwell and their
discovering that the FBI was smuggling listening devices into the compound

in a conversation with me. Thibodeau recalled Mark Wendell's recovering Peter Gent's body. FBI records recounted in the Department of Justice's 1993 report framed the timeline of March 9. Numerous newspapers and TV broadcasts carried images of the Davidians' WE WANT THE PRESS banner; the Department of Justice report drily noted the WE ARE THE PRESS reply in Satellite City.

14. TESTIMONY

Almost all of this chapter comes from interviews Steve Schneider conducted for the videotape the Davidians sent out on March 9. Many can be seen as "Branch Davidian home movies" and "footage from inside compound" on YouTube and in the University of North Texas's digital library.

15. TIGHTENING THE NOOSE

Noesner, the *Tribune-Herald*, and the Department of Justice's 1993 report tallied the number of children released. Many sources put the number of Koresh's biological children left in the compound at twelve; the *Tribune-Herald* reported the number was "at least thirteen" on September 24, 1994; Clive Doyle's friend and roommate Ron Goins told me it was seventeen. Noesner characterized the ongoing dynamic among FBI officials in *Stalling for Time*; he added details in phone and email exchanges with me. The Texas Collection at Baylor holds many of Vern Herschberger's clever editorial cartoons, which were collected in *51 Days* (Waco: Hilltop Publishing, 1995). Doyle recalled the privations inside Mount Carmel. Castillo recalled Greg Summers's plugging holes in a water tank with melted plastic in a letter to Moore. The *Tribune-Herald* covered attorney Dick DeGuerin's arrival; Haldeman's *Memories of the Branch Davidians* contributed details about the lawyer she hired. Noesner recalled urging Kathy Schroeder to come out (*"Bryan needs a hug . . ."*) in *Stalling for Time*. The *Washington Post* and *New York Times* reported on Koresh's banishing her for smoking cigarettes. Doyle and Martin told me about federal agents' offensive behavior. The army's March 11 memo on "refresher training" can be found in the Witliff Collections at Texas State University.

16. T-SHIRT HILL

Janet Reno's swearing-in on March 12, 1993, can be seen on C-SPAN and YouTube. The *Nation* (March 8, 1993), *Los Angeles Times* (November 23, 1986, and October 3, 1993), PBS (April 25, 2002), and many other sources detailed her "crusade" against child abuse as a Florida prosecutor. The *New*

York Times reported her quoting FBI advisors ("Yes, he's slapping babies around . . .") on March 8, 1993. Breault described corporal punishment at Mount Carmel in *Inside the Cult*; surviving Davidians and former Davidian Heather Jones added details that filled out my account. Koresh was the subject of *Time* and *Newsweek* covers dated March 15, 1993. The *Washington Post* reported Breault's talk of "human sacrifice" on April 25, 1993. A former Mount Carmel resident who asked not to be identified recalled the wounded Koresh's resurgent libido. FBI agent James McGee described Koresh's behavior ("He would literally sit on a window ledge . . .") in *Texas Monthly* (April 2008). Professor Tabor discussed his dealings with the FBI and Koresh in *Why Waco?* and the "scholars' summit" recording he sent me. Noesner related his views of the scholars in *Stalling for Time* and a conversation with me. The roles of UCLA professor Park Dietz, Syracuse professor Murray Miron, cult-buster Rick Ross, and agents Smerick and Young were detailed in the Department of Justice's 1993 report, which also records Breault's offer "to debate Koresh on a radio program." Surviving Davidians told me about conditions inside Mount Carmel as the siege wore on. Reno's opposition to snipers' shooting "someone who was not shooting at them" comes from an August 2, 1993, interview by attorneys at the Philadelphia law firm Morgan, Lewis & Bockius, part of the FBI's subsequent investigation, held at the Witliff Collections at Texas State. Sources including *American Terrorist*, the *Tribune-Herald*, *Dallas Morning News*, and *New York Times* to *Rolling Stone* and the *Daily Campus*, Southern Methodist University's newspaper, filled in aspects of the scene outside Mount Carmel. The *Dallas Morning News* described T-shirt Hill in a March 16, 1993, story. A YouTube clip, "Timothy McVeigh at Waco," shows McVeigh there. Sources, including *American Terrorist*, track his travels from Waco to Oklahoma City in 1995.

17. SIGNALS AND NOISE

Noesner recalled Dick Schwein's arrival at the Waco command post. Operation Nifty Package was described in the *New York Times* (January 6, 1990) and *Time* magazine (January 15, 1990). According to Meenekshi Bose's *From Cold War to New World Order: The Foreign Policy of George H. W. Bush* (Westport, CT: Praeger, 2002), national security advisor Brent Scowcroft was the diplomat who called the operation "silly, reproachable . . ." Numerous sources verify the playlist of songs and noises the FBI blared at Mount Carmel. Thibodeau recalled the "duel of the amps" in *Waco: A Survivor's Story* and a talk with me. Schneider's challenging talk with negotiator John Hyler was recorded by the FBI. Noesner and the Department of Justice's

1993 report noted the March 28 delivery of magazines and other materials to Mount Carmel. Noesner and Doyle recounted the tactical teams' clearing Davidians' vehicles from the front of the compound, which Koresh complained about on the phone to negotiators. Koresh's talk of enjoying "all the cigarettes . . . all the booze" is from his talks with negotiators, as is his characterization of those who had left as "weak people." Martin described her leaving the compound in lengthy talks with me. Noesner discussed strategy ("If you want to train your dog . . .") in *Stalling for Time*. Noesner, Thibodeau, and Tabor and Gallagher provide various views of Livingstone Fagan's exit, which Fagan has described, along with his still-strong Davidian beliefs, in Facebook posts. Reavis notes the FBI's use of flash-bang grenades on March 26. Doyle and other survivors related details of deteriorating conditions at Mount Carmel in *A Journey to Waco* and conversations with me.

18. REGIME CHANGE

Koresh referred to "my wives, plural" in a March 19 talk with negotiator John Cox. That exchange and the others in this chapter, including Steve Schneider's talk of his duties and memories of Hawaii, were recorded by the FBI. John O'Neill identified himself during talks with the Davidians. The Department of Justice's 1993 report related Louis Alaniz's arrival, which became a topic of discussion among Schneider, Koresh, and the negotiators. Noesner had brought in agent Dick Wren from Cleveland; Wren joined telephone negotiations on March 25, 1993. The Department of Justice report sets that day's clearance of vehicles at 4:00 p.m. and notes the Davidians' using mirrors to watch from their windows. Noesner described his last day on the job in *Stalling for Time* and in phone and email discussions with me. The Roper Center at Cornell University tracked public opinion polls on the standoff. Dennis's *Evaluation of the Handling of the Branch Davidian Stand-off at Waco, Texas* notes the FBI's concerns about the Davidians' possible use of cyanide to poison themselves. Koresh spoke of the fate of "top prophets" in a talk with negotiators.

19. BREAKTHROUGH

Attorney Dick DeGuerin's appearance and meetings with Koresh were discussed over the phone with negotiators and described by Reavis and in recorded conversations with Koresh and Schneider. Haldeman detailed hiring DeGuerin, who recalled his first meeting with Koresh in *Texas Monthly* (April 2008). Professors Arnold and Tabor detailed their efforts in *Armageddon at Waco*, *Why Waco?*, and the "scholars' summit" video Tabor sent

to me. Koresh described Jesse Amen and his reasons for leaving Mount Carmel as well as his own growing fury at the FBI in talks with negotiators. The
FBI's account of little activity on April 5 and 6 appears in the Department of
Justice's 1993 report. The *New York Times* reported on "defensive maneuvers" that DeGuerin and Jack Zimmerman called "destroying evidence"
on April 5, 1993. Koresh's April 10 letter, reported on by the *New York
Times*, *Washington Post*, and many other outlets on April 11, 1993, can
be found in the Ashes of Waco Collection at Texas State University. Joseph
Krofcheck and Clint Van Zandt's report to Attorney General Reno is sum-
marized in the Department of Justice's report. The *Wall Street Journal* and
Dallas Morning News reported the appearance of the FLAMES AWAIT sign.
Negotiator John Denton spoke of his service in Vietnam during a talk with
Schneider. Koresh's April 14 letter to DeGuerin was paraphrased in the press
by DeGuerin; there is a copy in the Texas Collection at Baylor.

20. PENDING JUDGMENT

Attorney General Reno's meeting with army representatives General
Schoomaker and Colonel Boykin is detailed in a May 13, 1993, army mem-
orandum in the Hancock Collection of the Witliff Collections at Texas
State University. Undated army documents, including one referring to the
upcoming meeting with Reno in Washington, detail Schoomaker's travels
that week and identify Dr. Salem. The Department of Justice's 1993 report
added details of that fateful meeting, another meeting the following day in
which Associate Attorney General Webb Hubbell conferred by phone with
Sage, and preparations to use CS gas at Waco. Judy Schneider-Koresh and
Steve Schneider described the wound to her hand in talks with negotiators. On April 14 and 15, 1993, the *Washington Post*, United Press International, and many other outlets reported DeGuerin's informing the press
of Koresh's April 14 letter. Noesner characterized the FBI's advising Reno
to use CS gas as "a sales pitch" in a phone conversation with me in which
he concluded that the Bureau "played on her background" and ultimately
"deceived" her. I relied on the National Weather Service and *Tribune-Herald*
for 1993 weather reports. Koresh's long discussion of scripture with Van
Zandt was recorded by the FBI. Reavis reported agent Bob Ricks's scoffing
at Koresh's promises ("What's next?") and Jamar's calling them a "stalling
technique." The Department of Justice report notes Reno's April 17 review
of Dietz's final report to her and Alaniz's departure in a DAVID KORESH/
GOD ROCKS T-shirt. That report also records Reno's worries ("Oh my God,
what if . . ."), also noted by the *Washington Post* on July 2, 1995. Koresh

and other Davidians described the FBI's April 18 clearing of their vehicles in talks with negotiators, as did Dennis in his *Evaluation of the Handling of the Branch Davidian Stand-off in Waco, Texas*. Dennis's report also notes the Davidians' dismay at the tanks' rolling over Peter Gent's grave, an issue Doyle discusses in *A Journey to Waco*. The negotiators discussed locating and delivering word-processing supplies to Mount Carmel in talks with the Davidians. *Newsweek* (October 10, 1993) quoted Koresh's poem "Eden to Eden," which Haldeman printed in full in *Memories of the Branch Davidians*. Professors Arnold and Tabor published it as part of "The David Koresh Manuscript: Exposition of the Seven Seals" (Houston: Reunion Institute, 1994). That document includes the work Koresh completed on the Seals with commentary by Arnold and Tabor. Doyle recalled Koresh's views in those last days in *A Journey to Waco*, adding details in a talk with me. Noise from the loudspeakers stopped moments before 6:00 a.m. on April 19; Schneider and other Davidians reported in talks with negotiators that Koresh had been "working all night" on the manuscript Ruth Riddle would save from the fire later that day.

21. "THIS IS NOT AN ASSAULT"

Sage and another agent noted the time before he announced the start of the tear gas operation at 6:02 a.m. on April 19. Thibodeau recalled the scene inside Mount Carmel in *Waco: A Survivor's Story*. Doyle and Thibodeau recalled Koresh's and other Davidians' reactions that morning. The Department of Justice's 1993 report tracks the use of "compromise" as the operation's code word and Reno's repeated instruction to the FBI to "back off" if children were in danger. Sage's off-mic comments were captured by the FBI's tape recorder and duly transcribed. Noesner described the SIOC in an email to me. The Department of Justice's 1993 report and the House of Representatives report *The Tragedy at Waco: New Evidence Examined* (Washington, DC: US Government Printing Office, 2000) confirm Reno's presence, the scene there, and her 10:00 a.m. departure. Reno discussed key elements of her thoughts and decisions before and after April 19 in her Morgan, Lewis & Bockius interview in August 1993. The Department of Justice's 1993 report confirms that the FBI's plan allowed the use of "deadly force" if the Davidians were to "open fire with any weapon." Doyle recalled the hissing of ferret rounds, the dog he fed in the siege's last days, and the Davidians' actions in the time before the fire in *A Journey to Waco* and a talk with me. The FBI recorded Sage's announcements over the loudspeakers. CNN's coverage, including a live interview with Bonnie Haldeman, can be seen on YouTube. The Department of Justice's 1993 report records the depletion of ferret rounds on the scene and the delivery of forty-eight ferret rounds from the field office in Houston. Sage described his surprise ("Hours went by . . .") to *Texas Monthly* (April 2008). Ricks's comments in an April 19 press conference, reported by United Press International on April 19, can be seen on YouTube. Thibodeau and Doyle added to their books' accounts in talks, calls, and texts with me. The FBI's, Texas Rangers,' and House of Representatives' investigations detail the insertion of tear gas into the vault. Koresh's and Schneider's talk of "Coleman fuel" was among the significant exchanges captured by FBI listening devices, as reported by the Knight-Ridder News Service on July 28, 1995, CNN on May 10, 2000, *Texas Monthly* in April 2003, and ABC News on January 3, 2018, and studied in depth by Liverpool Hope University's Kenneth Newport, who cited Scott Sonobe's recollection of a Bible study in which Koresh spoke of a tank attack ("It feels like dying . . .") in *Nova Religio* (November 2009). The *Dallas Morning News* (February 27, 2018) reported Craddock's hearing "Light the fire." Reavis's and Wessinger's descriptions in the "scholars' summit" video and Tarrant County autopsy reports showing that Davidian women and children died from blunt-force trauma and smoke inhalation support my account of what occurred in the vault on April 19.

22. APOCALYPSE

The first sign of fire is often reported at 11:59 a.m.; Reavis cited "independent fire examiners" specifying 11:59:16. Doyle's first-person accounts and TV coverage by CNN and other outlets contributed to my account. The Department of Justice's 1993 report noted firefighters' arrival at 12:34 p.m. and their difficulties due to Mount Carmel's being "not currently hooked to the town's water supply." Sage's account of the tanks' knocking holes in the compound, making "a funnel" for the fire, is from his 2021 *Vice* video. Doyle and Thibodeau described seeing Wayne Martin ("Wayne just slid down the wall . . .") and their escapes in their books, adding key details in a talk with me. Sheila Martin recalled her experience of April 19 in a talk with me. The Department of Justice's 1993 report and the *New Yorker* (March 31, 2014) tallied the federal force at Mount Carmel. Misty Ferguson described her ordeal in an April 25, 1993, interview with Texas Rangers. Marjorie Thomas recalled hers in testimony during the Davidian defendants' 1994 murder-conspiracy trial. Doyle recounted his escape and arrest in *A Journey to Waco*. Doyle shared details of what he'd learned about his daughter's last moments. I added information from autopsy reports. The

Department of Justice's 1993 report mentions "systematic gunfire" from inside the compound at 12:25 p.m. on April 19. Autopsies, the Department of Justice's 1993 report, and the Texas Rangers' forensics contributed significant details. Joe Robert, whose papers can be found in the Texas Collection at Baylor, interviewed medical examiner Dr. Rodney Crow, who described the deaths of Davidian women and children, "caused when the roof of the vault gave way, raining concrete and steel upon those who had sought shelter." Dayland Gent's autopsy, performed on May 29, 1993, established the cause of the boy's death. Ricks commented on the likelihood of Koresh's hiding in the vault in an April 19 press conference that the *New York Times* and many other outlets reported the next day. My description of Koresh's and Schneider's deaths relies on details of their autopsies. Both were performed by Tarrant County medical examiners, Schneider's on April 29–30 and Koresh's on May 2–3, 1993. Sage described being "in a daze" to *Texas Monthly* (April 2008). The Department of Justice's 1993 report notes that fire engines were allowed through the perimeter at 12:41. The tendentious 1997 documentary *Waco: The Rules of Engagement* features video of federal agents hoisting the ATF flag after the fire.

23. OUT OF THE ASHES

Accounts of the number of Davidians who died on April 19 vary from the low to high seventies. My count is drawn from the Department of Justice's 1993 report, autopsy reports, and subsequent investigations. It does not include Nikki Gent's and Aisha Gyarfas's trauma-born babies. Reports of the number of Native Americans killed at Wounded Knee in 1890 vary; my "more than 200" is a conservative estimate. Reno's April 19 press conference can be seen on YouTube; a transcript of her appearance on *Larry King Live* is available at CNN.com. Texas A&M professor Sylvia Grider's students' jokes and her view on them can be found in the Texas Collection at Baylor; Mike Cox's collection added to my list of Waco jokes. President Clinton's April 20 press conference can be seen on C-SPAN ("Texas Cult Standoff"). Doyle recalled his days in Parkland Hospital's burn unit in *A Journey to Waco*. ABC's *Waco: The Decision to Die* aired on April 20, 1993. *Time*'s second cover story on Koresh appeared on May 3, 1993. House Speaker Newt Gingrich shared his 1993 conversation with Reno with reporters on January 14, 1995. The *Oklahoman* (January 15, 1994) and *Austin Chronicle* (August 18, 2000) reported on Waco conspiracy theories. *This Is Not an Assault* noted the disappearance of an ATF camera. Larry King's CNN interview with Reno appeared on May 2, 1993. Koresh is buried in Tyler

Memorial Park in Tyler, Texas. His Tarrant County autopsy specifies his cause of death. Tabor described Koresh's burial and his mother's securing an Israeli flag for the coffin in *Why Waco?* An Associated Press photo dated April 30, 1993, shows the memorial (THEY WILL NOT FIND DAVID'S BONES!) to Koresh. *American Terrorist* recounted Timothy's McVeigh's views and his manifesto, "Constitutional Defenders."

24. FORENSICS

Robert H. Churchill quoted the Texas Constitutional Militia's Russell Smith ("Waco was the second shot . . .") in *To Shake Their Guns in the Tyrant's Face* (Ann Arbor: University of Michigan Press, 2009), which examines founder Jon Roland's role in the 1990s' rise of militias. Roland's influential 1994 essay "Reviving the Ready Militia" can be found at Constitution.org. The *New York Times'* "The Waco Whitewash" appeared on October 12, 1993; *Soldier of Fortune* headlined the government's Waco "whitewash" in February 1994. Reavis and Doyle provided detailed accounts of the Davidians' trial in San Antonio in early 1994. The *Times, Tribune-Herald,* and other news outlets provided details from the trial. Reavis's extensive documentation of the trial can be found in the Texas Collection at Baylor and the Witliff Collections at Texas State, which includes his editor's rejection note. Dan Cogdell was the attorney who sold his watch and Mustang to pay expenses, per Reavis. The *Washington Post* reported prosecutor Johnston's insulting defense lawyers. The *Tribune-Herald* noted Johnston's reference to "Methodists and Knights of Columbus." United Press International reported the jury forewoman's quote ("the wrong people were on trial . . .") on April 19, 1995. Reavis recounted the verdicts and defense attorneys' celebration at the Fairmount Hotel. The *Los Angeles Times* quoted jury forewoman Sarah Bain ("The federal government was . . .") on September 26, 1999. The *New York Times* reported her weeping after the verdict and alternate juror Mary Pardo's comments. The Witliff Collections at Texas State hold a copy of Bain's letter to the Senate Judiciary Committee. The *American Conservative* carried Senator Biden's October 31, 1995, quote ("The ATF had a legitimate . . .") on April 13, 2021; the hearing can be seen on C-SPAN. The *Austin Chronicle* noted Livingstone Fagan's decision not to appeal on September 22, 2000. Fagan described his alleged mistreatment by prison guards and referred to "vengeance" in the *Sunday Times* of London (December 14, 2008). *American Terrorist* recounted McVeigh's Gulf War experiences, sports betting, and Oklahoma City bombing. The Michigan Militia maintains a website, Michiganmilitia.com. Its history is discussed in

To Shake Their Guns in the Tyrant's Face and in Xavier University professor Mack Mariani's "The Michigan Militia—Political Engagement or Political Alienation?" in the journal *Terrorism and Political Violence* (Winter 1998). Its membership was noted in *USA Today* on April 17, 1996. Former Genesee County Volunteer Militia commander Paul Klinkenberger answered my questions by phone and email. The acquittal of two men charged with plotting to kidnap Michigan governor Gretchen Whitmer, with a mistrial declared for two others, was reported by Associated Press and many other outlets on April 8, 2022. The ATF released its five-hundred-page report in September 1993. Reavis reported Director Higgins's reason for not arresting Koresh when he was outside Mount Carmel ("They might have begun to execute people . . ."). The *Dallas Morning News* (August 24, 1999) reported on the FBI's using pyrotechnics at Waco. Filmmaker Michael McNulty's work with the Texas Rangers led to that story and the discovery that pyrotechnic rounds had been labeled as silencers. Reno announced naming former senator Danforth as special counsel to look into Waco's "dark questions" at a September 9, 1999, news conference; a transcript can be seen at Justice.gov. The *Washington Post* (July 22, 2000) and other outlets reported Danforth's findings, which were dissected by the libertarian Cato Institute's *Policy Analysis* (April 9, 2001). Danforth's report can be read at Wikimedia Commons. Thibodeau discusses Peter Gent's actions on February 28, 1993, and Gent's death in *Waco: A Survivor's Story*. He emphasized that Gent had been unarmed, a widely held belief among current and former Davidians, in a talk with me. Gent's autopsy, describing the hollow-point round that killed him, recovered "53 inches above the heel," was performed in the Tarrant County morgue on May 5, 1993. FBI records summarized in the Department of Justice's 1993 report describe Gent as "shooting at the ATF agents from the tower."

25. WEAPONIZING WACO

Alex Jones's documentary *America Wake Up or Waco*, detailing his views on the siege and fire and his "Phoenix Project" to build a new church on the site, can be seen on YouTube. His former radio producer Mike Hanson, a key figure in the project, posted a YouTube video called *The Phoenix Project: Up from the Ashes*, covering much of the same material. Hanson maintains a Facebook page, Remember Waco. Doyle read the names of those who died at Mount Carmel at the opening of the new church on April 19, 2000. He shared memories of that day and of Jones's involvement in a talk with me. Thibodeau and Ron Goins shared their reflections on Jones with me. The

Daily Beast noted Jay Leno's Waco joke on November 26, 2021. Bonnie Haldeman appeared that day. Her comments and Jones's, including his calling the Oklahoma City bombing "an inside job," appear in *America Wake Up or Waco*. The Supreme Court's ruling on five Davidians' prison sentences was reported by CBS News on June 5, 2000, and by the *Dallas Morning News* and many other outlets the following day. Fagan's story, including his years in prison and 2007 deportation, is told in the UK website *Left-Lion*'s "The Waco Siege: How a Man from Nottingham Became Part of an American Tragedy" (July 24, 2019). Thibodeau recalled speaking at militia gatherings in *Waco: A Survivor's Story*. Linda Tripp told CNN's Larry King of her views about Waco on *Larry King Live* on February 9, 2001. Roger Stone advanced his theory of Hillary Clinton's culpability in his book with Robert Morrow, *The Clintons' War on Women* (New York: Skyhorse, 2015), and subsequent comments to the *Austin American-Statesman* (September 25, 2018). Alex Jones propounded his views of the conspiracy in *America Wake Up or Waco*. *Rolling Stone* reported Jones's income from supplements and other products on January 7, 2022. Doyle told me about talking with conspiracists. Noesner described Waco as a "self-inflicted wound" but not a "massacre" on the phone and in emails with me. Michael German spoke with me about his undercover work for the FBI. Catrina Doxsee shared her views and CSIS data on the militia movement with me by phone and email. Fi "Monkey King" Duong's role in the Capitol riot of January 6, 2021, and his talk of "Waco 2.0" were reported by Washington, DC's Fox 5 television on July 6, 2021. Liverpool Hope University professor Newport explained his perspective on the fire in the journal *Nova Religio* (November 2009), which also included the opposing views of professors Wessinger and Wright. Newport spoke with me at length. So did Baylor professor Bill Pitts, whose opinion carries great weight in Branch Davidian studies and who told me he found Newport's views the most convincing.

26. SURVIVORS

Alexa Pace and Charles Pace were my guides on my first visit to Mount Carmel in July 2021. Pastor Pace was generous with his time. He shared reading material with me by email. Swedish filmmakers Emelie Svensson and Karin Oleander generously shared footage of their interview with Shaun Bunds. I met Doyle, Thibodeau, Kristin Hunsaker, and Ron Goins for several enjoyable hours at the Golden Corral in Waco; we stayed in touch. Sheila Martin met me for a long interview in Waco and answered many of my questions by phone.

EPILOGUES

Janet Reno expressed regrets about Waco ("Knowing what I do . . .") to NPR on November 7, 2016. Her interview at the University of Virginia's Miller Center took place on September 27, 2004. The *New York Times* (November 11, 2005) reported Bill Clinton's speech at Hofstra. The *New York Times* (March 29, 2011) carried McVeigh's calling Oklahoma City children "collateral damage" and his "tirade" about children who died at Waco. The *Guardian* reported his comment about the afterlife. Amo Roden corresponded with me by email. David Chipman claimed the Davidians had shot down a pair of helicopters in an "Ask Me Anything" Reddit forum in September 2019. United Press International reported Marvin Richardson's comments on the Waco raid on July 11, 1995. NPR's April 11, 2022, story on Dettelbach's nomination as ATF director was followed by the post asking if he was "at Waco too." Thibodeau spoke to me in Waco, by phone, and in texts. Heather Jones spoke to me on the phone. The *Athens Review* carried details of Bonnie Haldeman's murder on August 13, 2018. Gary Noesner spoke to me by phone and answered many emails. The *Dallas Morning News* reported Van Zandt's "iceberg" comment on December 30, 1999. Jim Cavanaugh testified during the House of Representatives' inquiry on July 26, 1995. His view of Koresh ("a two-bit thug") is from an interview for ticklethewire.com posted on October 28, 2009. San Antonio journalist David Flores interviewed Robert Rodriguez for KENS-TV on July 15, 2010; the *Dallas Morning News* (April 20, 2000) reported his visit to the new church at Mount Carmel. Sarah Bain's 1998 speech at Mount Carmel can be found at Speakingwhilefemale.co. Alex Jones and InfoWars' bankruptcy was reported by the *New York Post* and other sources on April 18, 2022. Thetrumpet.com (April 19, 2022) suggested that the FBI may have "orchestrated" the Capitol riot of January 6, 2021. The *New York Times* reported Mike Vanderboegh's prediction ("Waco can happen at any given time . . .") on July 12, 2015.

Acknowledgments

Meeting David Thibodeau, Sheila Martin, and Clive Doyle felt like stepping into recent American history. Many thanks to David, Sheila, and Clive, who were generous with their time, their memories, and their opinions. Kristin Hunsaker and Ron Goins joined us at the Golden Corral and aided my work. I'm also grateful to Heather Jones for sharing recollections that were often cheerful but sometimes painful.

Gary Noesner is one of the good guys—as sharp-witted, hard-nosed, and ethical as his FBI hero Eliot Ness. He helped me understand the Bureau's strategy and tactics, the context of the Bureau's actions at Waco, the negotiators' thinking, and clarified some of the links between events at Waco and today's headlines. His *Stalling for Time* and Thibodeau's *Waco: A Survivor's Story* are key resources for anyone intrigued by the story told here.

I am deeply grateful to current and former ATF agents who aided my work: James Balthazar and former ATF historian Barbara Osteika, Lowell Sprague, John Risenhoover, Dave DiBetta, Harry Eberhardt, Tom Crowley, and some who prefer not to be named. Here's a salute to Tina Bayless of the ATF Association, who helped me contact several of them. I won't forget the line Senior Special Agent Balthazar uses to close emails: "In God we trust. Everybody else, keep your hands where we can see them."

Dr. Bill Pitts served as my Virgil in Waco, introducing me to Branch Davidian history, to a wealth of research material in the Texas Collection at Baylor University, and to Ruth Pitts, his wife. Bill and Ruth became friends of the project and of mine. Ruth put me in touch with Clive Doyle and Sheila Martin; Bill served as a sounding board for a year's worth of follow-up conversations. I'm looking forward to joining them again at Ninfa's restaurant.

Baylor archivist Paul Fisher was a cheerful, resourceful ally. His arms may still be sagging from carrying Texas Collection files to the desk where I set up camp. Paul stayed in touch after I left town and sent me a trove of audio recordings and transcripts of Koresh's and the Davidians' talks with police and negotiators—more than ten thousand pages of invaluable transcripts. Baylor's Rachel DeShong and B. J. Thome provided advice and assistance at Baylor's Carroll Library, as did Katie Salzmann and Andres Vazquez at Texas State University in San Marcos.

I'm grateful to Charles and Alexa Pace, who welcomed me to the new church at Mount Carmel, which doubles as a museum dedicated to Branch Davidian history and the notorious events of 1993.

Dr. James Tabor, who played a role in the drama described here, sent me a video of a long, in-depth discussion he had with professors Phillip Arnold, Catherine Wessinger, and Stuart Wright. Their views and their years of work on the subject deepened my understanding of what happened in 1993. Dr. Wessinger's noteworthy contributions to Doyle's, Martin's, and Bonnie Haldeman's memoirs, as well as videos she made with other survivors, have helped keep the Davidians' stories central to chronicles like this one.

Dr. Kenneth Newport of Liverpool Hope University made his views clear in a long Zoom call and follow-up correspondence. His work and advice proved pivotal to my account of the April 19 fire and its likely origins. Eileen Kavanaugh handled the logistics of our Zoom call and later correspondence.

Paul Klinkenberger helped me explain the role of Michigan's militias and their point of view. Catrina Doxsee brought another perspective to that side of the story after Paige Monfort put us in touch. Ms. Doxsee's full title: associate director of the Transnational Threats Project at the Center for Strategic and International Studies in Washington, DC.

Michael German of the Brennan Center for Justice shared his experiences as an FBI agent working undercover and his views of Waco's continuing relevance. Filmmakers Emilie Svensson and Karin Oleander shared documentary footage with me—here's hoping their *Waiting for David* finds a worldwide audience. I also owe thanks to Boston University's Nancy Ammerman, the staff at the Forbes Library in Northampton, Massachusetts, the New York Public Library, the *Waco Tribune-Herald*, and Tricia Gesner at AP.

Some editors are brilliant; some are meticulous, tireless, shrewd, or a pleasure to work with. Conor Mintzer is five-for-five. He named the book and shepherded it from proposal to pub date. Holt's Amy Einhorn is a champion of writers and of this book. I'm grateful to her as well as to Holt's Sarah Crichton, Caitlin O'Shaughnessy, Pat Eisemann, Chris Sergio, Chris O'Connell, Vincent Stanley, and Meryl Levavi. Pete Garceau created a striking cover.

At the Robbins Office, David Halpern shaped the book's proposal and saw it through with his customary aplomb. I'm lucky to have an agent who is also my advocate and friend. I've been a Kathy Robbins fan for many years. I'm indebted to her and to Lisa Kessler, Janet Oshiro, and their colleagues at the Robbins Office.

Many thanks to Rick Paar and Jacqueline Sheehan, Helen Rosenberg, Phil Sullivan and Alexis Johnson, Tom and Kelly Cook, and Ken Kubik, the man my daughter calls my BFF.

Thanks to poet and scholar Lily Lady Cook I have texts, talks, and thoughts to prize forever. Thanks to Calloway Marin Cook, founder of Illuminate Labs, I have an example of what talent and hard work can do, and a great golf partner.

In the end, any story of mine comes down to screenwriter and author Pamela Marin, my in-house editor, partner, and muse. Every page of *Waco Rising* is better thanks to Pamela, whose *Motherland* is still the best book on our shelves.

Index

Entries in *italics* refer to diagrams and documents